CALATAFIMI

Angus Campbell has lived in Calatafimi for many years, after retiring from a career in the field of advertising in Rome and London. His wife comes from a long-established Calatafimi family. He has made many translations from the Italian.

Calatafimi

BEHIND THE STONE WALLS
OF A SICILIAN TOWN

by

Angus Campbell

dlm

First published in 2008
by Giles de la Mare Publishers Limited
53 Dartmouth Park Hill, London NW5 1JD

Typeset by Tom Knott
Printed in China
through Colorcraft Ltd, Hong Kong

A CIP record of this book is available
from the British Library

ISBN 9781900357289 paperback original

Contents

For Caterina

Acknowledgements

After it became known who I was (how I fitted into local society) and what I was doing, a huge number of generous people offered me help, in the form of snippets of information, answers to questions, spontaneous offers of documents, rumours about ancestors, visits to places of interest, talks with relatives, and anything else that they felt might be of use. It was overwhelming and I am truly grateful. My first thank-you, therefore, is to the citizens of Calatafimi.

In particular, I should like to express my gratitude to Gaetano Pampalone and Franco Maiorana, who gave up a great deal of their time to showing me around unusual aspects of the town and sharing their erudition with me. My thanks to Pietro Ancona, Vice-President of the Congrega della Carità, for permission to consult the archives. Giovanni Bruccoleri, the librarian at the municipal library for most of the time I was writing, was of immense help, as was his staff, and indeed his successor. My thanks to Salvatore Agueli for instructing me on the Carmine and the activities that went on inside it. I must thank the Stabile family for information concerning the Orfanotrofio Stabile, Elio Vivona for documents concerning Domenico Saccaro, and the pharmacist Antonino Gallo for an interesting old will relevant to the property in which we live.

Three men have been subject to a daily barrage of questions on matters varying from the dialect names for plants, to the intricacies of the guilds' role in the festa, and the number of hoopoes to be found here, etc. They are: Luciano Palmeri (and his wife Giuseppina), Nicola Laudicina and Luciano Garitta. I have thanked other people in the text, but, if I have inadvertently left someone out, I hope they will forgive a shaky memory and not blame an ungrateful author.

The extended Mollica family have been magnificent in their help, and I am deeply grateful to them all.

I must thank Fariborz Atapour for a valuable suggestion at an early stage in the writing. Also Vernon Hyde Minor for the enthusiasm he bestowed on the first draft at a time when anybody I approached with a view to publication said there was no hope. By the same token I must express my thanks to Giles de la Mare, whose expert eye and professional guidance have made the book possible.

Illustrations

Western Sicily

Introduction

When I told you recently that I was semi-retiring from Rome to the town of Calatafimi in this solitary corner of western Sicily, you were moved to ask me, from comfortable Kensington and somewhat peremptorily, the equivalent of 'What the hell do you think you are doing? Perhaps you might consider letting me know.'

Whether I'll be able to explain it satisfactorily, you will have to judge – as I'm quite sure you will. After stumbling from my normal Roman daylight into this sheltered spot, and my eyes becoming gradually used to the unusual light, I began to pick out some of the details and was more and more intrigued with the place. This attempt at explaining why I like what slowly emerged has generally delighted me, apart from a recurring irritation as it immediately became clear that Calatafimi inspires an utter lack of interest in the vast majority of those who accidentally run across it. Which put my back up. Uninvited, I felt drawn to its defence and I started peeling off some of the camouflage of ordinariness that makes the place seem so unnoteworthy. We share certain interests, so what follows will naturally be tipped in their favour, but you will also have to put up with the odd chunk of my daily life. Your fault: after all, you did ask me what I thought I was doing here.

Chosen from many, here are two bland examples of the complete lack of interest that my new home inspires.

After a very short visit to Sicily in the mid-nineteenth century, pompous old Vicomte de Marcellus, 'ancien Ministre plénipotentiaire' (French Ambassador to the Court at St James under George IV, at one point in his fat way through life, though his claim to fame was his part in securing the Venus de Milo for the French nation), dismisses the town and, initially, his generous host the priest Saccaro, too:[1]

Calatafimi n'a rien de curieux que son etymologie...

and he goes on to quote Dante with regard to its citizens:

Non raggioniam di lor, ma guarda e passa.

In other words Calatafimi has a quaint name that might intrigue us, but its inhabitants are unworthy of our consideration.[2]

And in his quite excellent *Companion Guide to Sicily*, Raleigh Trevelyan writes:[3]

> To Italians the name Calatafimi will forever be associated with the first victory of Garibaldi's Thousand over the Bourbons on May 15 1860. In fact the actual battle took place on the height opposite this otherwise rather insignificant little town...

I have now fully convinced myself that Calatafimi is not insignificant and have taken heart from what that exquisite scrutinizer of locality Gilbert White wrote in the Advertisement to his *Natural History & Antiquities of Selborne*:

> If stationary men would pay some attention to the districts on which they reside, and would publish their thoughts respecting the objects that surround them, from such materials might be drawn the most complete county histories...

In much humbler vein, I have been paying some attention to the district on which I reside.

Certainly Calatafimi will not wring gasps of astonishment from sophisticated globe-trotters or bowl them over with a savage magnificence, nor will it inspire intricate scholarly study by meticulous academics concerning its vital contribution to Sicily's tightly woven history; and Trevelyan was probably right in describing the outward appearance of the town as little and rather insignificant. But he did not have the time I have to get behind the camouflage and scratch at the apparently uninviting surface...

The place has rapidly metamorphosed me into a chicken. And since chickens scrape the ground at random in the ever-optimistic belief that they will uncover scraps to eat, what follows is the result of episodic scratching in hard though fertile ground that, thanks to its apparent insignificance, has managed to avoid the attention of resident, neighbouring, or passing fowls and has therefore been left alone to do what it had to do for a very long time.

One answer to your question, then, is that I have been scratching and pecking.

I

From Contrada San Giovanni into Calatafimi

You have of course met, either in Rome or London, some of the
people who live here in this family hamlet of San Giovanni outside
the small Sicilian town of Calatafimi, but you insist you are at a
loss to know why I came here or what makes me stay. There is
no straightforward answer, though ungoverned circumstances, as
always, played a part. So I suppose I do have a task on my hands to
explain myself, unless I can stir your settled urban spirit sufficiently
to entice you out here to discover for yourself. I had better begin
simply by giving you some bearings.

Caterina and I are in the west of Sicily in the Province of Trapani,
the proud owners of an unencumbered view of the valley below the
large windows of our small house, which is built over the stables
of what was once a medium-sized Sicilian country house that was
humbled, you may recall, in the earthquake of 1968. It stands half-
way up a hill that gives it a commanding view across the valley which
divides the family hamlet – resurrected from the ruins of the old
building – from the small agricultural town of Calatafimi, which is
unknown to the rest of the world though drummed into the minds
of all Italian schoolchildren as the theatre of Garibaldi's first victory
over the Bourbon troops of Naples in 1860 on his triumphant march
to forge the unification of Italy. It is also the nearest town to the
superb temple, the dramatic amphitheatre and the urban ruins that
constitute all that remains of the forgotten power that was Segesta,
a site which has enthralled so many centuries of visitors since it was
allegedly founded by the tireder remnants of Aeneas' followers
during their long flight from the destruction of Troy and on their way
towards the founding of Rome. The few outsiders who came to these
parts usually did so to see the temple, and they always seemed to be
en route to their next port of call. That has fortunately left this part
of Sicily relatively intact.

3

Calatafimi looks beautiful from this distance across the valley, pasted onto the hillside about five kilometres away with a Cézanne-like aggregate attractiveness that is not appreciable when you walk its steep narrow streets: I often wonder what Cézanne's villages were really like before he painted their bones in his own image. Calatafimi is not beautiful when you get there, but I react to it instinctively because it does not beckon. It has a certain private dignity, although it does not vaunt the eye-catching architecture of some of its neighbours, and much that is beautiful and interesting has been more or less wilfully neglected or hidden. Like all southern Italian towns it has a rich local history, jealously guarded and viciously defended by a long line of local historians that still flourishes. Also, being the nearest town to the ruins of Segesta, it was for centuries on the agenda of those foreign eminences who occasionally set their well-shod feet in the town: *en passant*, they left revealing glimpses of Segesta, Calatafimi and themselves. I find myself very much in sympathy with the place, partly I suppose because it does not attract attention, as I've said, and so becomes a personal discovery, and partly because a little trowel work is rewarding: you will be surprised at some of the things that turn up.

From these windows, the town is often caught in what Sicilians with their innate sense of poetry call an *occhio di sole*, an 'eye of sunlight'. Since it clings to a hill to the north of here, with taller hills behind, lower ones in front and nothing to the east and west, the sun often gazes at it drowsily in the morning and beams at it benignly in the evening while the surrounding country is in the dark. And it does look beautiful. If dark storms move in and the harsh Sicilian climate concedes some rain, the intervening valley enjoys far more than its fair share of rainbows – often two gory slashes at a time. Which brings painting to mind again: looking around here you realize that the trees outlined on the middle-distance ridges of *quattrocento* paintings are not as naively large as they appear to be: they are actually like that. There is no need for you to point out I could have seen that anywhere. But this undisturbed countryside makes it easier to see when you look. And anyway, that would never occur to you in London, would it?

All that is to be seen of the ruins of Segesta from our windows is the suggestion of a tiny mediaeval castle on the top of Monte Barbaro about ten kilometres off, which from here is so small that it tells you nothing of the wealth of Greekness on the other side of the hill.

The temple and the theatre are obscured from view, but you can feel them somehow even from here. Further down in the valley, on the road towards Calatafimi, the temple will draw majestically into view round a corner, only to slip away round the next. However, the theatre will stay hidden.

To the left, on top of a hill well before Monte Barbaro, you cannot help seeing the monument that shelters the remains of those who fell on both sides during Garibaldi's famous battle of Calatafimi in 1860: the Ossario, full of the contenders' bones. It is an obelisk with a squat base designed by the master Sicilian architect Basile,[1] who made Palermo the centre of Italian *art nouveau* together with Turin and Milan, a rare exception to the bleak north/south divide that plagues the united Italy Garibaldi's battle here was fought to bring into being. Inside the monument the bones of the fallen are no longer visible because they have been demurely bricked-up, and there is a dusty visitors' book that is just occasionally signed by lacklustre schoolchildren. But at night it is lit up and stands out as an incongruous, blazing exclamation mark in the indifferent rural darkness.

On the other side of the valley, to the right, sprawls the unprepossessing Pantano Municipal Water Works. It looks like an untidy medium-sized farmhouse with more than the usual number of shabby outhouses; but it is from here that Calatafimi is supplied with water. It was private property until quite recently, and the presence of water inevitably attracted litigation and attempts at regulation over the centuries. I have some interesting examples going back to the sixteenth century, which I shall almost certainly impose on you later on. Caterina's family, and other local families of long standing, had land here or hereabouts at various times and documentation still turns up or else has been kept. Documents are never thrown away because they can always be useful in an argument, and arguments are often useful and always entertaining. Some of them will make an appearance later, too. As can be expected from the presence of the Water Works, this area is an exception in normally parched Sicily; and, since our water is held to be particularly tasty, some of the locals in the know still beat a track to our hamlet to fill up their bottles because all Sicilians are connoisseurs of water and have their favourite vintages. We do not advertise it for obvious reasons, but we deny nobody. There was a time long ago, I suppose, when the water in Kensington was subtly different from Chelsea's, and barrels rather than bottles were carted from one village to the other.

The town is about five kilometres away, as I have said, and I tend to walk it occasionally, to the dismay of all because they think, or think other people will think, I am weak in the head. Nobody walks for pleasure in Sicily, and anyone seen doing it is at the least a needy foreigner. But I do it, and I'll tell you about some of the things I pass on my way into the village. The road looks just like any other run-down country road with very little traffic, but it is five kilometres of hidden delights, if you did but know.

The driveway from our hamlet down to the road is long, steep and windy, so I usually turn off it near the beginning and take a shortcut to the right, which was created and is maintained by the dogs who use it daily as they roar down to the road to bark wildly, if quite in-effectually, at Nicola, the neighbouring shepherd, and his dogs as he leads his sheep off to pasture, guiding them with little masonic cries that are quite comprehensible to the sheep and his dogs but in-furiate ours and intrigue us. Our brave dogs wish us to believe they are defending us, but they really just want a sniff at his ones, many of which are their close relations – although parentage does not seem to be an inhibiting factor in canine aggression or sexuality. All dogs and most people are closely related in this neck of the woods, which gives inspiration to some people with awesome memories and of many winters to dominate conversations about how exactly one family is related to another through the cadet branch of a third, fourth or fifth – who, like the mediaeval chroniclers (and even South Sea Islanders), can and do trace the family histories of the whole community back countless generations almost to the beginning of time. The canine equivalent is barking and sniffing.

This shortcut means I don't go past a burrow, den or sett (which is it?) of a couple of porcupines[2] further down the driveway. These animals are so shy they don't normally come out at full moon, though often the dogs find them at night and the noise is consider-able. When cornered by hostile animals, shyness deserts them: they turn their back on their foes and rattle their quills magnificently as a sign and siren of aggression and, if this does not have the desired effect, they charge their attackers vigorously in reverse and pierce them multiply. That had a devastating effect on one of our dogs re-cently. Around midnight it scratched wretchedly at the door with its body full of quills. A search party was mounted which had no diffi-culty in getting to the scene of the encounter as the rattling porcupine was now surrounded by the other baying but completely thwarted dogs. What could they do against this rattling thing that stuck spears in them if they got too near? I imagine you, who are militarily inclined, might theorize about how a small, well-trained and perfectly equipped force can easily decimate an undisciplined horde – something on the lines of the Roman legions or the British army surrounded by natives – but, be that as it may, the canine horde was no match for the lone rattler. The burrow/den/sett is evident to all, self-confident enough to dispense with camouflage or sentries. And yet they are afraid to come out in the full moon.

Anyway, when I walk into the village, I take this shortcut and as I get onto the road below the house I am immediately faced on the other side by a bee farm, though 'farm' may be too high-sounding a word for a small patch of land with a tool-shed and about twenty hives on it. The land belongs to a family with an agricultural equipment shop in the town, and so we do not see a lot of them except when the demands of this, their secondary calling, dress them in most un-Sicilian masks and white overalls as they look after their crop of insects. It is mooted that some eucalyptus trees nearby may be why the hives were sited there, but bee-keeping is a centuries-old occupation on the island (the Sicilian Hyblea honey is mentioned in Shakespeare[3] and has been compared to the legendary Greek Hymettus honey), and a lot of people keep bees in the area. If they were placed there for the eucalyptus, which I doubt, there are many other flowers around in profusion, so the bees have quite enough to keep them busy. They come up to us a lot, mostly just buzzing around for nectar, but occasionally there is a restless young queen who takes off in search of a place of her own. These swarms have been strangely slow and indecisive so far, so that we have had ample time to close the windows in case the young royal takes a liking to one of our rooms. Justinian's *Codex* lays down that bees (and strangely enough peacocks) are *feral*, and if they move terrain they change proprietors; but Sicilian custom has it that they can be claimed back within two days of moving.[4] (I mentioned peacocks because a fair number of them strut around locally in humble, muddy farmyards.) Fire struck at the bee-farm a couple of years ago and some of the hives were burnt, but nobody knows why. Mystery is common currency here and it is most unlikely that what happened will ever become generally known. Another mystery – at least it is for me – is why those superbly painted birds, the bee-eaters (*Merops apiaster*) who migrate here in the warm months, do not pay more attention to this area around the hives. They do sail languidly over us in the mornings and evenings, sometimes floating almost motionless in the contrary breeze a few feet from me if I'm quietly lying on the terrace, but during the day they conceal any sort of excitement about the hives in a most ladylike manner. Do you think that, unlike in the dog/porcupine encounter, the massed proletarian bee-troops confound the highly equipped elitist bee-eaters?

A word about the state of the road into town before I take you further down it. Until fairly recently a car would have found it adventurous to negotiate the track: conveyance was by cart, horse, mule, donkey or on foot, depending on the status and mission of the traveller. An idea of how it was can still be had if, instead of turning right at the end of our drive, you turn to the left, away from Calatafimi, and go up the valley towards the small town of Vita: there are deep water ruts and the occasional boulder in a dirt road that is fringed – depending on the season – with wild orchids, asphodel, daisies, dog-roses, irises and other marvels for quite a bit until bad, but welcome, asphalt is reached after about two kilometres. But when going towards town in the other direction, I walk on a road that has had to undergo three regulation surface changes at various points because in its wisdom the Provincial Government decided to build a Proper Road according to the Dictates of the Law. Coming down my shortcut opposite the bee-farm, I get onto a modern asphalt road hemmed in by concrete walls on one side, to stop water (and, with it, earth) seeping out of the hilly fields above. This first phase lasts for a few hundred smooth metres, until other legal dictates gain sway and the surface turns into dirt – rock-chips compounded with dirt, but dirt none the less. The reason for this essential change is that asphalt cannot by Provincial Law be used in the vicinity of rivers because of the danger of pollution, although this doesn't seem to pose problems elsewhere in the district. The 'river' in question is the Pantano, but, since the historic springs were converted into the Municipal Water Works, there is really no river at all, except perhaps a flash torrent after a rare rainstorm. Doubt about the existence of the river seems to have been registered by the Provincial Government because, after about two hundred metres, the rock-chip/dirt road turns into concrete. Both these surfaces are, of course, legal, but they have different characteristics. The rock-chip/dirt road deteriorates in next to no time (especially as it is on an incline) and becomes very, very bumpy. It requires continuous attention from an excellent road-mender who will patiently and philosophically discuss his being called out to patch it up all the time. The concrete part, though it works almost like asphalt, is less interesting than the dirt section and unfortunately creates no work for our philosophical road-mender. This civil engineering cocktail must surely have been the result of a Provincial Cabinet split and a hastily arrived at compromise. It is no exaggeration to say that politics and controversy worm themselves into every fibre of Italian life and especially into highly unimportant local issues in the south. Perhaps the road-mender was a relation of one of the leaders of the dirt faction and the other side had cousins in cement? After another hundred metres or so, however, the dried-up river-bed recedes to a safe distance, and the road reverts to asphalt that continues, albeit full of holes, right up to Calatafimi. A point of minor interest: all along this variegated road runs a major conduit carrying fibre-optical cable across the island. But although we in the hamlet are only metres away, we have no telephone land-lines and we have to use mobiles – *pazienza*! This, then, is how the road is constructed that takes me to the town – with its bees, mules, sheep, laws, cabinet splits, philosophy, water, it also rouses a fine sense of astonishment in me at all the plants and flowers that push up through the fertile soil that flanks it and the nonchalant birds that flutter, float and flash overhead.

To continue with my walk: a little further down the road from the bee-farm, and early in the rock-chip/dirt section, there is the establishment of Nicola, our nearest shepherd. Your romantic pastoral thoughts would be somewhat blunted by the absolutely genuine smell of the place, and the wrecks of cars and discarded washing-machines that always seem to accumulate in the countryside. There must be a niche market for these wrecks if Caterina's brother Paolo, as you know a respected lawyer, can exert such energy in searching out motors from old washing-machines for the contraptions he makes for slicing the quartz and jasper pebbles that he finds on the shores to the south of here, or if Caterina's father, retired judge that he is, can buy up any old Citroën of a given type and strip it of its spare parts to succour his own much-loved but ailing automobile. The countryside is beautiful despite these occasional wrecks, which anyway soon disappear under the exuberant vegetation. The shepherding business flourishes and Nicola, the heir to a long line of shepherds, is a daily part of our lives. He takes a lot of our puppies, which regularly get killed chasing the wheels of the few cars that pass. Those that survive are working animals, and that can make it a noisy affair to walk past; a pseudo-aggressive stance, however, induces cringing – something that has been noted by local politicians. In the morning the sheep, hundreds of them, have to be milked: they congregate outside a large shed and enter one by one; one by one they come out of a small hole in the wall at the other end, hopefully feeling lighter and happier; and when they have all been harvested of their milk (which is collected later by an outlandish milk-tanker) they are taken off to the daily grind of munching any greenish vegetation that can be found on the lands they are allowed to visit. From a distance they look like a scattering of white rocks because munching is a slow, almost stationary business. People who work the land look on shepherding as a life sentence, as sheep have to munch every day, come what may.

On Sundays, if the vegetation at the time of the year is green enough, if Nicola has the urge and if the sheep have given up good milk, ricotta or cottage-cheese is made. The operation would curdle the insides of any committed EU bureaucrat because Nicola, like his peers, does not comply with endlessly-debated compromise-ridden edicts but bows to tradition and makes something genuine. The making is almost by invitation and takes place on a Sunday morning. He does not make a lot, so you have to order and, as there is no telephone, the interested parties will gather in due time for an intense chat while the milk is being heated in a cauldron over a wood fire. It is stirred with a reed broom tied half-way up with an obviously old piece of string while the curds begin to separate from the whey; and at just the right temperature, determined by the shepherd plunging his hand into the concoction (stifled *oooh là là's!* can be heard all the way from Brussels), the steaming result is ladled out into a kitchen sieve and is best eaten immediately. Absolutely edict-proof. I suppose Fortnum and Mason might sell you a mild imitation in London if it were expensive enough.

Some sort of modernity has crept into the pastoral life, though: Nicola follows his sheep as far as he can on a motor scooter while listening to music on his walkman. But he still guides them by calling to them, and he counts them in the evening and will spend hours finding strays if any get lost, like good shepherds are supposed to.

Just after Nicola's establishment, the road cuts through what has remained of a *regia trazzera*, literally a royal sheep-track. These quasi-roads were cleared and guaranteed by centuries of so-called government so that animals could have legal passage through private property, and to this day they cannot be cultivated, even though many landowners try hard to believe they do not exist. The beginning of this one on the left still looks like a road, although it peters out now and then into a narrow path. I often use it, walking back from the town, as another short cut because it leads up to Paolo's house further along the road after the bee-farm. It is not now used by man or beast except perhaps by the odd hunter and it is flanked by large crystalline gypsum rocks that gleam in the sun.[5] I recently found some beautiful mandrakes growing there and transplanted them to our small garden. Shades of Donne's

> Go, and catch a falling star,
> Get with child a mandrake root,
> Tell me, where all past years are,
> Or who cleft the Devil's foot.[6]

The Sicilian countryside has that timeless, silent, shrieking mystery about it.

Walking a little bit further down on the rock-chip/dirt section of the road there is, or rather was till very recently, a somewhat bizarre form of alternative agriculture. It was all very secretive because I never saw anybody working the piece of land, which is squeezed between an orange grove and a vineyard. It was a snail farm. The fact that foreigners eat snails has always intrigued but disgusted Anglo-Saxons. However, snail-eating is a normal part of country life. It was a smallish field criss-crossed with black rubber irrigation-tubes that watered lines of vegetation enclosed by protective netting. The water was needed because snails react to rain; the netting was to keep the snails in and gourmet birds out. It was apparent that a fair amount of money had been spent on the scheme, but it does not seem to have worked as the land was ploughed up this year – destined for yet another field of grapes. Perhaps there had been a love affair with a European Union subsidy that was sadly broken off. Who knows? A pity, though no doubt success would have filled the local supermarket with plastic bags of snails, as they still buy some things locally. So people carry on searching for snails in their usual way with their plastic pails, prising the surprised gastropods from the wet vegetation. You can always tell when there has been an autumn shower from the number of abandoned cars along the roadsides.

I seem to remember you liked snails, but *escargots* not these small country ones. They are very good, you know.

Behind the snails, overlooked by rocky cliffs there is a *zubbia*, the name for those deep chasms or craters that are unexpectedly dotted over this part of Sicily. Some of them make you think of falling meteors, but probably their origins are simply volcanic. They are holes, big or small, that do not seem to have been formed by water, although if it rains hard they can become rather dangerous since they collect water very rapidly for later distribution underground. They are usually densely thicketed and a natural haven for birds and rabbits, and therefore attract men with guns, another source of danger. This one has been fenced off recently, presumably for safety reasons, and inside there is thick undergrowth and a tunnel at the bottom, which, so the locals say, leads to the *stazione* bridge over the *fiume freddo* (that is the part of the river Crimisus, of classical fame, before it gets to the hot springs and becomes the *fiume caldo*, the hot river), on the provincial road to Trapani some kilometres away. When much younger, Caterina's father went down it for about 100 metres, but he stopped when it began to get uncomfortably narrow. I always have a sense of awe when faced by these deep ravines. Strangely enough they are not looked on with any superstition by the country people, though the tunnels are supposed to link up with each other underground.

After the dirt section the road turns into concrete and about halfway into town, scarcely visible on the right and cocooned by palms and cypress trees, stands the house of Margi (which in Arabic means 'full of water'). It is a medium-sized country house and is where Caterina's grandmother was born and where she remembers playing as a child. It is now semi-abandoned and emblematic of what has been happening to almost all the houses and most of the land in the area since the laws of primogeniture were dismantled in 1861 and inheritance became governed by the *legittima*. Under that, all children have equal rights to half of the property, while legacies can discriminate on the other half, the *disponibile*, when – rarely – it may be deemed necessary. Each death in the family means that houses and land are cut up into ever smaller parcels, with abandonment and non-cultivation the inevitable result.[7] I do not know how many owners Margi has now. Nobody lives in the main house because it belongs to too many people, but one of the owners has built a prefabricated chalet on his small bit of the land where he spends weekends singing. One of the families that used to sharecrop there has bought out, or come to an agreement with, a few of the heirs and uses nearly all the land for market gardening under plastic greenhouses, producing, among other things, giant strawberries that really taste like strawberries. Nobody in Caterina's extended family takes any interest in the place because it is too complicated and would not be worth the trouble, so it is falling to pieces. Clearly the best solution would be for somebody to buy up all the parcels, but it is an almost impossible feat to get everybody to agree.[8] Thus, as always in Sicily, the situation is put into a 'wait-and-see' gear while more bits of masonry tumble down. I know you have always been taken by Garibaldi, so you might be interested to know that the litter that carried Garibaldi into Calatafimi in triumph after the battle, which took place just a couple of hundred yards or so away, came from this very house. Not so long ago even this disappeared.

After Margi the road regains its asphaltic respectability and climbs slowly up through orange groves, vineyards and prickly pears, past the sandstone cliff where the brilliantly coloured bee-eaters drill their dirty little burrow-nests, round the corner which momentarily brings the temple of Segesta into astonishing view, only to be obscured again at the next corner by the hill on which the *qal'at* or castle of Calatafimi rests. One has to be careful about the castle: the crenellations that spring to view have nothing to do with the castle itself, but are another manifestation of the Municipal Water Works that I have told you about – the high ground being useful for creating water-distributing pressure.

Before climbing up to the town, one goes over what was intended to be a railway bridge. The narrow-gauge track never carried trains: its building was part of a doggedly firm policy of Mussolini's to keep the idle young of the time in employment. It is in use today, though not as had been planned. The bridge now carries not rails but the road into the town, and nearby another bridge and piece of ex-railway track have become the impressive driveway to an unimpressive farmhouse on the left-hand side of the valley; and there is a tunnel, a hundred metres or so further on to the west, that now houses a flourishing mushroom business. There is also a station house, outwardly in good repair, which, as far as I know, has never been inhabited, no doubt for a myriad of bureaucratic reasons. Although Mussolini's railway never carried trains destined to arrive on time, he might have been mollified to know that much of it is in use.

On the other side, under the bridge that carries the road, there is one of those attractive watering places with animal drinking-troughs that are found in the most unexpected places all over Sicily. This one was used in the past by the women, before the Municipal Water Works got going, for washing and drawing water: they came down the hill from the old part of town under the castle with their washing and their ewers. In the early mornings and late evenings it was also used by the men to water their animals as they went to or came back from the country. Back on the ex-railway bridge, the road now begins to climb up towards the town and in the spring it is lined with intensely blue dwarf irises.[9] Way up to the left are what remains of the twelfth-century city walls: that is, very little. The locals call them the 'Saracen walls' and they enclose what was the oldest part of the town, the Borgo Vecchio, still sometimes called the Arab quarter.

There, you have had some glimpses of the road from our house into Calatafimi. It takes you through fragments of the past, the present and the future, and skirts scenes of stories, some of which sink from memory as quickly as the seasons; but at first sight it is just a rather ill-kempt lane of no particular note except for what fringes it. The country is, to use much-bruised words, startlingly beautiful. It changes colour with the seasons. In the early spring, after the orchids and asphodel, it is mainly yellow with wood sorrel, but it can also be white with four-centimetre-wide white daisies containing intensely yellow centres, which make them look like fried quails' eggs, interspersed with concentrations of intensely orange-coloured flowers and blotches of blue borage. Guarded by the tall fennel flowers, clumps of all these plants gather together naturally into formal arrays that would conjure a smile from the most demanding of gardeners. In the summer and early autumn, after the corn has been cut and safely stowed away, the colour is brown or burnt yellow as the earth's rib-cage takes the sun: only the vineyards and olives are left to stagger on in the heat. In winter, green and yellow take over, to be gashed at intervals where the tractor and plough have painted it red-brown – for a few days before it stubbornly reverts to green. You do get to know the dogs along the way: they lead such a boring life that they give you a rapturous welcome, particularly if they are chained. While you walk along, buzzards and swallows, bee-eaters and magpies, and finches and hawks, as well as the odd jay and hoopoe, peer down on you. Perhaps they also think I am mad to walk, as I am sure you do.

The first times I did the walk, I had a series of encounters, which are now things of the past. One of the earliest was with an elderly man on a mule with his son, two goats (they keep the mule company and anyway cannot be left alone in the country or they would be stolen) and a dog, who stopped me and earnestly enquired about what had happened to my car and whether he could help in any way. Wonderful. I was also often asked whom I 'belonged to' and, that established, whether the questioner could be of any help. Sadly, this sort of thing does not happen any more because people now know whom I belong to and that also I have not suffered a breakdown, except perhaps mentally. What is unchanged, however, and involves everyone, whether they use the road on foot, on a mule or in a car, is that everybody always hails everybody else with a wave. Even if they have no idea whom they belong to.

When were you last asked in London whom you belonged to?

2

The Town and
its Monuments

Having walked you into Calatafimi, I suppose I had better try and sketch it for you, as it is not a renowned tourist attraction and you cannot look it up usefully in a guidebook. Town, village or something in-between: at various times it has been each of these, but I think now it tends towards the in-between.

It has grown up over two not particularly high hills which must in the past have given it considerable strategic potential. They now just give some fine views. To the north, it dominates the Kaggera river valley: this river has an Arab name today, but was originally the Crimisus of classical times – traditionally its god in dog form emerged from the water and, presumably after shaking himself, came to love the beautiful nymph Egesta, which resulted in the birth of Acestes, the future King of the Elymians, friend of Aeneas and founder of the city of Segesta – the magnificent ruins of which have now been demoted to bureaucratic dependency on the Municipality of Calatafimi. To the west, lies the road which winds towards the provincial capital Trapani through flat, treeless land that for centuries disgorged immeasurable quantities of corn for Imperial Rome. To the south, you go down the road I have just walked you up and continue through the valley past our hamlet to the towns of Vita, Gibellina and Castelvetrano. High ground to the east overlooks the valley of the Belice which bulges with fine vineyards.[1] On the top of the western of the two hills, at 400 metres above sea level, stands what remains of the castle, the origins of which are more ancient than the present ruined Norman building. On top of the other is what is left of the forest of Angimbè where the Bourbon kings were wont to slaughter partridges and wild boar on their rare visits to this minor settlement, in what they undoubtedly considered very much the second of their Two Sicilies.

Like most old towns, Calatafimi grew down from the castle or huddled up to it, depending on what your political point of view may happen to be. The area just below the castle is called Terravecchia (still known also as the Arab quarter). You can see it in the only existing ancient print of the town, pasted on the hill under the castle: it was the original walled-in village where the agricultural workers crept wearily home to sleep after struggling with the land all day long; and some significant old street names survive – via Capre (goats) and via Mandrie (herds) for example, because both goats and cattle used to be herded back in the evenings to prevent them being rustled. This initial settlement went on to develop towards the southeast with the Borgo or Borgu quarter, the first buildings outside the walls. Then came the Circiara-Virdisca, which contains the remains of the Carmine Monastery with (until it fell down recently) its reddomed Arab tower, which was probably the mosque during the time the Arabs were around. This area also contained the first commercial piazza (now the Piazza Nocito, proudly named in the nineteenth century after a local lawyer and politician of some fame), where the market was held. Subsequent development crept up the hill to the east (it was mostly 'Spanish' and still shows some fine ogival arches), to the north towards the cemetery and the forest of Angimbè, and to the south a short distance into the valley that now leads to our hamlet. Inside the town, there are some pretty, steep alleys with the traditional surfacing of riverine pebbles framed in squares or diamonds of white marble, and there are many small courtyards leading off them that owe their sheltered existence to both the Arabs and the Spanish who had their time here. Despite the obvious outward signs of change, like satellite aerials and mobile phones, the spirit of the town now is not exactly modern. Change has come reluctantly, but at least Calatafimi's women are no longer avoided as witches, 'Calatafimare animalare' as they were widely known in the Province of Trapani.[2]

Recently, however, empty and dilapidated houses have been increasing in number, especially in the older parts of town: emigration has had much to do with it, even though remittances have been propping up the economy; but the major blow was the 1968 earthquake. As a result of it most of the inhabitants of the Borgo Vecchio quarter under the castle were moved to a newly built dormitory township called Sasi to the east, at the bottom of the second of the two hills, and pigeons flit in and out of the empty windows of their erstwhile houses, or just gaze blank-eyed from the windowsills. Doors stand ajar and you can wander gingerly in: I found one room frescoed with naive 'Caribbean' beach scenes and another piled up with coffins, for adults and children. Earthquake compensation has meant that the Municipality has become owners of much unwanted property. It could be argued, and it *was* vigorously, that Sasi New Town need not have been built at all, and the Borgo could have been restored. In the second half of the eighteenth century there was a bye-law in force which gave the municipal authorities the right to confiscate, without compensation, houses that were in a state of bad repair and assign them to other people with the means for repairing them, so that the town could show a good face. Times and systems have changed, but the Borgo definitely could have been restored rather than abandoned. It was just that there was a mountain of mouthwatering redevelopment money already earmarked and Sasi really had to be built – very slowly, very inefficiently and very late (the bath taps and, would you believe it, the tiles were ordered from the north of Italy). What is more, the buildings were, let's say, not of the highest quality, and no shops were envisaged in the initial plan: no chemist, no services at all. But it had to be, and, to make absolutely sure of it, the authorities had the Borgo area declared geologically unstable, an opinion incorporated subsequently and quite extraordinarily into a Presidential Decree (that can only be cancelled by another one). So Sasi went up and much of the Borgo will fall down.

Reading early local historians' descriptions of their town and their fellow townsmen is as intriguing as it is usually misleading. Naturally they tend to be apostles of local virtue and more concerned with what happened than how it happened, with what their prominent citizens did rather than why – which is perfectly reasonable and does not lessen interest in their work. Occasionally, though, the pressure to find new ways of embellishing their own backyard shatters the barriers between reality and wishful thinking. Our two leading ones, the notary Pellegrino and the priest Longo, are no exception: I'll talk to you about them in more detail soon enough. But, for the moment, let's ask: how did they, partisans that they were, look upon Calatafimi and its inhabitants?

Though they approach Calatafimi with different objectives, Pellegrino,[3] in the mid-eighteenth century, had the more traditional approach, setting down the doings of the notables for the enlightenment of future generations of citizens, even if he can stagger off this narrow, sober path. For instance: 'The inhabitants of Calatafimi are quick to talk, their tongues ever ready; in their speech they are vague, facetious, sententious and sharp-witted.' Some are sharp-witted, affable and honest; others are hot-blooded, offensive, arrogant and aggressive. Later on, he waxes rhapsodic about his fellow towns-people:

> one can describe Calatafimi as a superb Theatre in that it has had
> its children shining for Faith, smiling for Hope, burning for Charity,
> crowned with Roses, garlanded with Lilies, adorned with Violets and
> all Devout and embellished with every sweet-smelling Virtue.

Wow!

Longo,[4] on the other hand, at the beginning of the nineteenth century, whose avowed aim in his major published work was to prove the Trojan origins of Segesta, Calatafimi and the area surrounding, is more down to earth and bucolic in describing Calatafimi's situation in his time.

> Today's built-up area [in 1809] is on a medium-sized hill, which is
> surrounded by a crown of taller ones – which it seems Nature has
> so disposed as to moderate the fury of the winds and protect us from
> excessive cold. On going outside our City, the views are highly agree-
> able for the variety of the mountains, fields and woods and for the sea,
> which can be seen at a moderate distance. The air you breathe is fresh
> rather than cold, and is very pure, since there are no swamps nearby,
> or stagnant rivers which could infect it or make it damp. Visitors find
> it very salubrious and pleasant.[5] The springs of water, although they are
> scarce inside the city, are present just outside, and on all sides they are
> found to be limpid and fresh: among these the Anceli spring should be
> noted for the quantity of *Belzuarie* medicinal stones it delivers up.[6]

He goes on to describe the fertility of the land, the fruit, the vines (not too many at that period, but much more numerous now, you will be glad to hear), the justly famous *caciocavallo* cheese, the hunting (particularly partridges and rabbits: I suppose the wild boar were the King's prerogative); and he ends by mentioning that they had just discovered in a piece of land nearby called Sant'Agata a broad vein of 'alabaster marble, that is recognized by the experts as highly suitable for sculpture and work on the lathe.'

Sad as it may be, the Calatafimesi of today are neither embellished with every sweet-smelling virtue nor particularly hot-blooded or offensive, and the winds I have mentioned have brought little change, unless it be the disappearance of the partridge. They form a tight-knit agricultural community that deals pragmatically with each day as each day dawns. In the early morning, a surge of people moves out towards the fields (and even towards other occupations now, further afield); at midday the agricultural element sweeps back for a brief lunch. In the afternoon, until 4.30 or 5.00, the town sleeps, though the fields are being actively worked. Then the shops re-open as the returning tide brings the first cars and tractors back from the countryside, to be followed later on by the office workers. Those are the main movements. During the rest of the day the streets are only sporadically inhabited, and if there is walking it is confined to people with specific tasks. Otherwise, the town is characterized by clumps of people standing around and talking occasionally. Mostly they are men and mostly they are outside bars, not waiting for a drink (if they occasionally nip in it is just for a quick coffee), but because bars are appropriate places for meeting and being met. It is not a sign of laziness because the agricultural calendar has many days when nothing can be usefully done, and sometimes the weather impedes activity in the fields anyway. Whatever their status, these men form such clumps, stand, smoke and talk a bit, always at the same place, so that you can always find whom you're looking for. There are also clumps of women, although they are far fewer and disintegrate fairly rapidly: their snatches of talk punctuate outings for shopping; otherwise the women are usually at home. Mealtimes, of course, dissolve all these gatherings, quietly and at the appointed time.

The clumps of people can be a bit disconcerting for an outsider, as all eyes will be directed at him and conversation tends to fade away. But there are other less inquisitive variations on public socializing: the benches scattered around the centre of the town, for example, all seat their regulars. These seated people stay together longer and, though still male, are usually older. Quite a number sit on the benches donated by the Australian emigrants in the small garden with its statue of Padre Pio (always surrounded by fresh flowers); others in the garden near the Town Hall, or in the piazza in front of the bank. Just round the corner in the via Garibaldi there is a fairly large congregation of elderly men who meet, not sitting outside on benches, but inside at the cobbler's shop, and they talk about many things while he hammers and sews – he used to play with my father-in-law when they were children. This sort of gathering is a rung up the ladder that leads from the clump to the club.

There are three of these establishments near the cobbler's. The smallest is the Circolo Berlinguer, named after the much loved or much hated late leader of the Italian Communist party: it is hardly bigger than the cobbler's shop and consists of one minute window-less room giving straight onto the road, the inside plastered with political posters, a few chairs round the wall, and nothing else. There are seldom many people there, but it looks very cosy from the normally shaded road. Miraculously, at around 11.00 in the morn-ing, every corner of the little room is flooded with sunlight, trans-forming it for a couple of minutes into a glorious vision of the triumphant proletarian future. Across the road is the Circolo dei Lavoratori, but it does not seem to be filled with 'workers' although you can't really tell because the windows have curtains. There are usually a few chairs outside, but the main business takes place in-side. In the via Garibaldi there is the Circolo 15 Maggio, named after the day on which the Hero's battle took place: it was previously the misnamed Circolo dei Nobili and is now also known colloquially as the Circolo dei Ricchi, though it doesn't look wealthy at all. As the name implies, it used to be the meeting ground for the rich, a place where in not so far-off times rumour has it that fortunes were squandered at the card table with Dostoevskyan intensity. The door is usually left democratically ajar and inside there is a table on which newspapers are laid out. Nothing seems to take place other than newspaper reading and some desultory chat, but apparently cards are still played.

I discovered the other day, from reading an article by an eminent English philosopher in – of all things – the Italian equivalent of the *Financial Times*, that they still play Sicilian tarot games there, using a Piedmontese pack but translating the values and figures of the cards into the Sicilian equivalents, so that the card called La Papessa (the lady Pope) becomes I Piciotti (the young lads), and so on.[7] I even un-earthed the reason for it, which is this. In the early 1860s, after the unification of Italy in the wake of Garibaldi's generous exploits, a Piedmontese Pretore (a sort of local governing magistrate) was sent to Calatafimi by the newly installed Government. No doubt he, as a northerner speaking Italian with a Turin accent, felt something of a fish out of water in the deep, alien dialect-speaking South, but he turned up in Calatafimi with his pack of Piedmontese tarot cards and the local notables rallied round – whether to help him out or to curry favour I leave to your imagination, but I suspect the former. The fact is they played cards together and the use of the tarot cards survived the Pretore's departure. In time, however, the play underwent a metamorphosis and from strict tarot it turned into a mixture of two local games, *briscola* and *tre sette*, which is still played. It sounds exotic, but from the street outside you wouldn't know any better because nothing untoward seems to happen there, merely the reading of newspapers and desultory conversation, as I have observed.

In contrast, the young do not have such a choice of meeting places. In the summer they congregate at the Chiosco, a wooden pavilion in the small garden near the Town Hall, where they drink a bit, talk and get bored, so they say. In other seasons, they either wriggle to music in a tiny 'Pub' or squeeze into a pizzeria not far off. In all seasons they have the usual problem of reconciling citizens older than themselves to the volume of their music, but fewer and fewer of them are having to face that challenge as wilder shores beckon. The women of Calatafimi have even less choice: they must meet while they are out shopping or during visits indoors, visits which usually take place around 7.30 or 8.00 in the evening, as dinner is eaten late here.

Economic activity in the area is predominantly agricultural, as I have said, with the associated administrative, legal and commercial services. Many of the houses, even some of the recently built ones, still have facilities for storing farming tools and machinery overnight in high-ceilinged ground-floor storehouses with huge doors opening onto the street. Commerce, apart from foodshops and general stores which have all those little practical things you can't find in cities, reflects this economic bias, even if leisure shops are making timid inroads in the form of television and fridges, gifts and furniture. Shopping is almost always carried out on a first-name basis. There are no music shops, but clothes are sold and there is even a mobile telephone centre – the mobile phone is indispensable for country-based work. Agriculture involves tax-paying, boundary disputes and often litigation, so that the middle class have their share of lawyers and accountants, together with the doctors, the chemists and the clergy, who look after bodies and souls. Sunday is still spent in one's best clothes in clumps gossiping in the piazza or at the club; but more and more of the young are going to university now and doing nothing much in the piazza is becoming less attractive as a pastime. If they are successful in their studies, they will almost certainly have to leave Calatafimi because there is no work for them here. Society has changed and people are certainly better off – but at the moment there is no discernible future for the young. And agriculture, which the young no longer seek, is becoming ever more mechanized.

Although there is one enterprising citizen who imports furniture and bric-à-brac in containers all the way from the Ukraine, it would be wrong to see this as any sort of a trend towards commercial diversification: his dealings are very much against the current and, although I have been able to buy second-hand Ukrainian smock shirts for myself and even a gold-painted bust of Stalin for an eccentric Roman friend, he sells little in the town and relies on dealers from Palermo to keep his business turning over. The only 'industry' here is a very small one and, not surprisingly, agriculturally based: the Industria Siciliana Budella makes animal-based intestinal casings for the salame and sausage industry. Much of their limited production is taken up by a company called Fiorucci, one of the largest Italian operators in this sector, which exports to food shops all over the world. The next time you buy a Fiorucci salami in Harrods or Sainsbury's, do please spare a thought for Calatafimi, as the skin you peel off it may have belonged to an animal from around here.

While the architecture is not as attractive as in some other small towns in the area, as I've pointed out (they *will* plaster all the outside walls, hiding the stone), Calatafimi is a pleasant working town where tractors are driven back home in the evening and daytime traffic (apart from the working lorries) is usually in the hands of slow elderly drivers. A visitor not in the know will wonder why almost all the cars have Tuscan number-plates. This is because a local entrepreneur, perhaps with relatives in Tuscany, discovered that second-hand cars were to be had cheaper there, so he buys them up and brings them back, filling the narrow roads with automobiles from Florence, Pisa, Pistoia, Siena and so on. In the rare event of an accident, however, the torrents of abuse are in the dense Trapanese dialect, not in the language of Dante, and you wouldn't understand a word of it. Dialect is naturally in daily use, without inhibitions among the less educated or inverted snobbery in the 'establishment'.

If emigration has done something to sustain the economy with remittances, it has also pushed up the average age of the townspeople, and it is a lengthy business getting anything done at the post office on pension days – so much so that payments have had to be staggered by the use of the alphabet for surnames. A lot of letters come and go from Germany, Brooklyn and Australia to sons and daughters, and conversation in the queues often turns to those countries and correspondents, because everybody, of course, knows everybody else and their children. General friendliness is the order of the day, with forms being kindly filled out for the aged or the uninitiated when necessary. As I was passing by the other day, a clerk who was getting back after a coffee at the bar opposite, found it natural to cross the street and inform me that that there were letters waiting for me in my pigeon-hole, and on another occasion I was invited behind the public counter to look at some leaflets for a postal-service savings-bond scheme, though the conversation quickly shifted to the clerk's reminiscences about grape harvesting on my father-in-law's land forty years previously, which turned out to be enjoyable. There are, of course, drawbacks to this friendly approach: the sending of a large parcel of oranges to a son living in the cold north of Europe, by a mother who needs help filling up the requisite forms, can take time and try your patience if you are behind her in the queue. But it is widespread and *simpatico*. Recently a book being sent to me by hand from a neighbouring town was politely delivered to me in a butcher's shop by a man who did not know me: he had been on his way to leave it at the library, but an acquaintance of his had said he thought he had seen me and they tracked me down. The butcher now accepts books for me from the same source quite regularly.

Minor changes are filtering in. For instance there is a new version of 'basket-from-the-window' shopping: instead of hauling up from below what you have bargained for, in the new version a rubbish-filled plastic bag is let down and left dangling like a large bulging fruit until it is plucked away by the *servizio ecologico* van, leaving the line with its double-clawed hook swaying in the breeze until more rubbish has been accumulated and the process is repeated. If, however, the bag is lowered too far, it is sometimes the target of leaping, hungry dogs. Shopping is still done with the basket and the line, but mostly housewives do come out for provisions, specially for the once-a-week outdoor market which sells just about everything, but also on other days, as bread, at least, must be got in fresh daily. At certain given points, various types of local produce are sold directly by the growers from the back of their vans, which attracts groups of women; but shopping is mostly conducted quietly in the few shops scattered around the town. In establishments other than food-shops, and in the few offices that exist, nothing is rushed and attempts to get things done on time are doomed – 'it will be ready on Tuesday afternoon' is merely an indication. It will be ready, but all in good time and you will only get frustrated if you try to force the issue. Delivery of repairs, documents, orders or other services lies firmly in the hands of destiny. Or of agriculture: I have had to wait (more than happily) for the olive harvest to end before getting some expertly mended books back from a school-teacher who still practises book-binding. Even kitchen problems can affect opening times: I was once kept waiting a quarter of an hour for the Thermal Baths to open because the lady custodian had just plunged her dogs' *pastasciuta* into boiling water and could hardly have left it untended.

Some more than minor changes have occurred: witness the three railway-stations in the vicinity. The Calatafimi station proper, that was busy in the nineteenth and early twentieth century bringing visitors to Segesta, has had to deal with the fact that today's temple visitors wing in and out by coach (motor) and the locals now own cars. The decision was taken to eliminate station personnel completely and, although the trains do stop for the odd passenger, they must remember to buy their ticket at the travel agent in the town if they want to avoid a fine, or jump off the train at the next station where there is a ticket office and buy one quickly before it moves off again. Most of the very sparse local traffic now consists of undergraduates going to and from university in Palermo or Trapani. But that is not the extent of the station's transformation: its sidings have for years been crowded with goods-vans full of dangerous illegal asbestos – it is permanently dumped there because, I suppose, nobody has known what to do with it since it became illegal; and there it stays, conveniently forgotten. Gone are the days of station monkeys and red-capped stationmasters blowing their whistles importantly.[8] Two other stations in the area also demonstrate how railway fashions change: the buildings at the Segesta station are now occupied by a *trattoria* (restaurant) which feeds those tourists who happen to visit around lunchtime, and there is even a modest museum. Further up the track, at Bruca, the station hosts a full-blown, and apparently quite good, restaurant. The trains trundle past occasionally with almost no passengers on board.

There is some sort of precedent for these station changes, at least from the eating point of view. Louis Golding in his 1925 book, *Sicilian Noon*, describes arriving at Calatafimi station and being

offered wine, and indeed eggs, in the station-master's dining-room/
bedroom/chicken-coop. The wine was being replenished when they
observed an ancient Scottish lady ('a small black bonnet on her head
and an umbrella in her armpit') who, shouting in French with a
heavy Selkirk accent, was humbling a giant Sicilian carter, with only
his dialect to defend himself. It was over the cost of a ride to and
from Segesta, which had lost the carter a whole day's essential work.
During her outburst she even turned on Golding, who must have
looked Sicilian, and informed him 'in her terse Selkirk French that
we Sicilians were a race of thieves and pigs and a girl was not to be
trusted amongst us, our morals being as lax as our commercial hon-
esty.' Apparently, on her early morning arrival at the station she had
in French (all foreigners spoke French, of course) commandeered the
poor carter, who happened to be passing with a load of charcoal for
delivery to the neighbouring town of Alcamo, with the imperious
word 'trois' which to her obviously meant three liras and to him
equally obviously three dollars (all foreigners pay in dollars, of
course). Having kept him hours while she trudged dutifully around
Segesta and made him bring her back to the station, she offered him
his three liras and, in retaliation for his protestations, she proceeded
to deduct 30 centesimi 'to punish him for his contumacy'. The last
Golding saw of her was in the departing train – as she was settling
down, the knob of her umbrella was visible through the window.

Since Segesta has been mentioned, it's time I told you something
about Calatafimi's monuments. Place firmly in your mind a stout
wedge of distinction between the recent ones and those of an earlier
date, because Calatafimi has of late been the recipient of generous
amounts of public money which have been used to 'beautify' the
town. This is due to the energy, and indeed the ability, of the Mayor,
who is also a prominent Sicilian regional politician and probably
knows better than most how to manage the public pocket in favour
of local projects. So that we have quite a number of recently installed
monuments that are worthy of consideration.

My favourite is an extremely large one, which I pass every day, on
the *belvedere* of the Piano Perollo, a piazza that is being expensively
propped up because of its tendency to slip down into the valley,
which it did dramatically in a disastrous storm in 1933 (if you are in
the slightest bit interested). This monument measures about ten
metres wide by five high: on the left there is a tree flanked by two
prancing quadrupeds, lions or horses perhaps, but what fascinates is

the text. With difficulty, because it is uncoloured bas-relief on white marble, it can be read:

By the Law of the Region
Of Sicily n° 18 of 1st September 1998
And the Deliberation of the Municipal Council
N° 48 of 20th September 1999
Calatafimi
Symbol of the Glorious
Tradition
Of the Unity of Italy
Is Wedded to the History
Pluri-millenary of
Segesta
30/12/2000

It reads very much like the minutes of a Municipal Council meeting and commemorates the change of the town's name from Calatafimi to Calatafimi-Segesta, an event which caused no momentous change other than the construction of this striking monument. You would love it.

About five metres away on a plinth of white marble near the work-shop of Mario, who repairs the electrical works of cars, there is a three-dimensional marble sculpture of great interest. In the past you and I have had sometimes acrimonious discussions on what consti-tutes a work of art, but if we can forget all that and for the moment settle for a definition that requires a work of art to arouse active interest and cause people to think, then this monument has to be recognized as a genuine masterpiece. It has overwhelmingly suc-ceeded in arousing the curiosity of the whole town, and it is a source of much satisfaction to me to listen to their awed attempts at under-standing it. Even Berenson, who, sad to say, visited Segesta in 1908, long before its installation, would surely have embraced it as 'life-enhancing' for the invigorating debates it gives rise to.

A little further away, in the square with the bank and the post office, there is an obelisk. It has always seemed to me that most public obelisks in the western world are the result of colonial theft, but I am not aware of any Egyptian conquests having been carried out by the good townspeople of Calatafimi. However, we do have this large, white-marble, layered obelisk, its plinth fringed with beau-tiful marble balls. It isn't bad: it merely seems out of place. I must add a codicil, though. The other day, I was looking into a tiny de-consecrated church in the main street. It was dark inside, and after I had shaded my eyes to see what was in there, my gaze was met by two enormous menacing Egyptian sphinxes. When I had recovered from my surprise, the librarian, who happened to be passing, ex-plained to me that these and various other ones had been created in plaster by a school companion of his for a float (I presume the 'Flight from Egypt') that was used in the town's major procession, which I'll describe for you later on.

Per Carità, I am not complaining! Calatafimi is a great deal more interesting as a result of such energetic mayoral patronage.

A disturbing side to this laudatory eruption of administrative vitality is (or, hopefully, was) the attempt to create a 'Mystical Park', a sort of poor-man's Mount Rushmore with gigantic statues of the Pope, Mother Teresa of Calcutta and Padre Pio, a much revered, re-cently sanctified monk, right opposite Segesta's archaeological park. The site was chosen for its visibility and, if the plan were to go ahead, the rocky cliffs just before Monte Barbaro that face the lovely, re-cently revealed Mango sanctuary, would flash its mystical menagerie in Las Vegas neon to anybody using the road that connects Trapani to Palermo, and, without a shadow of doubt, cause fatal car crashes. With some effort, I can see that perhaps some of the basic objectives (presumably helping the local economy with a road, hotels, parking places and various bridges across the river Kaggera, and stamping Calatafimi indelibly on the minds of passing motorists) might be arguable, but the project is in fact preposterous. While there is no denying the blind enthusiasm these projects beget, especially when financial mysteries seem to be involved, the myopia in this case is acute – even if the nose for money is in excellent order. If it ever got through, it would terminally damage a very beautiful part of the world and produce yet another Cathedral in the Desert, because I have to believe that people would have the innate good taste to avoid the place at all costs. For the moment we are saved. But you can never be sure.[9]

Recently local elections were held, in which the issues this project stirred up were bitterly fought over. The incumbent Mayor won the battle and was quick to announce that the project would go ahead at all costs: its opponents, he declared, were of three kinds – those acting in bad faith, those acting in good faith but manipulated by the former, and imbeciles.[10] For a brief period, the press became involved fairly enthusiastically, television debated the question loudly, foreign concern was expressed, and accusations buzzed dangerously low in every direction like panic-stricken wasps. Unfortunately the clear-cut issue was soon muddied by humdrum considerations and the electioneering degenerated into a fight of a more personal and partisan nature. The Mayor's opponent in the elections had committed the cardinal sin for these parts of leaving his wife, which did not endear him to the conservatives. Moreover, an energetic citizen of some local note had done little to help his campaign by lambasting the Church's support for the incumbent pro-Mystical Park Mayor. For this, the noteworthy citizen complained he was made the object of a quite un-clerical reaction, although he immediately complained in writing to the President of Italy declaring that the candidate Mayor was illegal because he was (a) wearing the tricolour sash of office when not in office and (b) being accompanied for electoral purposes by the clergy of a religion that is, constitutionally no longer the state religion of Italy. All delightfully reminiscent of Don Camillo and the Communist Threat, but our Don Peppone did not win the election. Even if it appears that the reinstated First Citizen may be having second thoughts there is still talk of face-saving roads and parking spaces (for the Segesta tourist traffic), and the original idea has not actually been abandoned as yet, despite temporary desistance orders. The situation is entirely fluid and, since I know these sorts of things interest you, I shall keep you informed.

A week after those election results, I took part in a demonstration against the proposed 'Mystical Park'. I do not know how many people attended, perhaps two hundred, perhaps a thousand (how do you assess a crowd except by counting it?). They were enthusiastic and, although less colourful, looked rather like the peasant armies in Bertolucci's film *Novecento*, marching hopefully towards some new Future. They arrived at Segesta from afar, signed the book and were presented with the problem of what to do next. The plan was to follow the road outside the archaeological park up to the proposed site opposite the sanctuary of Mango, where buses had been laid on to bring them back to their cars parked near the temple. I managed to get myself into the official party of fifteen people, who were allowed to walk to the sanctuary on the internal road (to prove that a road existed, and that it was useless constructing another one). There were several elderly ladies, who were incomparably stronger walkers than the men, and an important individual, who would go on talking about environmentalism. During one conversation, I made the mistake of suggesting to him that certain modern artefacts, like the motorway in the valley below, which had been built for many kilometres on stilts just like a Roman aqueduct, was an example of acceptable progress. It was not. Not at all. It should at least have been made out of natural local rock. He did, however, eventually accept that this would hardly have been possible without slave labour, and that the modern world actually did need swift transport, although he then retreated to the position that, if, for socio-political reasons, there was the unfortunate need for a concrete motorway, it should at least have had plants down the middle to make it blend into the environment. I remarked that you could not easily put oleanders in the middle of a concrete motorway suspended thirty metres above the ground, in an almost tropical climate, and even if you could, it was difficult to understand how floral centrepieces would blend it into the dramatic, harsh environment – and remembered that it is always interesting and generally instructive to talk to enthusiasts, but useless to argue with them. You will understand that he was a good man.

It was a beautiful, hot, sweet-smelling walk below the sheer cliffs of Monte Barbaro with its Mediterranean scrub vegetation, past a large semi-walled-in cave where till quite recently people reminiscent of Cyclops had lived with their sheep, to arrive next at the truly magnificent sanctuary of Mango,[11] which I had vaguely thought was Christian but was in fact the massive ruin of a Greek place of worship – that was just pushing its brows above the ground. Superbly simple: overlooked by ancient grey-white slabs of rock with prickly pears and fig trees thrusting out between them; patches of arable land with tufts of reeds and the smell of sheep droppings which was the only hint that live beings might have been around. A real mystical park, if you like. Bits of fluted columns, vast slumbering stones. Just opposite, a towering cliff of ancient whitish rock, clung to by prickly pear, fig, capers and scented bushes and swept past by doves and birds of prey. That is where the concrete or plastic statues of Pope Paul, Mother Teresa and Padre Pio may still be erected. The hawks were mewing.

But I now have to move you back into town for a consideration of its older monuments, which are decidedly more dignified and humbly attractive than their recent rivals. I shall only expose you to a few of them, so as not to overtire you. They tend to be straightforward local thoughts put onto canvas or into stone by piece-work artisans without names. But some I shall leave till later, like the bas-relief of the Madonna di Giubino, the town's patron saint, whose cult deserves more attention.

Many were known to have existed but are no more: they have vanished, been covered over or digested by time, as was the case with the first one I tried to identify. In a fairly recent local historian and pharmacist's publication (1936: his name was Mazzara and his family farm the valley below us) there is a description of the grand portal of the Palazzo Alvarez de Toledo as being 'perhaps the best work in the Renaissance style that Calatafimi has'. The haughty ring of the Spanish name (it was some cadet offshoot of the ducal Alba family who, among other things, were and are the Counts of Modica and Barons of Calatafimi) and Mazzara's description of the work as an eighteenth-century copy of a sixteenth-century original was inviting. So I found the street and...and there was nothing. I asked the greengrocer and he confirmed that the buildings at the beginning of the street, now anonymously plastered, were where a Spanish count used to live, and he pointed out where the stables had been; but he could remember nothing of the noble gate. And that seemed to be that. But I did go back later with somebody who knew a little more, and the remnants of the palazzo could just be discerned, wedged between the two streets that meet at the early seventeenth-century church of San Isidoro Agricola, with the high relief on its facade of St Labrador and oxen ploughing and finding water. What is left of the outside of the palazzo is difficult to make out, as it has been divided up into private houses, and although there is not much to be seen of the famous gate, there are still traces of arches and fine doorways into the street. My friend told me that, inside the houses, there are still some of the columns and arches that graced the original building. There used to be a private door from the palazzo into the church, which the Alvarez de Toledo considered their family chapel. But the palazzo...has been digested.

Not everything has been appropriated and put to other uses, however: the first sight on approaching Calatafimi is the castle, in Arabic the qal'at. I know you like castles, and so here we are faced with a now silent shell of a castle watched over by hawks. The Normans built the present fortress 'Normanly' as the architecture shows, but Norman King Roger's Arab geographer[12] said it had been built over a much earlier building. It was obviously a strategic holding post. But now its only crenellations defend the local water works, as I have already told you. I keep toiling up the hill to visit it and I can report that it is well maintained; but I have never encountered anybody else up there, with the exception of the people who look after Calatafimi's water supply, and, once, two German tourists whom I surprised there. For some centuries after its military usefulness had faded away, the castle became a prison and it has a number of small windowless rooms which were presumably the cells; but with the melting down of the cannon (in 1848, for revolutionary purposes[13]), the abandonment of the various grottoes beneath it that had been used for storing grain and even illicit card games, and the grassing over of the odd Arab tomb, it has reverted to being a simple visual symbol of what must have been Calatafimi's past standing. It has, as I have mentioned, been well maintained of late and the three towers have been fortified with sustaining mortar. It is always a pleasure to see monuments that are well looked after, which suggests people care sometimes and occasionally spend money altruistically. If you take the trouble to climb up and inspect the castle, however, you will soon see that not everything has been made good. You will realize with a Gothic shudder that if you go to the far side of the ruin, you could very easily tumble, or indeed be pushed, into the gorge below – because there are absolutely no safety rails.

Just down from the castle in the old Terravecchia quarter, which had been walled in the eleventh century, I recently paid a visit to what was until the 1960s the old town hospital. It involved asking a lot of people for permission because it is still classified as a charity, and the key had to be got. The building is near to collapse; the floors are covered in pigeon excrement; there are rusting hospital beds, medical instruments, an operating theatre and a dental chair; and frantic pigeons try to get out, full-speed at head level. I was with a friend who suffered from an atavistic fear of birds ('you know women are terrified of rats, but I have birds'), which caused some problems. The reason for our visit was that a mutual friend had, some time previously, looked at the hospital chapel and surmised that there was something behind the plastering. He was right. He began chipping off the plaster and, lo and behold, a perfect early Norman gatehouse began to emerge. The vaulted ceiling was criss-crossed diagonally with sandstone ribs with simple decorations at their four ends. The gate out into the town was a simple Norman arch, but for you to enter the tiny gatehouse from the outside there was a much larger arch, to the right and left of which there were sentry cubicles with archery slits pointing in. Longo (*Ragionamenti*, appendix VII, page 345) describes a chapel 'in our existing hospital' which had originally been the site of the church of Santa Maria dei Miracoli – itself in the past the seat of a noble confraternity, the Bianchi. He goes on to quote from a manuscript written in 1615 by a certain P. Gaetani which deals with the old church: 'It was an ancient gate of Terravecchia (the name given to that part of town) in the form of towers (*turrigghiuni*) with two doors, within which there was a painting of the glorious Virgin Mary with her Son in her arms.' There is no painting there now, but the two sites are one and the same, and the tower can be seen in an old print of the town. This was the Porta Palermo (the Palermo Gate). Traces of the arch of the inner gate out to the town are still visible on the outside of the hospital wall and, on the road opposite, you can discern the arches of a stairway that led up to the castle and the Matrice church. An official attempt was made to demolish the hospital, which was blocked by a protest from the man who uncovered the gatehouse. Strangely enough, soon afterwards accusations of illicit excavation were to be heard. Few people know the gate exists and it may fall down, as the rest of the hospital is about to.

It was unexpected, this almost-discovery, but there is apparently (although I did not see it) yet another gate a little to the west, almost under the church of the SS Crocifisso, called the Porta Trapani and also visible in the same print. The authorities have fairly recently built a new road flanking the Crocifisso church and it covered what few traces were left of this gate and almost all the houses by it. One of the owners of these houses, while doing necessary plumbing work in his lavatory one day, saw some odd masonry and asked for advice from the man who had unearthed the Porta Palermo – who was able to inform the surprised owner that it was the Porta Trapani. Nothing deterred, he proceeded to re-excavate it, and the Porta now adorns his lavatory. Somewhat overwhelming, I should have thought.

Next to the hospital is the ex-convent of San Francesco: after its time as a convent, it was used as a prison for a while before being taken over as a school for boys; but even that phase did not last long and Calatafimi's local government is currently restoring it as a School for Dance and Drama – for reasons beyond the power of my paltry imagination to decipher. By chance, as it is almost always locked up, I managed to get into the church the other day: the building was much older in origin than the convent and its apse is pure Norman-Arab. It looks as though it was uncovered yesterday – which, it was.

Further down the hill, in today's via Colombo, used to be the Baronial House of the Counts of Modica[14] that was built around the end of the fifteenth century, for storage and accommodation for the Counts: they were still occasionally making an appearance, if rarely, to assess their tithes. The house was enormous. There is a plan of it in the Archivio di Stato in Palermo, after it had been restructured for King Ferdinand's hunting trip in November 1806, showing about forty rooms on the first floor. The whole of the ground floor was given over to the storage of all the grain and agricultural produce that they had procured from feudal taxes, while the first floor was for human habitation. It had been taken over by the crown after the death of Maria del Philar de Silva in 1802; and Ferdinand's hunting trip in 1806 was clearly a success because he used it again, for the same purpose, in 1808 and 1811. After the unification of Italy, the palazzo was sold off by the state to private individuals and divided up into separate establishments. From the street little of it is visible now: practically the only thing you can see is a massive corner-stone opposite the church of San Francesco, and there are also the large rooms and hints of solid masonry I have seen in the private houses that have surreptitiously swallowed and digested it – just like the palazzo Alvarez de Toledo. You may be relieved to hear that I was about to slip into *sic transit gloria mundi* gear, but I stopped myself in time.

Behind that street you come to what is left of the church and monastery of the Carmine – the latter built perhaps in 1430, though the church is much older: Pellegrino in the eighteenth century says he saw a roof-beam with the date of 1114. It was constructed around the mosque I have told you about, but over the centuries it has been added to, subtracted from and propped up at intervals. According to Pellegrino, it was particularly beautiful and was the church of the local rich: hence the presence of sarcophagi containing their bodies and chapels built with their donations. It had Caterina's Mollica family arms in a chapel; and in his will dated 13th February 1617 Vincenzo Mollica was described as 'Padrone della Capella dell' Udienza, oggi capellone dentro la nuova chiesa' (i.e. 'Master of the Udienza Chapel, now called the big chapel in the new church': nobody has ever seen it or ever will, but I get all this from Pellegrino on pages 93 and 94). The church has had a chequered life. Already by

1574 it was on the verge of ruin; in 1641 it was reported to have been 'long ago demolished'; it was restored, but in 1764 the roof fell through and nothing was done about it. In 1785, on the abolition of the monasteries, the convent was used by the Counts of Modica to store the grain they collected from their illegal feudal grain-tax. Then the state, which confiscated it after the person who was considered to be the last legitimate Modica heir had died, sold it to private individuals, many of whom slipped into debt. After which the banks moved in.

When Mazzara[15] described the Carmine, it was a collection of shops, storehouses, stables and garages. It is now mostly boarded or cemented up. I went with a friend to see the underground grain stores, which had still been open until the other day, but we discovered they had been sealed with fresh cement. A carpenter's shop had a bit of the ruin and next to his room stands the main entrance to the church with its lateral pillars though no pediment. The old stone gutters are still there, sticking out. There is almost nothing left of the church itself, which has been gutted and divided into three spacious garages. I saw inside the middle one but found no ecclesiastical remains. The garage furthest from the main door is sealed, as there are inheritance squabbles. Unfortunately that is the one that leads through to the garden and the *cuba*, or red-domed Arab tower, which had recently, after endless warnings, finally collapsed, so that I did not manage to see it close to.

Flanking what had been the church, at the end furthest from the main door, there is what is left of the cloisters with two sets of eight columns and capitals on either side: they are roofed and bricked in now but, according to my friend, the left-hand aisle originally opened onto the garden and *cuba*. This walled-in cloister is empty except for high-flying pigeons, and you can see the sky through the odd hole in the walls. As you go in on the left, there is a small door leading today to a lavatory for people involved in commercial activities in the ruins, but in the past down to a crypt complete with sarcophagi, which I suppose must still be there. From a side door outside in the street there is a staircase that leads up to a floor, built over part of the cloisters, which housed the offices of the local bank, the Cassa Comunale di Credito Agrario. It incorporated the Banca Agricola Saccaro,[16] and was complete with railed-in guichets for three tellers, but is now completely abandoned to pigeon droppings. Outside, on the side wall of the original church, the central one of the three garages, which I was able to enter, has a pedimented renaissance door complete with bas-relief columns that flanked a central winding metal shutter, on which is painted the equivalent of 'Garage – Do Not Obstruct'. As there is a sort of piazza in front of it, this entrance makes an ideal goal for children exercising their talents at soccer, and a particularly satisfying one for them, too, because the metal shutters register the shooting of a goal very audibly – somebody, I cannot remember who, suggested this was the reason why the whole mediaeval complex was falling down.

Then there is the Chiesa Matrice, the Mother Church or Cathedral, high up near the castle. The original church was probably coeval with the Norman castle, but, because it had become too small for the growing population, enlargement and modification began in the sixteenth century, and subsequent works have left little of its original architecture, except for a barely visible window on the north wall. It has some nice things in it, such as a large marble altarpiece, by Bartolomeo Berrettaro, 1512, with the Madonna and Child and Saints in polychrome and gilded white marble relief, and the apostles underneath; a fifteenth-century wooden statue of St Agatha and an early-sixteenth-century marble cone, 4.65 metres high, sculpted by two craftsmen from Carrara in Tuscany. It has a nave and two transepts 36 metres long which are divided by eight monolithic Trapanese marble columns. In the right transept lies the sarcophagus of Giuliano Truglio, who died in 1611 after leaving money to restore the church, bolstering the finances of Calatafimi's hospital and a host of other charitable deeds. His statue has him in a beautiful white marble Elizabethan-type ruff, with a black and white skull and cross-bones underneath. In the left transept is a red and white marble font from 1602 and a monument to Francesco Vivona who died in 1936. Vivona was one of the most important twentieth-century Italian Latinists: he was Professor of Latin at Rome University and translated the *Aeneid* into modern Italian. He is merely one, conspicuous, example of the enormous amount of erudition that is so often to be found in small cities in the south of Italy.[17]

I have the records of an organ restoration that took place in the church in 1888, with a detailed breakdown of all the costs, making a total of 5,800 lire, which seems quite a hefty sum. It may have been the organ for the playing of which Giulio Mollica sent in a bill in 1882 – Christmas and Easter, 42.27 lire; festivals and funerals 7.73 lire; which makes a nice round 50 lire; plus a further charge of

8.50 lire for the *alza mantice* or bellows-boy, whom I suppose Giulio provided for out of his own pocket. The 1888 restoration was also accompanied by a technical assessment of the instrument signed by a certain Paolo Terranova of the city of Trapani. The instrument was 'well constructed, solid, strong and "da maestro"', which justified his short assessment of one page. The instrument has a 'magnificent clarinet, difficult to find in other leading instruments; the imitation is extremely beautiful with surprisingly natural effects...not very effective, however, in the intonation of string instruments. The bell tones also leave something to be desired: they are all discordant and not in keeping with the sounds they should be transmitting...' He goes on to say that 'I deplore it that the organ is situated in such a narrow space compared with the size of the church' when it would be so easy to find a better position; and Judge Alessandro, who agreed with him, had undertaken to find a better position. He ends up by recommending that, 'since almost all organists are ignorant concerning musical art' (presumably they were knowledgeable about engineering or mechanics), a copy of the repairs done and of his assessment should be transmitted to the makers of the organ 'so that the organ should not deteriorate in the short term...among other things due to the frequent changes carried out by the organists themselves.' So there! Incidentally, you might be interested to know that these manuscripts came to me from the son of the owners of one of the local supermarkets.

I went up to check a couple of points in the Chiesa Matrice the other day, a Friday morning. It is almost impossible to visit churches in Calatafimi because they are nearly always closed (although I am sure that is not peculiar to this town), so I was delighted to see the door open. As I came near I saw that soapy water was flowing out of it: I was met at the threshold by a lady with a mop and the following conversation took place:

'Oh, I'm sorry. You're cleaning.'
'Yes.'
'Can I come in?'
'No.'
'Why?'
'Because the day after tomorrow is the festa of San Giuseppe and I'm cleaning the church.'
'And I can't come in?'
'No.'

'That sounds rather un-Christian.'
'No.'

And that was that. Had it been Rome I think I should have insisted on seeing the Bishop or some such idiocy, but not here. She was absolutely sure of the necessity of preparing the church for San Giuseppe, and who am I to say she was not right? I only wonder whether the church was totally closed for the rest of Friday and the whole of Saturday. I should in my city way have checked.

I have already described the monument to Garibaldi's victory, and no doubt it will stick its obelisk through other pages, so I shall be brief. It is very useful as a point of reference. Driving back home at night, its floodlit presence reassures you that home is just round the corner, and it helps guide people visiting us for the first time. You might even use it one day. It was built as a worthy resting place for the bones of the soldiers that fell at the battle, both Patriots and Bourbons, which had been housed in a rather more spartan way beforehand. It was erected in 1892, a mere thirty-two years after the citizens of Calatafimi, organized by the wealthy banker Saccaro, had started collecting funds for it. Even then it was not absolutely finished, as the obelisk was in wood at first. The design is by Basile, as I have said, a famous Sicilian architect whose fame travelled beyond the island's shores. It is said by many that he made two identical monuments to this design, but I do not know where the other is, or if it is identical, or just similar, or even if it exists at all. Inside and under the thirty-metres-high column there were the two glass-covered reliquaries in which you used to be able to see the bones, but they have been closed in now. No distinction was made between Patriot and Bourbon bones, and Garibaldi himself always said the Bourbons fought well.

Since the subject of bones has come up, I must mention a recent incident involving them, though it concerns the remains of an ancient monument, the Capuchin Monastery founded in 1581 by Salvo Amuruso, which had been taken over, in the second half of the nineteenth century after disestablishment, by the banker Saccaro and transformed into a home for the poor – which I shall tell you about fully in another context. Some of the original adjuncts to the monastery had been allowed to run to ruin, including a burial ground, and towards the late 1950s it was decided that these areas should be cleared up and made use of for public recreational spaces.

A friend of mine with an enquiring turn of mind was in elementary school at the time and receiving his first lessons in human anatomy from a benign middle-aged schoolmistress. Since skulls and tibias were being explained in his textbook, he decided to bring along some similar pieces that he had picked up from the land that the bulldozers were in the process of levelling in preparation for public flowerbeds, thinking that they might prove useful in his lessons. Sadly, this commendable initiative backfired: his benign schoolmistress became severely hysterical and the Carabinieri had to be called in for an investigation. If nothing else this incident shows how close history lies to the surface in Calatafimi, and with what ease it can be disturbed or erased.

Another minor 'disappearance' occurred about a week ago when evidence of a more recent war finally surrendered in via Guido Sylva no. 6, a side street that flanks the municipal building. Until then I had seen, in black on a white enamelled plaque that was chipped and somewhat the worse for wear, this comforting message:

Opera Nazionale
per gl'Invalidi della Guerra
(legge 25 marzo 1917 n° 481)
Il Delegato
[National Organization
for the War Wounded
(law no. 481. 25th March 1917)
The Delegate]

Clearly the Delegate, had one still been in office, would have had nothing to do for some considerable time. But I wonder whether a municipal council debate was necessary before they could finally take the plaque down. It has left a slightly lighter, fresher rectangular space on the cracking paint of the door. I suppose that will disappear soon as well.

I suggested earlier on that Calatafimi was a private, even shy, sort of a town and this is borne out by the number of things that you just cannot see. Apart from digested Spanish and Bourbon palaces, there are water cisterns and caves under the castle, grain storage areas under the Carmine ruins, the Roman theatre under a church in piazza Nocito, another one under the former church of Santa Caterina near the old hospital, the cache of arms buried under the convent of San

Francesco, the crypt under the Carmine, the ancient church underneath the dentist's consulting rooms, and the Roman baths under the houses adjoining the Carmine opposite the chemist. And no doubt hundreds of other things. But they are all invisible. They have just been built over, forgotten, relegated to the underground. Although this has been happening all over Italy for centuries, I find Calatafimi's cover-up frustratingly complete.

3

A Potted History of Sicily and Calatafimi

Now I know this is going to bore you to death because you enjoy a most respectable knowledge of Mediterranean history. But I am going to pencil in a bit of historical background, if only because I at least am always aware of the embarrassing gaps that exist between what I know I have read and what I can effectively remember without some sort of stimulus. I mean, what do you recall of the War of Jenkins' Ear, except the poor Captain's ill-defined plight at the hands of the Spanish somewhere in the West Indies – the mention of it, however, wafts back the smell of blackboard chalk and a rush of other thoughts, including something of what the war was about. So I write this for myself as much as for you and, in any case, we both know that Sicilian affairs must be set in an historical context to keep the hyenas of snap-generalization at bay. Please bear with me and listen briefly once again to what Sicily has had to suffer, digest (that word again) and make use of from what other peoples have thought expedient to impose on her.

Branded above the main door in the unprepossessing twentieth-century front of the Church of San Michele, which is dedicated to that military Archangel of Christianity, is the message that 'Only God Is Great'. Despite its Muslim ring (quite justified in this corner of Sicily), it is reputed, perhaps with reason, to be an irate ecclesiastical reaction to the overwhelming popularity of Garibaldi and his deeds in and around the town. After the battle he had rested in a house, which is still known as the Casa di Garibaldi, right in front of this church, while the jubilant townspeople waited expectantly outside. To the left of the church is a small bar which roasts good coffee. To the right, one of the three banks in the town and a small municipal garden with a recently installed 'artistic' fountain, a monument to Garibaldi and another one to the fallen of the First World War. There are palm trees in between. Attached to the church, on the right, is the Municipal Library, which was the object of one of my first visits in the town.

I caused some consternation. The few callers are usually confined to young people anxiously consulting the *Gazetta Ufficiale*, *Concorsi* or other specialist periodicals that list competitive examinations for job openings and hence slender hopes for their future, a sad comment on the outlook for school or university leavers in southern Italy. The arrival of an unknown foreigner – by now I have become better known – in a town off the tourist track caused a minor stir, and that this unheralded stranger was interested in local history was greeted with surprised appreciation. It opened up a better than expected library with a most collaborative librarian, himself a local historian.

The library is well stocked with all sorts of books and some manuscript material. It owes the nucleus of its collection to a local peasant-boy made good, Natale Maria Macaddino (1788-1846), whose evident early intelligence brought him to the notice of a local notable and philanthropist, Don Vincenzo Stabile, who sent him off at his own expense to study in a seminary at nearby Alcamo. Don Vincenzo unfortunately met a premature death soon after, which clearly would have meant the end of the funds for Natale's schooling had not the sad event happily coincided with the rare hunting trip to Calatafimi by King Ferdinand of the Two Sicilies in 1806. This sovereign, mainly known to the world through his wife – Maria Carolina, the sister of Marie Antoinette – and her drawing-room friendship and mischievous plottings with Nelson, Sir William Hamilton and, above all, the famous Emma, was only really interested in hunting, eating and church matters; but he was, at the instigation of Cavaliere Vincenzo Mollica,[1] somehow persuaded to desist from slaughtering wild boar long enough to grant further funds for Macaddino's studies, thus paving the way to his becoming an eminent doctor with a practice in Palermo. There he later died in the palace of the Prince of Resuttana (where he had received hospitality all his working life), embittered by the petty rivalries of his fellow doctors, but with memories of Calatafimi benign enough to move him to bequeath all his books to the town when his work was done.

The librarian was quick to introduce me to the two essential books on local history. The first has already been referred to: it was by Vito Pellegrino, a notary (1697-1773), who wrote 377 manuscript pages under the title *Calatafimi Scoverto a' Moderni* with the subtitle *Alla Novella Segesta Oggi Calatafimi* ('Calatafimi Revealed to the Modern Generation', subtitle: 'To the New Segesta, Today's Calatafimi'). The manuscript was discovered and bequeathed to the library in 1950 by another local historian, the pharmacist Nicolò Mazzara. It was subsequently published by a local bank as a gift book. It is a welcome anomaly that many Italian banks have non-profit statutes and devote some of their proceeds to publishing lavish and interesting books that would be wholly unalluring commercial prospects for normal publishers.[2] The second book, which I have also mentioned, was by Pietro Longo (1756-1825), priest, academic, politician and fighter for local rights, who wrote an erudite work on the Trojan origins of Calatafimi and Segesta (*Ragionamenti Istorici sulle Colonie de' Troiani in Sicilia*, or 'Historical Dissertations on the Trojan Colonies in Sicily', Palermo, 1810) which was dedicated to the Vincenzo Mollica mentioned above. He also wrote the only biography of the Blessed Arcangelo Placenza, the nearest Calatafimi got to a saint, whom we shall meet anon. This humble priest dedicated a large portion of his life to amassing an amazing amount of documentary evidence from the fourteenth to the nineteenth centuries, which formed the basis of the long legal battle against the Counts of Modica for the abolition of certain centuries-old feudal dues that had been illegally imposed on the harvests of the good citizens of Calatafimi. The case, which I'll take you through in time, was finally won in 1846, after Longo's death. But his memory is still alive in Calatafimi.

A third area for research emerged when I got to know of a series of visits here by an eminent Victorian, whom you well know: Samuel Butler. His visits have lived on in Calatafimi's memory, even if in a rather deformed way. His book *The Authoress of the Odyssey* (Longmans, 1897) was to a large extent written in Calatafimi and was dedicated to a local schoolmaster, Biagio Ingroia, who donated his own personal copy, that had been given to him by Butler, to the library. He wrote an inscription in it in English in his fine handwriting: 'to the young students who like anybody, everything honouring our fatherland' (sic).

There are other works, of course, but for me these three set the scene, which is not so different from that in other parts of southern Italy, where local history is very much alive and a jealously guarded tradition that is vigorously defended against all comers. This is manifest in Longo's book on the Trojan origins of Segesta and Calatafimi, in which he mercilessly attacks, among others, the eminent seventeenth-century Polish geographer Philippus Cluverius (1580-1622) for a series of appalling topographical and historical blunders in his *Sicilia Antiqua* (1619), almost as if he is defending Calatafimi against hordes of invading Saracen pirates, out to wreak plunder and rape on the town and its innocent inhabitants.[3]

The mainstream of Sicilian history sweeps majestically past Calatafimi without causing so much as a ripple, apart from Garibaldi's wave, of course, but a potted history of the island here is nonetheless in order. Although what follows is a wildly oversimplified account of an island that has contributed so generously to the human story, I'll be happy if it suggests that the overall flow of events involving Sicily has left behind significant alluvial deposits which Calatafimi's inhabitants have grown up in, and on which their lives still unconsciously feed.

I am about to distort history by squeezing the Sicanian, Trojan, Greek, Roman, Byzantine, Carthaginian, Vandal, Gothic, Arab, Norman, French, Spanish, Neapolitan, Piedmontese and English contributions to Sicily's history into a few paragraphs. Worse still, I am going to squeeze what little is known of Calatafimi's history in between that of two eminent ladies – the Greek Helen of Troy, the aftermath of whose troubles caused Aeneas to travel to Trapani on his way to found Rome, and the Spanish Duchess of Alba, whose ancestor was for a long time erroneously thought to have been the model for Goya's *Maya Desnuda*, and who, among her many other titles, is still the Baroness of Calatafimi today. I know this is in no way justifiable, but that's what I am going to do.[4]

The colonization of aboriginal Sicily by the various branches of the trading Greeks began around the eighth century BC, and they found a whole collection of peoples there – Sicans, Sikels, North Africans, Elymians, etc. Time and local successes gradually gave them pre-eminence, particularly in the east of the island, and made them independent, warlike, tyrannical and highly motivated intellectually, and avid players on the treaty chess-board. They gave the world Empedocles, Pindar, Dionysius, Theocritus, Diodorus and Archimedes, to mention but a few of the ancient names that are quintessentially associated with Greece but were actually those of people from Sicily. Syracuse, Gela, Agrigentum, Selinus and Segesta (that's us) made a habit of war and involved Athens, Sparta and the Phoenicians in an ever evolving web of alliances and interests. Inevitably, because of the strategic position of the island, North Africa became increasingly involved, which affected the interests of Rome (traditionally founded by Aeneas who, according to Virgil, knew this part of Sicily well) and caused her to intervene and wrest Sicily for Rome in 210 BC after the Punic Wars – and with the help of our very own Segesta. The no-nonsense Romans set about exploiting the fertile island by turning it into a granary: all agricultural activity was dedicated to the whole-sale cutting down of trees and the clearing of land for the growing of corn on oceanic farms worked with the labour of Asiatic slaves. One of these estates has left a unique picture of how life was for the rich at that time: it is the Roman villa at Piazza Armerina with its magnificent mosaics, including the first depiction of a girl in a bikini; and the legacy of the *latifondo*, the large estate owned by people living far away, remained a *leitmotif* in later Sicilian agriculture, and in the society and outlook of Sicily, over the centuries.

With the shrinking of the Roman Empire and after an under-energetic Byzantine presence which left the island invitingly weak, the Vandals and the Goths were the next to move in, Theodoric establishing his rule there in 493. They gave and left us very little, as was their wont, as also did the Byzantine Bellisarius who won back Sicily in 535 as a peripheral limb of the already ailing Eastern Empire. It remained more or less attached to that Levantine body while waves of Arabs started raiding the island from the North African coasts as early as the seventh century, although their first real settlement was not established until much later at Mazzara in the year 827. That was engineered by the rebellious Euphemius of Messina, the Byzantine naval commander. Although Euphemius' rebellion was probably motivated by crude political issues and personal ambition, the traditional explanation has it that he fell in love with and forcibly married a nun named Homonizza. When the Byzantine Strategus took exception to this and ordered Euphemius' nose to be cut off, he, understandably valuing his nostrils, and looking for a way out of the situation, rebelled and proclaimed himself Emperor. He also came to an agreement with the Arabs under Ased-ibn-Forat for a bit of help in a tight situation. I suppose that at a pinch this could be dubbed the 'War of Euphemius' Nose',[5] but anyway the first perma-nent Arab settlements were the result. The Byzantines kept trying to get back into Sicily, encouraged by numerous revolts and rivalries among the Arabs, who only fully established themselves there in 902.

I have never had much sympathy for Byzantium, perhaps because I lost an early girlfriend to a future professor of Byzantine studies. You may remember him.

The Arabs, on the other hand, did make a permanent contribution to Sicily. Despite more than their fair share of internal uprisings, tribal jealousies, plagues and locusts, they flourished everywhere on the island, but particularly around Palermo and in the Val di Mazzara, the Calatafimi/Trapani/Mazzara area, until the arrival of the Normans from the Italian mainland in the eleventh century. They brought a degree of practical civilization to the island which lived on long after the demise of their eventual conquerors. They brought with them their architecture and poetry and the desert-dweller's reverence for water which, for a time, diverted agriculture from the vast Roman grain estates to the more intensive, irrigated farming and hill terracing that was carried out by themselves and the Berber settlers. Their love of water and of a life of pleasure can still be appreciated in a distant way by visiting the Ziza Palace at Palermo and reading the descriptions of its gardens, though the palace itself was actually built by the Arab-influenced Norman King William I. Their building and decorative talents in marble and mosaic inter-twined later on with the solid rock masonry and round arches of Northern Europe, and the fusion testifies both to their civilized con-tribution to the island's way of life and to the intelligence of the nomadic Normans who accepted Arab ways at the start and then adapted them to their way of government.

The Normans took time to establish themselves as a central government and exploited what they found on arrival until they were able to make Sicily, relatively slowly, into the jewel of Europe – in time the richest and most cosmopolitan society in the known world, or so it seemed to visitors. Palermo swarmed with Christians, Muslims, Greeks, Turks, Slavs, Germans, English, French, Lombards, Jews, Arabs, Berbers, Persians and African negroes. Norman ad-ministration, cooking, learning, building and worldly pleasures (just look at those mosaic hunting scenes and peacocks in the Royal Palace in Palermo and the dazzling architecture of the Palatine Chapel) were all highly influenced by the Arabs.[6] This essentially cosmopolitan melting-pot lived on until the royal house's increasing Imperial interests – it had become Imperial Hohenstaufen by then, through the marriage of Constance, which I will shortly tell you about – and papal influence (the Pope was desperately afraid of being encircled by the Germans) reinforced the move towards latinizing the island, which edged the remaining Muslims back into the interior of the island, where their influence is heard to this day in the spoken dialect and seen in some basic water-systems and agricultural methods that have remained embedded. I know you know all this, but *pazienza*.

The Normans began their occupation of Sicily around 1060 under the Great Count Roger I, 'the most dazzling military adventurer between Julius Caesar and Napoleon,'[7] and acquired royal status in 1130 when Roger II was crowned King of Sicily by the Pope: that doyen of Sicilian-Arab historians, Michele Amari, described him as a 'baptized sultan'. They set about adapting their northern military habits to the governing of the island, endowing some of their warlords with landholdings, many of which lasted for centuries. They also established an English connection which, after a long period of Spanish domination, was given a boost in the eighteenth and nineteenth centuries. Gualtiero Offamilio must surely not be forgotten here, if only because his Sicilian name is held by some to be a transliteration of Walter of the Mill: he was the English Archbishop of Palermo from 1168 till 1193, and it was he who in 1177 married the Norman King William III to Joanna, daughter of King Henry II of England. As the royal house grew in international importance, Sicily became of less interest in the context of its increasingly European vision of things. But the flower of the house – the Holy Roman Emperor Frederick II, the son of the Norman Constance (daughter of King Roger II) and the German Emperor Henry VI (son of Barbarossa) – was probably the most enlightened monarch in mediaeval Europe. Known as Stupor Mundi for his all-encompassing magnificence, his power base was in Sicily. However, *après lui* the dykes disintegrated and his world was washed away. He left the island of Sicily in possession of an admirable administration, but with the succession to his Empire in considerable disarray.

After complex claims, counter-claims and bloody fighting, the curtain creaked up on a less glamorous Sicily. Charles of Anjou, a Frenchman, was crowned King in 1266 with papal and civic support; but his mindlessly harsh administration, on top of the background of turmoil he had inherited, built up inexorably to the explosive Sicilian Vespers in 1292. The Sicilians, backed by the old Norman feudal lords, could take no more and massacred the French wholesale. Calatafimi showed magnanimity towards its French

Governor Porcelet, who had behaved honourably – I shall come back to him – but it was practically alone. The resultant bloody wounds were eventually bandaged up by Frederick II of Aragon, who became King of Sicily in 1302.

This marked the beginning of the Spanish influence, an 'influenza' which, if you will allow me, without too much wincing, quickly developed into an endemic sleeping-sickness that lasted for centuries, first under Aragon and then in 1503 under the royal house of Spain. The Spanish had other more important concerns, e.g. the New World, the Turkish threat and the Low Countries to mention but three, and their consequent lack of interest in Sicily, except of course as a cash-machine, meant that conservatism held sway, with the aristocracy safely chloroformed by a life of luxury in Palermo. Far from their lands and from the practice of agriculture, these noble puppets abandoned their estates to rent collectors and tenants, and any form of land improvement was discouraged by punitive taxation which the nobles did not pay (neither did the ecclesiastics) and which was ruthlessly passed on down the line to anybody else, principally the royal towns and the long-suffering peasants. There were no signs of movement for centuries until the European powers decided to give Sicily to Piedmont as a small thank-you present for their part in the Spanish War of Succession in 1713. That arrangement did not last long.

The Habsburgs were not satisfied with the carve-up. Portions had to be altered: Sicily was blithely exchanged for Sardinia by the Piedmontese who were probably happy because it was nearer Turin; and the Habsburgs came in, eventually ceding the island in 1735 to the Neapolitan Bourbons; and, despite some mercantilist reforms on the mainland, bad governance continued to be Sicily's fate for many wearying years. Towards the end of the century a *philosophe* Neapolitan Viceroy, Domenico Caracciolo, began the awesome task of dismantling the surviving feudal system; and Napoleon's military intervention on the mainland as far south as Naples forced the Bourbon royal family from Naples to Palermo for a short time, and created some partisan English activity during and after Emma Hamilton's bad advice to her friend, Queen Maria Carolina, and Nelson's heavy-handed and bloody intervention in Naples against another Caracciolo, an admiral who was ignominiously hanged on board his ship. English backing of an emerging, though fragile, reformist movement even brought about a Westminster-type constitu-

tion that was briefly foisted on the bemused Sicilians by Lord William
Bentinck in 1812. But the reaction after the Congress of Vienna soon
stamped on that and the old conservative regime settled back again
into its old routine.

Revolutionary movements followed later, here as elsewhere in
Europe. Revolts against reactionary Bourbon rule erupted in 1820
and 1837 (complicated by the outbreak of cholera, which was generally considered a 'poison' spread by government officials), and also
in 1848, when the Sicilian revolt was the first in the series that broke
out all over the continent: Calatafimi sent the cannon from the castle
and seven church bells to Palermo to be melted down for cannon
balls. But nothing durable came of these sincere protests for the
moment. The revolutionary movements were put down and Glad-
stone, after a visit to a Neapolitan prison in 1850, described the
Bourbon government somewhat exaggeratedly as 'the negation of
God erected into a system of government', exaggeratedly because
the Neapolitan Bourbons at that stage had never managed to erect
anything and their government had never resembled anything
approaching a system. A head of steam was steadily building up,
however, even if the situation remained sullenly stable until Garibaldi
– in the face of serious obstructionism from his Piedmontese so-called
sponsors and enormous political debtors, whose interests lay in the
north of Italy and not the south – finally managed to begin the process of removing oppressive governments and setting Italian unification into motion in the famous battle of Calatafimi in 1860.
Nothing really changed after the arrival of the Piedmontese as Kings
of United Italy, except that Sicily acquired a new role as a leading
victim of Italy's increasing north-south divide, and many people
began to think the northerners were even worse than the Bourbons.
This *plus ça change* school of thought has, as you know, been
masterfully expressed in the fictional works of De Roberto and
Tomasi di Lampedusa.[8]

That is nearly three thousand years of history crushed into a few
superficial sentences. What I have wanted to suggest is the sheer
wealth and variety of the experiences that Sicily has enjoyed or
endured through its succession of invaders and their resultant
aristocracies, and that, though Calatafimi was decidedly on the side-
lines, life here today still carries traces of it all. As a result of this
foreign interference, Sicilians feel profoundly different, exploited,
mistrustful of any form of authority, worthy of the best in life but

resigned to the fact that better things will never come their way, however much they exert themselves.

But what about Segesta and Calatafimi, or Calatafimi-Segesta, as it is called today?

For the few references that have survived, one must again go back in time. Such as they are, they shed light on the Trojan origins of Segesta, on Greek, Carthaginian and Segestan diplomacy and skirmishing, on a little of what the Romans were doing in the area and of what the Arabs contributed, and on very little relating to the Normans except what can be deduced from their architectural and organizational footprint. They give a glimpse of how Calatafimi showed a sense of justice to their Angevin governor during the Sicilian Vespers; they reveal the town's long-lasting preference for direct royal rule rather than seigniorial domination; they chronicle their victory over an iniquitous latter-day feudal malpractice; and they end up briefly with Garibaldi's impulsive exploits on the wider historical canvas.

Act one: the aftermath of Helen of Troy. Longo, our local historian, argues at some length – and strenuously – for the Trojan origin of Segesta and also, though less convincingly, of Calatafimi. With admirable energy he marshals Dionysius of Halicarnassus, Virgil, Strabo, Diodorus Siculus, Ovid, Cicero, Livy, et al. to his cause. The story is that after the fall of Troy, the flight of Aeneas and his followers brought them at a certain point to Trapani, where, after the burial of his father and the conclusion of his North African *affaire* with Queen Dido, he left behind some of his men and most of his tired women – Virgil says they were so fed up they went to the length of trying to burn his ships to make their point – as he made his way up Italy to Latium to found Rome. This is the Classical contribution to the normally accepted eighth-century origin of Eryx and Segesta as settlements of the Elymians, a hotchpotch of Trojans, Greeks, Phocians and Sicanian exiles from Libya.

Segesta was perhaps the Sicilian city that was least subject to external political and military influences, for the founders became pastmasters at playing off the various Greek communities in the east of the island against each other and against the Carthaginians. An interesting example of Segesta's diplomatic dexterity is nicely illustrated in Freeman's late Victorian study *Sicily*.[9] He describes how in 415 BC Segesta sent envoys to Athens to seek help in their continuous struggle against Selinus down the coast, which was allied at the time to Syracuse. The matter was debated at some length and the Athenians prudently decided to send envoys to Sicily to assess the situation at first hand and discover whether Segesta really possessed the riches it claimed, before making a decision. In order to convince the Athenian envoys, the Segestans gathered together all the gold and silver plate in the city and all that they could borrow from elsewhere, and proceeded to arrange a series of showy feasts in honour of the Athenians that was hosted by the various leading citizens – each one of whom passed off as his own all the collected plate when it was his turn to entertain them. The judicious Athenians were gulled, and they were induced to embark on what turned into a disastrous campaign against the power of Syracuse: they sent a great invasion force to Sicily which, despite a considerable reinforcement including Demosthenes, failed in its objective and met defeat in 413 BC, with many of the Athenian troops ending their lives as slaves.

But alliances came and went and only slightly later Segesta managed to annihilate its rival Selinus, not with Athenian but with Carthaginian help – though 'help' is hardly the appropriate word as the North African army they involved was far superior to Segesta's and the result was not only the spectacular destruction of Selinus in 408 BC, the smashed ruins of which you can see today scattered along the coast half an hour or so from here, but also Carthage's complete hegemony over its ally. The wheel of fortune continued to turn, however, and Segesta itself was destroyed later on, in 307, with appalling cruelty even for those rough times, by Agathocles, one of the worst of the Syracusan tyrants, who had been persuaded by Segesta to attack the Carthaginians in Africa and had failed. If you have the stomach, you can read the details of Agathocles' vengeance in Diodorus Siculus.[10]

While the Elymians were not pure Greeks and claimed to be Trojans, they were highly hellenized and the coins and the architecture they used were Greek in spirit. Segesta was an important city. The theatre with its spectacular view, which would take your breath away if you would bother to come, could seat 4,000 in its heyday, and the area now set apart for excavation amounts to 180 hectares and is being increased. In the end, when the Carthaginians were clearly becoming too dominant a power in the area for Roman comfort, the Segestans, so versed in diplomatic dexterity, wisely sided with the Romans during the Punic Wars, gaining allied status and thereby exemption from Roman tribute when the Romans took over Sicily. Incidentally the pompous and rather snobbish Romans changed the original name of Egesta to Segesta around that time because *egestas* means 'poverty' in Latin. Would you believe it? Rather like newly rich burghers turning up their noses at living in Cheapside.

Longo argues that Calatafimi was also of Elymian origin. He maintains that the third city that the Trojan Acestes built, after Eryx and Egesta, was Aceste, that is to say Calatafimi. He backs this up with the Greek coins found in ancient grottos near the castle. But his theory apparently does not stand up: most probably the strategic hill became inhabited gradually, though more rapidly after the razing of Segesta by the Saracens in the ninth century.

There are, or were, numerous theories about the origin of the town's name. One of the earlier ones, bandied around until the eighteenth century, was that the town was brought into being by the union of Calatafo the son of Ceres, who was living on Mount Eryx, and Ima, the daughter of Gesta, one of Aeneas' generals who built Segesta. On the marriage of the two, Gesta is supposed to have constructed a walled castle on top of a hill as a sort of dowry and so it became known as Calatafimi. It is a romantic theory and seems euphonious but it is not, I think, to be taken seriously.

Two theories now compete for the origin of the name, both of which accept that *qal'at* is the Arabic for a high fortified place or castle. One is that it was named after Euphemius (Fimi in Arabic), the Byzantine naval commander based in Messina whose nose business and anti-Byzantine rebellion, that we have alluded to, brought about the first permanent Arab settlements in Sicily in 827. While there is something to be said for this theory etymologically and historically – it was first quoted from Arabic sources by Rosario De Gregorio in the eighteenth century – Messina was a very long way from Calatafimi for the latter to have been given Euphemius' name and although the crucial naval invasion when Euphemius brought the Arabs into Sicily did take place on the coast at Mazzara, not too far off, the army turned to the west, away from Calatafimi and towards Syracuse, after their initial success, Euphemius with them.[11]

More convincing is the theory that stems from Cicero's denunciation of Verres' malpractices when he held sway as the infamous Roman Governor of Sicily after the Punic Wars. He writes of a prominent landowner in the Segesta area in *Verrine Orations* 2,3,92-3: 'Diocles was from Palermo, his surname Phimes, an illustrious and noble man: he cultivated land in the territory of Segesta.' Cicero decribes how Phimes was illegally and brutally taxed by Verres despite Segesta's allied status, which gave it exemption from tribute. This theory has it that Phimes was a major landowner and that his family either held the land for centuries or in some way bequeathed their name to the area. In Roman times the town was probably called Castrum Phimes, which could have been changed to Qal'at al Fime under the Arabs, who arabized everything they could lay their hands on. For what it's worth, I much prefer this second version.

The first literary reference to Calatafimi, is contained in *The Book of King Roger* written by Edrisi, King Roger II's Arab geographer, in the early twelfth century. The book describes a voyage around the world as it was then known. It is quoted by the eminent Sicilian historian Amari:

> ...from the castle Al Hammah [now Alcamo] to Qal'at al Fimi is about eight miles. Calatafimi is an ancient castle, without known origins, and a fortress to be reckoned with. It is populated and has arable and wooded land, [but] little water in the area.

Strange about the 'little water', as there was and is quite a lot of it in the area, although not inside the town. This view that Calatafimi was an ancient site is also maintained by Longo, citing as evidence both the Greek coins and some Roman ones that were found there. There are traces of troglodytic grottos which, when deserted, were used as grain stores, even one where, in his time, illegal card games were played. Pellegrino, our other local historian writing before Longo, also supported this thesis and he even talks of a leather coin found there depicting a serpent sucking at a woman's dugs. The Arabs left deep traces in the Calatafimi area. Probably the only un-Christianized mosque left in Sicily, with its *mehrab* indicating *qiblah*, or the direction of Mecca, was recently unearthed at Segesta; and the Muslim dome, which was incorporated into the Carmelite monastery in Calatafimi, and which collapsed the other day, was likely to have been the town's mosque – as, according to custom, it was outside the town walls at the time it was built. The present castle is twelfth-century Norman and was built on an Arab site where many Arab burial grounds have been found.

Calatafimi appears briefly on the pages of history with its perhaps unique example of the exercise of tolerance during the Sicilian Vespers in 1292. While the whole of the island was given over to the enthusiastic slaughter of anybody French, only two towns went against the current: Sperlinga (which gave rise to a saying still used today, *sulu Spirlinga nigau*, a dialect phrase used to describe somebody who obstinately insists on swimming against the tide) and Calatafimi. Calatafimi was lucky to have had as its French Governor a good man in Guillaume Porcelet. According to the chronicler Bartolomeo da Neocastro,[12] he distanced himself from the iniquities of his fellow countrymen and when, during the Vespers uprising, a bloodthirsty rabble arrived in town hell bent on the destruction of the French, the townspeople stoutly defended him to the extent that his would-be assassins not only spared his life and the lives of his men but gave him comfort, showed him honour, and arranged for him to be sent back to Provence. The chronicler used this case as a moral lesson to the effect that when men revolt violently they usually do so with some good reason. I should imagine Porcelet was merely relieved.

For 250 years after the arrival of the Normans Calatafimi was part of the Royal demesne, and over subsequent centuries it strove to remain crown property and thereby escape some of the iniquities of feudal domination. It succeeded but rarely, the kings breaking their promises and continually giving it back to greedy barons. Frederick II of Aragon left it to his third son, Duke William, by his will in 1336. And, with only short gaps, it remained feudal until the nineteenth century. The story is long and intricate, but, by marriage, it ended up as a small part of the County of Modica, one of the principal feudal powers in Sicily; and over and above the usual tithes it was forced to pay illegal dues to the Counts from about the middle of the fifteenth century until the long-lasting legal battle, based on Longo's painstaking evidence, was finally won in 1846. I'll tell you the story of this feudal dispute on another occasion.

Although Calatafimi became a part of the County of Modica much later, the way that county first came into being under the Chiaramonte, a family of great importance in Sicilian history, might shed light on some of the less pleasant aspects of the establishment of illustrious families in ancient Sicily. The story is brutally simple and Pellegrino, in his Calatafimi MS, describes this family's arrival in Sicily thus:

Henri Chiaramonte, who was a Frenchman, having fallen foul of
St Louis and his son King Philippe, came to King Charles in Naples

in the year 1271. Charles, having noticed that Chiaramonte's wife was very attractive, raped her. Whereupon Henri Chiaramonte raped Charles' daughter and came to King Peter of Sicily...from whom he received the County of Modica with the privilege of 1283.

When, later on, I deal with Calatafimi's illegal feudal taxes, I shall return to the vicissitudes of the ensuing period of its history. For the moment I should like to note that Donna Violante de Prades, of Calatafimi's now Spanish ruling family, married her tutor and uncle, Don Bernardo Caprera, in 1420. Their daughter married an Enriquez in 1480 and the County of Modica, the second largest landholding in Sicily, of which Calatafimi was a small part, belonged to a family that lived in Spain. Much less violent times ensued, the Enriquezes intertwined with the Albas and in 1741 the Baroness of Calatafimi was Donna Maria Teresa Alvares de Toledo Haro Enriquez de Cabrera e Moncada, Duchessa d'Alba de Havescar e de Montery, Marchesa del Carpio e de Villanova de Rio, Duchessa di Medina de Riosecco, Condessa di Modica e Baronessa d'Alcamo e Calatafimi. What a contrast to the grinding conditions then obtaining in tiny, quivering Calatafimi! However, she would have known little or nothing about them, as she never set her haughty foot on Sicilian soil. The current Countess of Modica and Baroness of Calatafimi is still the Duchess of Alba, one of whose illustrious ancestors, Dona Maria Teresa Cayetana Silva y Alvarez y Toledo, had her portrait wonderfully painted by Goya and was for a long time, perhaps wrongly, thought to have been the model for the *Maya Desnuda*, as I have said. She did certainly have a close relationship with the painter, and her rings in the portrait have 'Goya' on one hand and 'Alba' on the other, as well as 'Solo Goya' traced in the sand in front of her. She seems aeons removed from Calatafimi, though Goya, had he known about the town, might have been inspired to paint some of the harshness of life here at the time.

Calatafimi is only remembered in literature, or at least in books of travel, because it is the nearest town to Segesta, and over the centuries a host of visitors have left their impressions, both favourable and otherwise. I will be quoting you some of their opinions.

Like the rest of Sicily, Calatafimi suffered from repressive taxation and government, as we have seen. During the period of the town's famous fight against illegal feudal taxation, on 8th December 1815 the already familiar Cavaliere Vincenzo Mollica, the *prosegreto* of

Calatafimi and one of Caterina's forebears, ordered, in the name of Ferdinand III, the imposition of a milling tax, that most hated of all duties. Political awareness was stirring by now and there was some unrest in 1820. The town also played its part in the Europe-wide uprisings of 1848. The capital Palermo rose on 12th June and Calatafimi, together with other Sicilian towns, rose on the 22nd, to cries of 'Long live Pius IX, Palermo, Sicily and the Italian League'. Four cannons, together with a team of honest patriots under their leader Filogramo, were sent to help in the defence of Palermo, as I have described. The local arch-priest D. Francesco Avila (the civic leader in the fight against the 'Terraggiolo', the unjust feudal tax I will tell you about) was elected to the Lower House of Parliament in Palermo and, as the oldest deputy or 'Presidente d'età', had the honour of presenting the duly elected President, the Marchese Fardella di Torearsa, to the house in 1848. The Municipality of Calatafimi was authorized to levy a tax on meat, fish, horses and donkeys for the upkeep of the Provisional Government and the town formally adhered to the Government's bid to elect the Duke of Genoa, Alberto Amadeo of Piedmont, as King of Sicily.[13] But, as elsewhere, the momentum of the movement petered out in spite of hectic international politicking, particularly by the English, and the *status quo ante* was harshly reimposed on the island.

I will also deal with Garibaldi's activities in, and his impact on, the town separately. Everybody in Italy knows that a Calatafimi exists somewhere in Sicily thanks to the activities of this impetuous revolutionary, and it may be of interest to mention here that his famous speech 'O Roma O Morte' ('either we win Rome, or we die') was delivered in Calatafimi as in other places, in 1862, two years after the battle, during his unsuccessful second attempt to march on Rome. The town always held a place in Garibaldi's heart. The hopes that Garibaldi's actions and promises had raised in the hearts of all Sicilians were betrayed by the actions of the Piedmontese Government and by the early 1890s the anti-establishment syndicalist movement of the Fasci Siciliani (not to be confused with Mussolini's Fascists) began to take action, and even Calatafimi was marginally involved. One of the earliest socialists in this part of Sicily was Vito Vasile, a native of Calatafimi, whose outraged revolutionary invective against the bosses, social injustice and (later) the Fascists was packed into hundreds of volumes of manuscript diaries, which, in keeping with the undemonstrative character of his home town, lie peacefully unconsulted in the local library.

Calatafimi had a population of 3,375 in 1570. It rose to 10,000 in 1798, only to fall thereafter, particularly over the last hundred years, during which emigration has taken a heavy toll: Government statistics show that its population fell by 26% in the period 1951-71. Officially, it stands at present at just over 7,400 (though those actually living here are nearer to 3,500) and there is little or no industry, the small middle class preferring the professions to any sort of commerce, industry or improvement of the land that it owns. It is still a close-knit, happy, if fatalistic, rural community, and so greatly interested in local events that it only takes about half an hour for an insignificant rumour to reach the ears of all and sundry. The town has a long and exceptionally interesting tradition of looking after its fellow citizens through works of charity, which I shall try to explain to you in due course. That charitable instinct is still alive and flourishing, and I can hear you muttering that this is probably why they put up with me.

4

A Day

If everybody knows about light pollution, fewer are aware of its noise equivalent: wipe out general hum and sound-stars will emerge. The silence that usually reigns here means I can get the grumbles of a sleeping dog at 100 metres and the hoeing of an early worker at two kilometres. Since I wake up early, those are some of the sounds that say good morning to me before the first tractors growl past on their way to the fields. You would probably still be snoring and there is nothing wrong with that, but my day begins with such. Since you did ask me to explain what the hell I was doing here, I shall now tell you briefly about an average day.

I can easily live without coffee. My favourite early morning stimulant is listening to baroque music, a pleasure akin to munching fresh grapes; but Caterina really needs coffee, so I have it as well. Nor do I often indulge in breakfast, but I always find it fascinating that adult Italians, who seldom eat it, are convinced that breakfast is a secret Anglo-Saxon weapon, that eating it every morning is a strange, Masonic rite that is essential for successful Empire-building, and that not eating it has let greatness slip from Italy's grasp in recent centuries. I repeat: they almost never eat it in the classic 'English' form, while prescribing it for all and sundry as a physical and moral restorative. To be perfectly frank, I should quite enjoy wandering down in the morning to kidneys on the sideboard and to leisurely discussion on the latest political developments in Westminster or Delhi, although I suppose I shouldn't say that. However, when I make breakfast myself the menu becomes inexorably simpler, immensely less Imperial, and the fast is seldom actually cracked. I sometimes eat an orange, and the other morning, when reaching for a particularly nice one in a tree, I came face to face with a lovely little black kitten with green eyes. The colour combinations in the early morning sun were far more stimulating than coffee.

When I do manage to make it, it usually consists of that morning's freshly laid eggs and some bread and marmalade, this latter being made by myself from our oranges to a recipe of Mrs Beeton's. I know you will think I am trying to pass off as some sort of Somerset Maugham character, reading his three-month-old, ironed copy of *The Times* in his tent in the middle of the monsoon in a Malayan jungle. No. The reason I eat marmalade is because I make it, reducing the kitchen to a sticky yellowish cubicle in the process, in reality a Laocoön-like struggle. The reason I do is that we have far too many oranges that are never picked. In fact you can be unnerved here when walking along without a thought in the world by thudding and crashing in the undergrowth behind you which, unless you are used to it, suggests that some savage animal is about to get you. The noise is unwanted oranges falling off the trees. That's why I make marmalade. Almost all of my life has been happily lived without marmalade, but I do now enjoy my *Thin Sliced Clear – San Giovanni*, unabashedly, because it's mine. It is a bit like making your own wine: the process is extremely expensive, the result seldom good, but it is, dammit, absolutely yours and has to be appreciated by all and sundry, cost whatever it may. I make so much that most of our friends are saddled with bottles of it, whether they like it or not.

A quick check in the flower pot outside the door to see if the toad has come back after his nocturnal ramblings – he spends the day burrowed in the earth with no shred of respect for the plants that are trying to grow there – and it is time to deal with the dogs. They require bits of bread, even though they do not really want them and usually just sniff at them dismissively before conceding a token crunch, unless of course one of them is really hungry and tries to muscle in on a crust not meant for him, whereupon all hell is let loose and canine feelings are hurt. You are going to get dogs now, although I know you don't like them. They take up a great part of our day one way and another. So it would be in order to introduce them here. They are not house-dogs and it would never occur to them to come inside. They consider the purpose of life to be making as much noise as possible in exchange for food. The noise is ostensibly in defence of their masters and it does have an effect on strangers. But they are not aggressive, preferring the eating part of their contract and relishing a good patting.

The chief is Garibaldi, a large dog that actually used to be called Bobby, believe it or not, and lived at a nearby smallholding: he came because there was more food over here than at his place. He is getting on now and is beginning to be challenged in his role as the pack-leader; but he more or less manages to fill the position, especially at mealtimes when he loudly lays claim to all the food bowls he chooses, particularly when other males are eating. He was recently operated on for a large growth on the knee of his right front leg: he had to be drugged to get him into the vet's car because he had never been in one, but he came back after being pampered for a fortnight looking much younger than when he went away. His principal mate is Munni (the dialect word for *immondizia*, or rubbish, because she was found as a puppy tied up in a plastic bag on a rubbish dump – though incidentally *munni* in Hindi means 'pearl', which she is). She is not well, but was an excellent hunter and was often to be seen coming back in the morning with a rabbit, which she promptly buried so that it could be eaten later by her two remaining offspring. Munni did try to teach them how to hunt, but they were hopeless. They are a black one called Balù, who is testing out becoming the head of the pack, and Ciccio who, like his mother, has no tail and is not very well – on odd occasions he harmlessly nips strangers for some esoteric reason. There were many other puppies, which have been sent elsewhere, because Munni has the reputation of being a hunter and so it is easy to find homes for them. We occasionally see some of them if they have not been run over while mindlessly chasing the spinning wheels of passing cars. But of course they don't remember us.

Next comes Percy, who was the last to arrive, again drawn by the fact that there was food here. Great attempts were made to drive him off because there is a limit to the number of dogs we can feed, but he would not be dissuaded and eventually won acceptance against considerable odds, earning the name of Percy which stands for Perseveranza. He has the unique distinction for dogs in this part of Sicily in being the object of electronic correspondence with the University of Colorado, because some friends of ours from that university were staying with us when he was in the process of being accepted and have become interested in his career. He is still very young and has a penchant for chewing plastic, particularly mobile telephones. Since Garibaldi is getting old, Munni has been giving Percy lessons on how to make love, but it does not seem to mean a lot to him yet. However, her eldest surviving puppy, Balù, did not need lessons and two new puppies are now with us, Orso and Orsetta, who are still into intensive playing. Orso, the male, becomes so excited with life that when you get near him he instantly lies on his back and pees copiously.

All of them without exception lie on their backs when you get near, waiting to be patted and scratched – but they have moved beyond the peeing stage. Orso is, strangely, the victim of identity confusion on the part of three small black kittens who think he is their mother. I suppose they were neglected in early days and they have identified him, a large black furry animal, as their mother: they sleep with him, look for his teats and knead his belly. He looks very sheepish, but is very fond of them and licks them in a proprietary way.

I usually go to Caterina's parents' house early on to see what is happening. Caterina's father will probably be involved in feeding and letting out the chickens, ducks, guinea-fowl and turkeys, and gathering whatever eggs there may be – mysteriously it is never enough. The duck eggs are important as they are bartered for lettuce at the local supermarket, usually for the previous day's lettuce. But that is still excellent food for the artificers of the eggs who, by pecking it up, set in motion a closed production cycle that would be frowned on by conventional capitalists, as there is no profit at the end.

The turkeys had to be moved from the ducks' enclosure because one of them, when young and romantic, believed he was a duck and drowned in the pond. The guinea-fowl are dark, mysterious and very cacophonous – a bit like peacocks, of which there are quite a few in the neighbourhood. The ducks are commonly referred to as the *signorine* because they chatter incessantly as they waddle around collectively. The chickens are more martial: the roost used to be firmly ruled with Bonapartean vigour, by a diminutive, now culled, cockerel called Napoleone, to the frustration of a much larger and more beautiful one who has taken over the reins now since Napoleone's demise. Another interesting feature of the chickens is that one of the hens, called Anita (after Garibaldi's wife, of course), was genuinely in love with Caterina's father and followed him everywhere. She is now in the deep-freeze and nobody eats chicken because it might be her. During the night (because of the foxes) and when they have young (because the magpies carry them off), all these birds stay in pens covered by nets. Such is his blind hatred of magpies that Caterina's father not only protects his animals with these nets, but strives to keep enemies at bay with an airgun and very noisy fireworks, which terrify all the animals including the ones he is trying to protect. The explosions blend in with the firing of shotguns during the shooting season and if you have ever read D.H. Lawrence's short essay *Man is a Hunter!* (*L'Uomo è Cacciatore*), you will appreciate the ruthless energy of the Sicilian peasant with his gun when faced with anything that flies or even moves. Incidentally, this normally indiscriminate aggression leads one to the conclusion that magpies must taste disgusting as there are so many of them blithely flying around.

For a certain period each morning I usually do something that passes for work, though there is nothing stoical about it, before finding out if collective tasks, like buying food or taking rubbish into town, are called for. The shopping does involve some forbearance, as a general delight in gossip among Calatafimi's citizens spins out an activity I am not over-fond of, but *pazienza*! After instructions have been given by others to the man who helps outside – sometimes a formidable task as he loves the land as his very own and has firm opinions on what has to be done: it normally involves the small tractor or indeed anything faintly mechanical – Caterina's father and I often drive into town to buy necessities: during the winter in a conventional car; in the summer in a red beach-buggy which makes us very visible in Calatafimi. I am now the proud owner of a scooter on four wheels which, when not under the mechanic's scalpel, carries me into the town equally visibly. I never did get round to obtaining a driving licence, which according to all Italians is a sort of *vice anglais* and beyond normal Latin comprehension.

The trip usually leads first to the baker because bread must be bought fresh every day from the best baker, the right to which title is hotly debated by all. Our best baker, just like his rivals, uses a wood-fuelled oven, and stacks of vine and olive prunings are to be seen outside his establishment, ready to convert the dough into loaves of a variety of forms and sizes. If the bread is still hot from the oven, you must remember not to close it up in paper or plastic bags or else it becomes soggy, and the first chunks are usually being munched within twenty seconds of our getting back into the car, it smells and is so good. It must be said, however, that the bread from Calatafimi is not as good as they make it in the neighbouring village of Vita, and far less tasty than the bread from Palermo – a subjective view if you like, but a legitimate part of the great bread debate. A couple of times a week we also get a large, empty flour-sack filled with old bread to mix with the pasta and the rest of the food for the dogs at home. Unlike duck-eggs-for-lettuce this is not a barter operation and money changes hands. Next comes a visit to the newsagent for the papers, and then we cross over the road to buy provisions from the supermarket and exchange the eggs for the duck-sustaining lettuce. Greetings and short conversations are indulged continuously, often with people whose names and even faces are unknown. Just down the hill there is the small piazza with the obelisk that I have told you about, which hosts the bank and the post office. A ritual visit to P.O. Box 4b has to be made (we live outside the postmen's circuit so we have the right to a free P.O. Box) to pick up sometimes strange things from strange countries: often books and seed catalogues.

Occasionally bank services are needed, usually for swift and easy transactions. I have had difficulties, however. Trying to cash a US bank cheque became a lengthy business when the essential form was found to be missing and had to be sent for from Central Office. And quite recently I went to cash a personal cheque to be greeted with abject apologies that for the moment they could not negotiate it as they had practically no money that morning. They even showed me how little they really did have left. It would not, however, be a problem for long, they hoped, as the armoured car with its provisions would arrive in about half and hour and, if I would care to take a coffee in the meantime, they could deal with my cheque afterwards. I thought this experience delightful and mentioned it to Caterina's father, who had no trouble in capping it. A similar incident had happened about six months previously. He had just received *in cash* the EU subsidy money for his organic wheat crop (why it was in cash I shall never understand) and was trying to bank it. The bank, when he went in, naturally assumed that he wanted to receive money rather than pay it in and came out with the same apologies that I heard. The situation being different, he suggested that he might be able to help and put the considerable amount of cash onto the cashier's desk. The reaction was immediate and heartfelt: 'Oh, thank you, thank you,' came the relieved chorus, 'Now we can get some work done, thank you.' I must, in fairness, state that our bank is very efficient and helpful. It's just a long way from where most of the money is.

Meanwhile, at home the food for the dogs and the twenty or so cats – the cat population changes mysteriously as it does with cats – has been prepared: a thick soup of that old bread with pasta, meat and left-overs. Since it is usually Caterina that gives them their food, around midday they congregate at our house in anticipation. When it is time, she is preceded, flanked, jumped upon and followed by a hoard of ravenous quadrupeds, towards the spot where they are fed. This may conjure up a new vision of her for you, but that is what happens – and the animals' love for her reaches a peak during that short walk. She does not consider this work and is untouched by stoicism. This major animal gathering means that pack-supremacy among the dogs needs to be dealt with, so that there is a lot of barking and shouting, and sometimes the weaker of the dogs have to wait a bit. The chickens were excluded from the culinary rout long ago, as they are surprisingly aggressive when confronted with food of any kind and can baffle even large dogs, who are a conventional lot and not quite sure how to deal with these outsiders.

And then it is time for us to eat. During the week, this is a fairly normal procedure, but, at weekends, more often than not it erupts into a celebration of eating, way beyond the demands of simple sustenance. However, as I say, on a normal day it is contained within reasonable limits and ends part one of the day: the pleasure of eating gives us an effortless conviction that the morning has been well spent.

In the winter afternoons I usually 'work' or read inside, and in the summer I often do the same on the terrace – a matter of some concern to everybody here. You are, of course, well aware that people born in hot climates spend most of the summer taking the greatest possible care to avoid all contact with the sun, and look askance at anybody who does not do likewise; and you also know that, far from being romantic, Mediterranean people are the most down-to-earth people in the world: it is only the northern peoples that want them to be romantic. People who cover themselves carefully and shun the midday sun at all costs are the pragmatic southerners.[1] Those who dress in shorts and take their shirts off to read in the blazing sun are the northerners. I am from the latter group and am misunderstood, not that that worries me in the slightest.

Naturally, not all days follow the same pattern and more energetic things are also undertaken, like swimming in the hot sulphur baths nearby, thwarting nature's intentions by some form of gardening, or introducing guests to the delights of Segesta, for example, or trips to Palermo, Trapani and the sea. We are quite flexible, you know, and there are so many intriguing places within easy reach of here. I might even take you around in my so-called car, if you have the courage.

If work has been done during the day on the land, or odd jobs around the place, a civilized sit-down discussion among those involved usually takes place around five or six in the evening to debate what has been done, who did it, why it was done and how it was done. This, a very democratic *conversazione* that is normally accompanied by coffee or water, is often peppered with the lapidary philosophizing that categorizes and simplifies the workings of the weather and the earth in a series of set phrases. One of my favourites is 'la terra è a palme', which means that the nature of land changes over a distance as little as the span of a man's palm, and it serves as an definitive explanation or excuse for any sort of unsuccessful cultivation, brooking no discussion. The next day's plan of action is worked out in detail, though this does not mean that it will not be gone over again the following morning and assessed during the evening. The odd person will come up to fill their bottle with our water. Preparations for dinner get under way.

We sometimes have visits in the evening. Talk takes place. Sunsets are looked at. Glasses of wine are enjoyed. Music is listened to. Dogs are played with. Birds broadcast their evening feelings. Food is savoured. Mosquitoes are fought. Television is looked at. Books are read.

And so to bed.

5

Samuel Butler and Calatafimi

I suppose I have to accept your gratuitous sniping at the potted history I have served up to you, even if I am still convinced that an awareness of Sicily's historical stratifications helps you to categorize some of your daily discoveries. However that may be, I will be on safer ground if I move on to a Victorian iconoclast who appeals, I know, to both of us and who, unlikely though it may seem, spent a considerable time in Calatafimi, actually becoming a sort of honorary citizen. I know you don't like *The Way of All Flesh*, but the rest of his work still retains a fine cutting edge, however neglected it has become.[1]

Samuel Butler apparently loved Calatafimi. As a luminary he may be dimmed now, but no one can deny the astonishing influence he exercised on many of the greatest names in twentieth-century English literature: George Bernard Shaw, H.G. Wells, E.M. Forster, Ivy Compton-Burnett, James Joyce, W.B. Yeats, D.H. Lawrence, Robert Graves, George Orwell – to name but a few.[2] He spent time here almost every year towards the end of his life and found himself among friends.

This grandson of a bishop, scourge of accepted Victorian standards, one-time successful New Zealand frontier sheep-farmer,[3] musician (rigidly Handelian), writer of utopias, theologian, translator, antagonist of Darwin's, satirist, failed capitalist, moralist, painter and quiet gentleman, came to the conclusion in 1891 that Homer's *Odyssey* could only have been written by a young inexperienced woman, and, in the following year, that it had been written in Trapani to describe a journey round the island of Sicily. He became interested in the *Odyssey* while writing, with his friend Festing Jones, the libretto and music for a 'secular Oratorio' entitled *Ulysses* (rigidly Handelian, of course), and the germ of the idea came to him as he was translating *The Odyssey Rendered into English*

Prose for the use of those who cannot read the original (James Joyce was one of these, incidentally). He wrote most of *The Authoress of the Odyssey* in an unprepossessing inn in Calatafimi and dedicated it to Biagio Ingroia, an ex-priest who had lent his Calatafimi church pulpit to Garibaldi in 1862 for a patriotic outburst including the 'O Roma, O morte' speech, when the Hero returned here during his second, thwarted, attempt to march on Rome. As a result of this gesture, Ingroia had to leave the priesthood and he went on to become the local schoolmaster and eventually Butler's firm friend: they met every year, and Ingroia worked indefatigably helping him with the book.[4] A brief but interesting glimpse of their collaboration is given by the British Library's copy of the Trapani magazine *Quo Vadis* dated 4th October 1901. The article in Italian is entitled 'La Nuova Quistione Omerica. L'Autore dell'Odissea è una Donna?' ('The new Homeric question. Is the author of the Odyssey a woman?') and it has been corrected in ink for typographical and textual errors by Butler himself. It is signed Samuel Butler, London, September 1901, but Butler has added in his elegant handwriting at the end, in Italian: ' No. This article is a translation of an MS of mine done years ago by the deceased Captain Messina-Manzo, with additions of mine that were corrected by Cavaliere Professore Ingroia.' Strange to be reading Butler's hand-written comment on the Calatafimi schoolteacher a hundred years later in London.

Not being a classical scholar, I cannot comment on his theory, except to note that he argues it vigorously and is magnificently angry at not being taken seriously by the establishment ('How can I be other than dismayed at the magnitude, presumption and indeed utter hopelessness, of the task I have undertaken?...However much I may deserve stoning there is no one who can stone me with a clear conscience'). In August 1891 he wrote:

> It was during the few days I was at Chiavenna that I hit upon the feminine authorship of the *Odyssey*. I did not find out its having been written at Trapani till January 1892,

on 30th January of which year *The Athenaeum* published a letter from him containing a detailed geographical case for Trapani being the original Scheria. Few people engaged with him in London, but the pros and cons of the theory were actively debated in Sicilian publications and still are, the latest being published in book form in 2003.[5]

The Authoress, which was published in 1897, was subtitled 'where and when she wrote, who she was, the use she made of the *Iliad* and how the poem grew under her hands.' In highly simplified form, his thesis is that the *Odyssey* must have been written by a woman because the female characters in it are numerous, credible and strenuously defended (in particular, Penelope's dealings with the suitors he saw as a whitewash, a woman's attempt to defend the honour of women), while the male ones are far less well defined. Also the author showed considerable understanding of domesticity and comparative ignorance of 'male' things such as sheep, ships, the sea, timber, hawks and axes. One of the first pointers to this was his noting that

> Polyphemus was made to milk ewes in the morning, though they had had their lambs with them all night, and [I] concluded that the writer was young and town-bred.

He came to the conclusion as well that she was in fact Nausicaa, the princess who helped the stranded Ulysses on the beach at Scheria in the saga, and was in reality the daughter of the King of Scheria/Trapani. His theory that the *Odyssey* was a voyage round Sicily, beginning and ending in Trapani and Eryx, is built up with Victorian thoroughness from the study of mythology wedded to geography, a considerable amount of research in the Map Room of the British Museum,[6] and meticulous on-site inspections carried out by Sugameli and other friends in Trapani, such as the Calatafimi schoolmaster Ingroia and Butler's friend, fellow musician and biographer, Henry Festing Jones.

It was never likely that the subject matter of his book, written in English – apart from anything else – would become the talk of Calatafimi, but his memory still lives on today, if imperfectly. Strangely enough, a Circolo Culturale Samuel Butler was opened a few months ago. It is true, I swear it, though as an institution it has so far been dormant. Before coming here, I had had no idea that Butler had been in Calatafimi, and my first inkling was early on when I was told that Calatafimi had been the meeting place for a famous English writer, a de-frocked priest, and another local de-frocked priest: Ingroia, I discovered later. My informant also said there was a secretary (Festing Jones) who published all his work, the implication being that their stay in Calatafimi was some form of Victorian sex tourism.

Butler was never of course a priest although he had been destined for the Church, and he would probably have ended up as a bishop, like his grandfather, had he not lost his faith. He could not accept the dogma of infant baptism. As a consequence he also lost his father's support, which forced him into making a success of sheep-farming in New Zealand. Although he never married, I can find no evidence of his being homosexual. Indeed Festing Jones talks of his friend 'Madame': 'Madame had had predecessors, but during the twenty years of intimacy with Butler she had no rivals,'[7] unless one counts Miss Savage, whose opinion was sought on all he wrote, but about whom Butler felt guilty because he could not bring himself to fall in love with her. Ingroia, having allowed Garibaldi his pulpit in 1862, clearly had to leave the Church, but he stayed on in Calatafimi as a happily married teacher and subsequently a *cavaliere*, an esteemed pillar of society. Festing Jones did have an allowance from Butler, after his father Canon Butler died and his son's finances had improved, but this was so that he, Festing Jones, could give up trying to be a lacklustre solicitor and help Butler, principally with his music. The allowance ceased at Festing Jones's mother's death, when he also had an inheritance. He promptly proposed to restore the money to Butler but it was refused. He continued to visit Sicily after Butler's death, writing about Sicily and Butler, though he was not his literary executor.

The book, which was originally to have been dedicated to a Trapanese friend called Emanuele Biaggini, who had helped Butler and introduced him to Trapani and its men of culture but who had died, was actually dedicated in Italian to 'Professor Cav. Biagio Ingroia, Prezioso Alleato, L'Autore riconoscente' ('Prof. Cav. Biagio Ingroia. To the Precious Ally. From the grateful Author').

This produced a beautiful thank-you letter from the 'Precious Ally' in Calatafimi, written in his picturesque English to the 'grateful Author':

My Dearest Friend

I have not any expression and want word suitables to signify my wonder in reading your most kind postcard on 21 istant. The undeserved hight of honour with which you regale me, inscribing your justly dearly book to my poor name and in such a manner joining it to your deserved renown, way so unexpected and much precious gift that I have been strongly struck and affected with it and wept for joy together with my wife. It is and will be for ever my better title of honour in which I will take pride only angry to not deserve it.

Thank you most heartily my dearest friend – no more friend but my true brother in love, if you please, for I have not neither could never met or find another gentleman so good-hearted and so dear to my soul on the world.

My wife send you her kindest regards; likewise the family Adamo with Giulio; the family Mollica with all our friends. Give our salutations to Mr Jones and you take an hug from truly always yours, B. Ingroia.

The standard of Ingroia's English suggests that Butler might have communicated in Italian when he was in Calatafimi. Apropos of this letter, Festing Jones noted that Butler felt it to be quite something to accept a hug from one who had been hugged and kissed three times by Garibaldi (after the 'O Roma O Morte' incident, when Ingroia had still been a priest). The 'family Mollica' mentioned was Caterina's great-grandfather's, and the Adamo family were relations.

Appropriately, I read the book for the first time in the Calatafimi library. The fly-leaf has the following dedication in Ingroia's fine handwriting:

> This book
> Has been restaured
> To the municipal library
> Of
> Calatafimi
> And Inscribed to the young students
> Who like anybody, everything
> Honouring our fatherland
> By
> Biagio Ingroia
> Today seventh of March
> Of the year (A.D.) 1901

Although he made a lot of noise as a public iconoclast, Butler left practically nothing he wrote about his time in Calatafimi that I have been able to find, although Festing Jones fills in some gaps.

Butler and I were together in Italy nearly every year from 1878 to 1901 inclusive. He went alone to Sicily every Autumn from 1892 to 1895 inclusive, joining me afterwards in North Italy. In the three years 1898-1901 he went to Sicily in the Spring and I accompanied him. He went alone in the Spring of 1902 and I shall always regret that I was not with him on what proved to be his last journey.

Not all of these visits were spent in Calatafimi, and what happened when he was there one has to glean indirectly, as in private matters Butler was very private. Only brief glimpses of him in Sicily survive. Here is one of him in his shirt-sleeves:

> He is of a happy frame of mind and speaks Italian well, though with something of an effort. He is a good eater, like the Polyphemus in his *Odyssey*. A worthy son of Albion, while he drinks his coffee he smokes, reads the paper and drinks wine...[8]

Not a picture of the Victorian moralist that springs naturally to mind.

He and Festing Jones invariably stayed in the Albergo Centrale, owned by Sebastiano Renda, a legal man, which was run by a much appreciated elderly couple, Don Paolo (in the intervals when he was not mending shoes) and his wife Donna Maria, both of whom were most attached to him. It was thought that Donna Maria had been very beautiful in her youth, and when this was mentioned she allowed herself a smile. When they first met, she still had one rather long tooth in her mouth, and when, subsequently, it had fallen out, Butler commented, perhaps with Mrs Jupp of *The Way of All Flesh* in mind: 'Si può suonare una bella melodia su un violino vecchio' ('You can play a good tune on an old violin'). She appeared to appreciate the compliment. This was a far cry from 15 Clifford's Inn, Fleet Street, London EC, where his ordered life was looked after by the all-capable manservant Arthur Caithie.

After Butler's death, Ingroia wrote to Festing Jones that the Municipal Council had adopted by acclamation a motion naming a street after him, and Renda followed suit by changing the name of his hotel. Festing Jones called in at Calatafimi in the spring of 1903 on his way to Trapani to leave the MS of *The Authoress of the Odyssey* to the town. He had lunch with Ingroia and his family, after which 'I gave him a card-case of Butler's and a sketch made by him the last time we were in Calatafimi, also the negatives of several snapshots Butler took at different times in the neighbourhood.' They then visited the Albergo Centrale, now called the Albergo Samuel Butler, and the via Samuel Butler. Ingroia had obtained the stone for the road-sign and had it cut in Trapani at his own expense; but the Municipality did at least pay for putting it up. (This municipal deliberation, which also expressed friendship for the English nation, was 'undeliberated' later on by the Fascists in 1935, and the road became known as the via Segesta; the hotel had been closed down by 1908 after Don Paolo's death). Festing Jones saw the old couple and told Donna Maria that she was 'sempre giovane e allegra' ('ever younger and happier-looking') which, as it was her own opinion, was received with another smile. The last glimpse of her comes from Festing Jones in 1908, by which time Don Paolo was dead and Donna Maria had been reduced to selling newspapers – she died the next year. These were Butler's worthy hosts when he was in Calatafimi, and they turn up in other people's quests to discover what Butler had been up to in Calatafimi, too.

Festing Jones was not alone in visiting Calatafimi after Butler's death. His literary executor, R.A. Streatfield, was there in June 1903. I know this because he gave Ingroia a copy of *The Way of All Flesh*, in which he had written an introductory note. In the fly-leaf there is this dedication: 'To Biagio Ingroia, in memory of our friend the author, from R.A. Streatfield.' This volume was later passed on to a young student, Giovanni Autuori, who became a pharmacist in Calatafimi, and whose grandson is one now. Another of Giovanni's grandsons, a cousin of my father-in-law's, has it today, as well as another book, Butler's biography of *his* grandfather, the *Life and Letters of Samuel Butler 1790-1840*, which was also given to Giovanni Autuori by Ingroia – to whom it was thought to have been given by Butler himself. After having a good look at both of them, I gave them back to the proud owner.

Festing Jones does have some other vignettes of Butler in Calatafimi, but they are very simple, almost domestic, and based on picnics and snap shots – Butler was an accomplished amateur photographer. It might be worth mentioning just one of them. In 1894, when he was fifty-eight he went with Ingroia and other friends by horse to Mount Inici, beyond Segesta, to find the remains of a castle that had once been used for hunting by the Emperor Charles V, and where he had been told there were prehistoric ruins. The ruins did not materialize, and they had their picnic lunch in the shade of some trees which shielded them from brilliant blue skies and scorching Sicilian heat. After a reflective silence he announced quite unexpectedly, shaking his head sagely: 'It will not snow today.' A moment of perplexity, and then everyone burst out laughing: why I cannot begin to understand. The laughter was probably nervous – at least I cannot see anything funny in his remark – but it became part of local folklore. He was known in the town as the Englishman who held that the

Odyssey had been written by a young girl in Trapani, and who had announced that it was not about to snow in September. Apparently, the remark was a private joke of his, from his New Zealand days, though I have never got to the bottom of it, as I say. It does very occasionally snow in Calatafimi, but when it does it will be around February.

While Butler himself wrote practically nothing about the town, there is a passage in the Note Books which illustrates something of the poverty of Calatafimi at the time, as well as his own curiosity.[9]

> Jones and I at Calatafimi saw some children who had got a mouse to whose hind leg they had tied a string. They kept letting it run away and then pulling it back again. Ingroia and two or three others were with us, and said we had better not interfere. On our return an hour or so later we saw the boys pouring some stuff that looked like water over the mouse, but which on enquiring we found to be petroleum, which they were about to light. Having burnt the poor wretch alive, and thus partly roasted it, Ingroia said they would eat it. On pursuing the subject I was told there was another, much larger kind of mouse nearly as big as a rabbit, with a long tail, which was a much greater delicacy. 'Ma sono proprio coneglie' (sic) (i.e. they really were rabbits) was repeated over and over again. On enquiring still further at Trapani, I was assured that the peasants in the country eat rats whenever they catch them. The son of the landlord of the Hotel Centrale (at Calatafimi) told me that once in a peasant's cottage he found them eating, as he thought, a sparrow pie, and had some. On asking what birds the pie was made of he was told they were mice not birds.

The man who flayed Victorian ethics and some of its heroes – he had a long public argument with Darwin – who maintained that an egg was not a hen's attempt to create another hen but an egg's attempt to create another egg, who foretold that men will become to 'machines what the horse and the dog are to man', and who influenced countless distinguished writers, although he made almost no money out of his own writing during his lifetime,[10] lived a simple and unchronicled life here in Calatafimi, writing a book he knew would irritate the English academic establishment – a fact that mystified many people. That he came so often can only mean that he liked the place, because it was hardly a Homeric site.

Among the various people who arrived in quest of Butler was one Louis Golding, who came here in the early 1920s to look for the hotel.[11] Climbing up the hill towards the town with a rucksack on his back, he was offered a mule by a group of villagers and some children gave him flowers and a thorned twig to use as a goad:

> So I rode into Calatafimi with roses in one hand and a goad in the other, to pay my obsequies to the shade of Samuel Butler, not knowing which of those two offerings his shade would appreciate most. I required them to take me to the hostelry named after him, but I was led to so reeking and cavernous a place that I cried, 'avanti'! This cannot be it!...They took me to another hotel,[12] named of Garibaldi, and dispiritedly I entered its not much more joyous portal, letting the thorny roses drop from my hand. For though I had hardly expected the inhabitants of Calatafimi to have formed Samuel Butler Study Circles and to be standing at the street corners with copies of *Alps and Sanctuaries* and *The Authoress of the Odyssey* under their arms, I had hoped at least to find his name green, to find it more than a foreign gibberish on the plate of a street...[at first the hotelier could not work out the Albergo Samuel Butler, but]...Then of a sudden he suspended the shakings [of his head] and bade me repeat the name. This time he recognized it as an attempt upon the curious collection of sounds which constituted the name of one of the principal streets of his city. He remained buried in thought for some minutes, then ventured the information that this very hotel was called by that name twenty or thirty years ago. It was the name of some forestiere, a commercial traveller who used to come to this inn and make up his accounts. He had a feeling that he travelled in books and stationery, but it was all so long ago, before his time as landlord, and he could not be sure.

While a certain amount of artistic licence must have been woven into the above, Butler never forced himself on the attention of the town; nor does he now, although for some considerable time Simone Agueli, a local educator, did nurture his memory, and, as I have just told you, a Study Circle has recently been dedicated to him, which would no doubt have pleased Golding. All the same there is still a vague awareness that a famous English writer was somehow connected with the town a long time ago.

The last word, though it preceded Golding's account by ten years or so, should go to Israel Zangwill,[13] who arrived in Palermo by sea from Tunis to find the customs in the port were unable to compute the customs duty on bicycles, and describes his cycling trip in Sicily as 'to pedal backwards in time' (what about Tunis, for Heaven's sake?). He also came to Calatafimi:

I was not aware that any English writer had achieved the distinction
of stamping his name on a Sicilian street, or even – quainter, if lesser
glory – upon a Sicilian inn. Yet at Calatafimi, a little town so obscure
(despite its heroic Garibaldi memories) that it had not yet reached the
picture-postcard stage, a town five miles from a railway station, up one
of the steepest and stoniest roads of the island, I lodged at the Albergo
Samuele Butler, and walked through the via Samuele Butler.

He met Donna Maria, then a septuagenarian, who showed him
photographs of herself with Butler. She said to him that he called her
'la bella Maria'. Festing Jones later told him that 'he [Butler] always
remembered all about everybody and asked how the potatoes were
doing this year [most unlikely: potatoes are not common], and
whether the grandchildren were growing up into fine boys and girls;
and he never forgot to enquire after the son who had gone to be a
waiter in New York.' He was struck that this

British iconoclast...was hail fellow well met with the cottagers
of Calatafimi...[and] how the first century and the fortieth [were]
lodging under the same roof – for Butler was at least as far ahead
of the twentieth century as his hostess was behind it.

He slept in the same bed as

perhaps the subtlest wit since Swift...The walls of his bedroom in the
formerly yclept Albergo Centrale are whitewashed, the ceiling is of logs,
the washstand of iron, and even if the water jug is a lovely Greek vase
with two handles, and the pail a beautiful green basin...The bed is of
planks on iron trestles. The Albergo itself, with its primitive sanitation,
is in keeping with its best room. For Sicily it is, perhaps, a Grand Hotel,
embracing as it does an entire flat of three bedrooms on the second floor
(a cobbler occupies the ground floor, and the mystery of the first floor
I have never penetrated)...All the same the attraction of Calatafimi for
Butler is difficult to explain. It is one of the dingiest of Sicilian towns,
littered with poultry, goats, children and refuse, though, of course, you
are soon out of it and amid the scenery of Theocritus. But the view from
Butler's own balcony – often of paramount consideration for a writer –
was not remarkably stimulating: hemmed in by the opposite houses,
though rising into hills and a ruined castle.

He goes on to describe the hotel's arrangements when he was there,
which changed in accordance with the number of the guests; he gives

a sympathetic picture of Donna Maria; and he wonders that such a complex character could have reduced his demands on life to the simplicity of living in that way.

Butler just liked Calatafimi.

Zangwill ends on a note that would please Butler even now. The theological side of Butler was expressed in his belief that the only afterlife for the dead lies in the hearts and minds of the living, and Zangwill quotes a sonnet of his published in *The Athenaeum*:

> We shall not even know that we have met,
> Yet meet we shall, and part, and meet again
> Where dead men meet, on the lips of living men.

> It is strange to me, who lived – as chronology would say – in the same age as Butler, and in the same London, and only a minute's walk from him, to think that I should yet never have met him save on the lips of the peasants of Calatafimi, lips that spoke only Sicilian.

You also have just been conversing with the late Samuel Butler in Calatafimi.

6

Foreign Travellers on Calatafimi

I have an Intrepid Travellers corner for you now. There were scores of them, and intrepid they surely were. Most eighteenth-century travellers in Italy thought themselves brave to get as far south as Naples, and so many of them in fact did that the British Envoy Plenipotentiary, Sir William Hamilton, became a trifle fed up looking after them, however much they appreciated his 'vases' or the 'attitudes' of his wife. Only a small proportion made the journey on from Naples to the second of the Two Sicilies; and, in those early days, most of them were satisfied with a glimpse of the monstrously interesting Etna and vastly pleasant Palermo with its social rout. Those few of them who reached as far as these wild parts came to see Segesta, and some of them put up briefly in, and with, Calatafimi, leaving their impressions, some sympathetic, some mightily uncomplimentary, and all of them revealing as much about themselves as the circumstances they experienced. None of them tarried more than was necessary.

Though the son of the poet John Donne got there exceptionally early on,[1] most visits to Sicily were set in motion by that enormously popular eighteenth-century trail-blazing travel book, *A Tour through Sicily and Malta*, written by the Scottish borderer Patrick Brydone in 1773.[2] Before its appearance, educated opinion had been decidedly negative about Sicily, even if we are only to judge from that sacred repository of European Enlightenment, the *Encyclopédie*, which was largely ignorant of the island and dismissive to a degree: 'Abrégeons: la Sicile n'a plus rien aujourd'hui de considerable, que ses montagnes et son Tribunal de l'Inquisition' ('In a nutshell: Sicily has nothing more of interest to offer us now, except its mountains and its courts of the Inquisition'); and, *voilà*, that was that. The Philosophes were not interested and it was left to Brydone to edge the veil off Sicily's dangerous face. His book was also avidly read in French and

German, thanks to immediate translations. Some read it at home and fantasized about the savagery of Sicilian life (Anne Radcliffe used whole bits of it[3]); the more adventurous came to the island to experience what Brydone had so intriguingly described, some of them criticizing his many colourful inaccuracies. Brydone never went to Segesta or Calatafimi, but he played Pied Piper to generations of travellers who did go. The Sicilian travel industry really ought to have commemorated him in an appropriate way.

I am only going to expose you to a few of these intrepid travellers, stepping over names like Goethe (who wasn't anyway over-impressed by Segesta and thought that Calatafimi across the valley looked like a 'mycological colony'), as well as a host of others. If they stayed at all, they used the town to find something to eat and a bed for the night, so that there was not much what you might call in-depth analysis, and their thirst for philosophizing was usually assuaged at Segesta. Some of them hated Calatafimi, and I therefore detest them. Some liked it, and my heart opens to them.

Jean Houel, a painter who had Caravaggio's eye for drama, dirt, horses and chiaroscuro and spent four years in Sicily from 1776 to 1780, said that he did not enjoy Calatafimi much, although he was a highly adaptable traveller and spent a long time on the island. That calm, balanced gentleman Henry Swinburne, who travelled in Sicily with his large family between 1783 and 1785, spent Christmas Day here and approved in a patrician sort of way. Chamier and Warren, who were not permitted to pay for their excellent board, found the company agreeable. Douglas Sladen rather liked it, perhaps because he found a good ready-made story in Segesta. Louis Golding enjoyed describing the station and defended Calatafimi against the superficial insults handed out by the famous motorized-tourist Maurice Maeterlinck. W.A. Paton painted a far from picturesque portrait of Calatafimi in a time of poverty which marked the first phase of Sicilian emigration to the United States. René Bazin, who was there just after 1900, stayed in the 'Albergo Centrale' of Butler fame, also quite liked it and discovered a delightfully romantic lady who decidedly did like it and indeed espoused it. These were just some of them.

But I shall begin from the negative corner, at least as far as the town is concerned, with none other than the young Rev J.H. Newman, well before he became famous and donned a Cardinal's hat. Despite the fact that, during his visit to Segesta in 1833, he met a 'few rude intrusive men, who would have robbed us, I fancy, had they dared', and 'a savage-looking bull prowling amid the ruins' of the theatre, he declared the visit to have been an essential event in his life:

> In all Sicily the chief sight has been Segesta...by contrast with the misery of its population, the depth of the squalidness and brutality by which it is surrounded. It has been a day in my life to have seen Egesta.

That was written to his sister Jemima on 9th February. For his mother on the 28th he concentrated on the misery:

> but Calatafimi, where we slept, I dare not mention the facts. Suffice it to say, we found the poor children of the house slept in holes dug into the wall, which smelt not like a dog-kennel, but like a wild beast's cage, almost overpowering us in the room upstairs. I have no sleep all night from insects of prey; but this was a slight evil. The misery is increased from the custom of having the stable on the ground floor and the kitchen on the first. The dwelling is on the second floor.[4]

Newman was thirty-two at the time, still involved with the Oxford Movement, and still highly critical of his future Church: in the same letter to his mother he writes: 'The state of the Church is deplorable. It seems as if Satan was let out of prison to range the whole earth again.' I do not feel any sympathy towards Newman, though I don't suppose you – or anybody else – will care two hoots about my opinion of him.

A few years earlier in 1828 a Frenchman, Louis Simond, did dare to mention the facts, and in doing so he illustrated the innate, if rudimentary, hospitality that was willingly bestowed on visitors by the citizens of Calatafimi. After a tiring visit to Segesta, and while waiting at Calatafimi for one of their horses to be shoed, the inhabitants invited him and his fellow travellers into their houses to rest. Simond judged the houses too dirty to accept, but some of his companions did, and his comment was as follows:

> Those of us who accepted the invitation gave us a frightful description when they came out of the absolute destitution and filth that they had encountered, and the vermin that ran all over their clothes gave energetic testimony to this report.[5]

Dirty, poor but hospitable would be my comment on the house-holders, even if you may think I am a fraction partisan.

Less negative but much more dramatic was Jean Houel's much earlier visit to Segesta and Calatafimi in the 1770s.[6] This French court painter and student of architecture spent his first day roughing it at Segesta and, when the time came to find somewhere to rest his limbs in the evening, he made his way to Calatafimi over paths that were horrible even though it was almost May. He says that it was a little town about four miles away on a very high mountain (which is simply not true, although all early travellers talk of the steep road up), that the people were not rich and it had nearly as many churches as houses. He mentions one church in particular, the church of the SS Crocifisso (designed by Giovanni Biagio Amico and built between 1741 and 1759) which, according to him, was one of the most beautifully decorated interiors in Sicily with gilded friezes and sculptures on a white background, 'without parallel, I believe'. This description, which seems exaggerated, is much quoted by local historians, though they fail to reveal what Houel goes on to say: 'However, it inspires more a sense of joy than respect and seems more suitable as a ball-room than a place of worship.' Our local historians, mostly clerics, naturally tend to gloss over this last phrase.

Unlike most travellers, he did not carry any letters of introduction, which were almost a necessity at the time because hostels were few and badly organized, and also because the tinder of Sicilian hospitality was set ablaze by letters of introduction. Houel's normal practice when arriving at a new place was, as he writes, to seek out the doctor for information about local amenities. In this case, he could only find a pharmacist, who showed him some limestone that split horizontally when broken, and insisted on giving him too many samples. It is a stone which is still used today as dressing, and indeed our house is faced with sheets of it.

Without introductions, Houel had to fend for himself. 'When night fell, I went to a dim tavern, where my servant and the *campieri* were waiting for me.' The *campieri* were a sort of armed guard, used by absentee landlords to protect their property, and by visitors to buy their safety from the bandits who were supposed to be as common as rabbits though not as retiring. The Governor of nearby Alcamo had given him provisions for which he was thankful, as the tavern only sold wine and had no space for sleeping. He was directed to a nearby *fondaco*, which he described as a miserable doss-house for muleteers; but it was in fact an institution that he must have been used to, as it was widespread all over Sicily as a sort of post-house for people who needed to travel.

So after he had eaten he went to this *fondaco*. 'My men had got hold of the best bed which, with some difficulty, they had managed to keep hold of and for which the many travellers envied me': it was, he explained, a shelf of stone in a stable. Behind the door, muleteers and their women were cooking.

> I got to bed vainly hoping that my weariness would let me sleep on the stone, but the noisy euphoria of the other guests who sang while they ate and excesses of wine and high spirits that degenerated into the horrors of arguments, swearing and fisticuffs, meant that I could not close my eyes. Suddenly everything went calm. It was quite late. My men were lying on the ground in the stable near me. The men snored, the horses munched, the haltered mules rattled the enormous bells round their necks. In the end, I managed to get to sleep, but then something worse happened. A horrible noise broke out, with neighing and loud banging, which shook the whole house and woke everybody up, with shouts from all sides. A horse which wanted to lie down on the straw had got caught up in its halter and was running the risk of strangling itself.

All hell was let loose. Finally

> I was no longer able to sleep and so contemplated the picturesque sight of men and beasts lying down together and sharing the floor as a form of bed. I was impatient and got up; the sun had not risen as yet, but the sky where the sun would rise was getting light. I woke up my men; I wrote the story of my night's experience, jumped on my horse and went back to Segesta.

That was Houel's reaction. One suspects he was well used to the conditions, and was being a little dramatic for literary reasons. They were more or less the same all over Europe in out-of-the-way places – what about Dr Johnson's travels in the Highlands and Islands, described by Boswell in 1785? Almost all travel at the time was driven by necessity rather than choice, and tourists had to adapt to the available conditions, complain as they might.

A much more benign reaction flowed from the pen of Henry Swinburne, who was travelling in the area around the same time as Houel, in 1777.[7] Reading him gives one the impression of a calm, quintessentially English travelling Gentleman, even though as a Catholic, he and his family were destined to live a life of exile.

Segesta was on his itinerary, but he arrived first in Alcamo, some miles from Calatafimi to the north-east, after giving an interesting if flawed description of the geography and the agricultural techniques of that part of Sicily. He talks of the custom of digging trenches around the roots of the vines in winter so that 'the plant acquires fresh health and vigour by having its roots thus exposed to the air.' It was and is of course a simple technique for collecting rainwater. Unlike Houel, he was carrying letters of introduction, and on arrival at Alcamo

> I lodged at the Archpriest's, a very polite clergyman. He invited the principal gentlemen of the town to supper, which was good, and served up, in handsome plate, no mean sample of the richness of the benefice. The company was well bred and appeared conversant in various branches of literature; one gentleman had a numerous collection of medals, which he would not part with for money, but according to the Italian custom, pressed them on me as a present.

He describes the cultivation of corn, vines, olives and sumach (*Rhus coriaria*, an important export from the district for the tanning of leather and also for the dyeing of Persian carpets).

After they had fed and rested, the family party (wife, children and servants) moved on, and:

> December 25th [1777]. A hilly deep road over high arable country, ten miles to Calatafimi, a large ugly town, belonging to the proprietor of Alcamo [the Count of Modica] and containing eight thousand souls. The environs are well cultivated, and some vineyards and orchards enliven this large tract of corn land. Its castle, now in ruins, stands on the summit of a hill in a commanding situation. Having deposited my baggage, and ordered my supper, I rode down into a low valley, by a disagreeable dangerous path, which was scarce practicable even for my cautious mule. At the foot of the mountain, I forded the river of San Bartolomeo, supposed to be the Crimisus of the ancients, so famous for its god, who, in the shape of a dog, found favour in the eyes of the nymph Segesta, and is represented in that form upon the Segestan coins. I then proceeded about two miles over moist pastures to a place called Barbara [Monte Barbaro], where stood the city of Egesta or Segesta founded by the Trojans.

You might be amused to know that 'at the foot of the mountain' there is now a bridge over the former Crimisus with a large monument erected in the IVth year of the Fascist era, on which Benito Mussolini urges Italians to ascend the new road to the glory of Segesta.

After examining the ruins and musing on what little was left of the city, describing the temple in detail, and noting that

> The clear colour and the majestic disposition of so many columns, on which light and shade are cast in various directions, and the insulated situation of so grand a building on a bold eminence in the midst of a desert, have something singularly awful and sublime in their effect,

his mind began to turn to more mundane things.

> Having spent the best part of the day in examining, measuring and drawing this noble building, I hastened back to Calatafimi, as eager for refreshment as I had been in the morning for antiquities. I found the best fare provided for me that the place could afford; the lodging, however, was old, crazy and cold, but the owners so civil and attentive, that it was impossible to complain of any inconveniences; the master of the house was a notary and his wife one of the prettiest women I have yet seen in Sicily; I was afterwards distressed beyond measure to learn, that they had not suffered my man to pay for the least thing, and had sitten up all night to accommodate us with beds. To enliven the evening conversation, they invited the principal people of the town with their wives, who were very free and sociable; this rather surprised me, as many travellers, and those very modern ones, tell us that the Sicilians are so jealous and severe to their wives, that they never suffer them to come into the company of strangers, much less to join in the conversation with them. I suspect these persons have copied authors who wrote in times, when such mistrust reigned more than it does at present, or have formed general inductions from partial evidence. There seems to be very little constraint laid upon the intercourse of the two sexes among the nobility at Palermo, and none among my visitors at Calatafimi, people of a lower class; the observation, therefore, does not hold good in every instance. The assembly was very attentive to all my words and motions, that they might anticipate my wishes and save me trouble; but their civility was of an unpolished kind; I was frequently the subject of their discourse, and those that knew anything about me, either from the Archbishop's letter or from my servants, communicated their knowledge

aloud to every new comer, as if I were deaf or did not understand their language [did he really understand strict dialect, which they would have spoken among themselves?]. An old gentleman, the wit of the circle, put many questions to me, and in return acquainted me with the politics and scandal of the town; he was possessed of great cheerfulness and native humour, but so totally ignorant of every thing and place beyond the limits of Sicily, that I could never make him comprehend where England is situated, or how circumstanced with regard to its colonies, of which he had learned something from the gazettes. Finding my answers to his questions were incapable of conveying instruction, I gave myself no farther trouble, but suffered him without interruption to smoke his pipe, and in the intervals of his long puffing to run on in a long string of stories, confounding times, names, places and persons, in so ludicrous a manner, that the most inflexible features must have been betrayed into a smile – fortunately he took my laugh for a compliment, and joined very heartily in it.

That says a lot about Swinburne and the provincial society here. As a loyal citizen of Calatafimi, I am proud they treated him well, if perhaps in an unpolished way, and I should certainly have liked his hosts.

On 26th December 1777, the family set off towards Castelvetrano, travelling along the same route I traced for you earlier, when walking you into Calatafimi: there are more trees now, but he would have passed by the old house in a part of which we now live. This is how he describes it:

> The next morning being, as the night had been, cold and stormy, the peasants went to Church in short dark surtouts with capuchin hoods, which, added to their swarthy complexions, sour looks, and greasy frizzled hair, composed the blackest congregation I ever beheld. The road from Calatafimi is extremely steep and clayey; a few inclosures surround the town, but at a small distance commences a very mountainous country covered with grass, and destitute of trees. The temple of Segesta makes a noble appearance on a verdant knoll embosomed in the lofty hills...the rocks lie here at day shining like diamonds, being composed of chalk and gypsum...

And so he went on in his leisurely way with his numerous family.

Like the Swinburnes, another large party in the middle of the next century had similar problems over paying for the hospitality they received. Chamier and Warren[8] were a party of six: Captain and Mrs

Chamier, Warren, Polehampton, Mrs Chamier's French maid and 'Tilly'. The Viceroy at Palermo, the Prince of Satriano, had given them an introduction to Father Pampalone of Calatafimi ('Pampeluna', according to both Chamier and Warren), and the Chief of Police, the infamous Maniscalco, had arranged for an escort. They carried in their 'large carriage with rumble…besides six bottles of porter, and another containing something more potent…enough oranges and biscuits to have regaled a half-starved boys' school.' After a trip of forty-two miles from Palermo, they arrived at Calatafimi and, although their host had never even travelled as far as Palermo, Chamier judged that there was in Pampalone 'an elegance in his simplicity, and character in his manner, which stamped him as an unpretending but true gentleman'; his house was 'elegantly, comfortably and usefully furnished'. There were language problems, but the ladies proved helpful and

> Pampeluna [curé of 6,000 souls], his brother and the curé of the other two thousand seemed a trinity of excellent companionship. Kindness, hospitality, generosity, seemed to pervade them all; and how any kitchen in Calatafime could have supplied so excellent a dinner, I cannot conceive.

Next morning, after a very early visit to Segesta with horses and guides provided free for them by their host, they were given an equally excellent breakfast. They were aware that it was unethical to offer money in return for priests' hospitality, so Chamier mentioned that he had noted the poverty of the parishioners and wondered if he could offer some funds to help the poor. Any sort of payment was resolutely and lengthily refused, on the grounds that the two parishes were quite able to look after them, and it was only when Chamier claimed that it would be on his *conscience* if he did not contribute something to the well-being of the parishioners, that Pampalone accepted a fraction of what they were offering (the guides and horseman had fewer scruples). Despite being mobbed by the poor when leaving and being rescued by the vociferous trinity of their hosts, Chamier left this judgement on Pampalone:

> This man [was] as happy and contented as if the whole world was concentrated in his parish, and listened to and obeyed his exhortations, to love one another, fear God, and honour the King.

I am now going to push you forward in time – towards another mentality. Douglas Sladen[9] came from Castelvetrano in the opposite direction, on his way to Palermo, at the beginning of the twentieth century. On arrival at the railway station, he had the usual trouble with the price of the coach, but paid it because there was no alternative.

> We had been informed that the district had a bad name for brigandage, and appearances appeared to confirm the idea; for the road wound up to Calatafimi round the edges of wild looking hills, and we saw so many villainous-looking sportsmen, mounted as well as armed and accompanied by dogs. When Mr Forbes-Robertson [the famous actor] made the journey in 1900, he was compelled to have a carabiniere in the carriage with him, who, on starting, loaded his revolver with most disquieting ostentatiousness.

For some extraordinary reason, probably because he had written a book on that country, he compared the countryside to Japan. They came into sight of Calatafimi and

> just before we came to the town we passed a shallow almond-fringed valley, with a picturesque washing pool, and many men in their dark blue, hooded cloaks, and flocks of striped goats, while on the hill there was a ruined convent with a dome like a mosque.

The carriage left them at the bottom of the valley from where they walked up to Segesta. They encountered a large number of lizards at Segesta and a distinguished German couple 'being shown around by quite half a dozen people'. After a lengthy visit to the ruins, both they and the German couple realized they had misjudged the time and had to rush for the train, with the result that the German lady

> slipped and fell. Instantly the rough-looking men who had been eyeing them from above in a most suspicious sort of way, though they had not even gone so far as to beg, rushed down. But all they did was to lift her up quite gently and help her down to her carriage. We had visions of heavy blackmail, but saw no money pass.

For the way back to the station came this description.

> We decided we should have liked to stay at Calatafimi. That chimneyless

town in the clear mountain air stood out like a piece of carving, especially the ruined Saracenic castle and the ruinous convent with its brown battlements and mosque-like dome. In the little valley below there were gebbia's [an Arabic word for water cisterns] and wells, and nowhere else had we seen such groups of women drawing water into antique-looking pitchers, and gliding away with them balanced on their shoulders. As they came up from the valley they walked in Indian file up the narrow, stoney paths, as if they had been as smooth as the roads, but on the road they walked two or three abreast, and when they were on a rise in front of you against the sky they looked as though they might have been taken from a frieze on the Parthenon. In different parts of the island they carry their pitchers in different ways; here it is always on the shoulder.

By then the fear of bandits began to creep in on them again:

Haven't you noticed that hardly any of the people we are passing know the driver?...Well, I think all these men with asses and mules and guns and these goat-herds in their skin clothes are brigands...Some of the men in their top boots and spurs, and blue, hooded cloaks falling in elegant folds on their mules, certainly did not look like peasants out to shoot small birds...as we neared the railway station a cart drew up suddenly in front of the coach and brought us to a dead stop, while two of the armed men on mules clattered up. But a second later I caught sight of three 'bersaglieri' [a crack Italian regiment recognizable by the feathers in their helmets] with their rifles at the port guarding nothing on earth but the station monkey.

They arrived at the station, and

the first use we made of our safety was to get out our tea-basket from the cloak-room, and monopolize the table and most of the seats in the tiny waiting-room. Presently the Germans...came into the waiting-room [and] we noticed that all the people who were with them waited outside. We were glad. We had only to make room for two people. Directly she was seated he went out and fetched a chair for her to put up her sprained foot...So we finished our tea, and in the falling dusk glided out of the valley with its picturesque vines...No one, not even the stationmaster, dares sleep in the valley below, for it is one of the most malarious spots in Sicily and the kindly railway people warned us to close our windows, as sunset is the deadly hour.

When they got to Palermo they were informed that

there was quite a regiment of bersaglieri guarding you today...Not all for us?...No, not all for you. Some of them were for the brother of the German Emperor and his wife, who have also been to Segesta today.

They were actually only the Emperor's cousins.

Calatafimi's station also plays a part in Louis Golding's 1925 book *Sicilian Noon*. He came up by train from Alcamo (just one stop), to be met by

> the stationmaster at the halt of Segesta [who] gave me wine and eggs. So fiercely the sun blazed that he invited me into the shade of his dining room. It was also his bedroom and his hen coop. He had a wife, for he presented her to me, and an assortment of children, who presented themselves. But the bed was as narrow as an operation-couch. Where did the wife and family dispose themselves at night?

These speculations continued for 'half an hour or more' when this relatively tranquil gastronomic self-questioning was sharply interrupted by the sound of a female voice with a strong Scottish accent shouting angrily in French at a defensive male speaking dialect. I have already told you about this incident of the old woman who commandeered a carter to take her to Segesta. There was never any doubt of who would win.

> He was the sort of man who, had he asked for ten liras, would have received twenty-five, he was so strong and savage to look upon. The little old lady from Selkirkshire was stronger and savager. She took her seat in the Palermo train as if it were the afternoon slow to Selkirk. The knob of her umbrella appeared for a moment through the window.

We have heard that there is no stationmaster now. Golding was in Calatafimi on the quest for the hotel that Butler had stayed in which I described to you some time back. Although he did not like the town, he took great offence at the superficial and derisory remarks that had been made about it just before his visit by Maurice Maeterlinck, the noted playwright and Nobel prizewinner for literature in 1911, who had briefly visited Sicily in a new-fangled motor car with a Baedeker, publishing his experiences in the first issue of the French review *Demain*. He felt strongly that the citizens of Calatafimi in no way deserved phrases like 'curiosité de negrillons ou des grands singes' ('curiosity of black men or large monkeys') and that he would

write a refutation of M. Maeterlinck's 'calumnies'. So I enrol Golding as a Friend of Calatafimi. But I can find no trace of his refutation.

A much less romantic, if equally animated, description of Calatafimi is provided by W.A. Paton,[10] an American traveller of Scottish
origin, who saw a depressing side to Calatafimi around 1897, when
extreme poverty had already set the rush for America in motion.
After an hour's journey from the station, straining up the hills and
rushing down them at breakneck speed

we arrived at the crest of the hill, and just below it, on its further, its
southwestern slope, beheld Calatafimi, a city of ten thousand people.
Down a stretch of badly paved highway we plunged, the old vettura
rattling like a hundred pairs of castanettes, and swaying from side to
side, and entered a narrow and untidy street, through which we
careered, reckless of the consternation, not to say terror, we occasioned
to children, pigs, fowls and mangy cur-dogs, that fled screaming,
squealing, cackling and yelping promiscuously into dirty houses or
down filthy side-streets, or still filthier alleys, pell-mell, in mad struggle
to escape from our onward charge. Suddenly the vettura drew up in
front of an albergo, at sight of which we instantly congratulated
ourselves that we were not dependent upon its hospitality for
entertainment. Indeed, the squalor of the town, the filth accumulated
in the streets, the sickening odours which polluted even the mountain
air, the poverty-stricken appearance of the inhabitants, the loathsome
aspect of hosts of beggars who crowded around our conveyance,
mumbling, whining, some boldly demanding alms, grimacing idiotically,
gesticulating wildly, as they exhibited gruesome scars or hideous
deformities…all these sights and sounds made us impatient to continue
our journey with as little delay as possible. On taking our departure
from the albergo we were compelled to go on foot, owing to the
steepness and roughness of the streets, to a gate of the city at the
opposite side of the town from that by which we had entered. It is
needless to say that we were followed by a crowd of beggars, who
limped and hobbled after us, plucked at our garments, ran before us,
and stood in our way, crying 'Muore di fame, signori! Muore di fame,
signori!' (Dying of hunger, your worships! Dying of hunger, your
worships). We hurried on, utterly disconcerted by the awful spectacle,
dropping half a handful of soldi in hopes of delaying the mob, that
seemed ready, in the recklessness of despair, to lay hands on us, and
we dared not look behind to see the mad scramble for the coppers.[11]

Such is the milk of human kindness, and what a difference if we compare this with the town and hotel Butler was describing at around the same time and his untroubled pleasure.

I began with a Frenchman, so let me finish with one and allow him to introduce you with gallant aplomb to an English Gentlewoman.

One day in about 1900 René Bazin, a member of the Académie Française, came with a friend from Palermo to see Segesta, and it was not on the first train.[12] This created problems because arriving at a late hour it meant that a visit to the ruins would be late in the afternoon, and to get to them you had to go through the valley at a time when malaria was known to come out of the mists and strike. Somebody had been detailed to look after them, a certain Bommarito, who had arranged for a coach to meet them at the station and for donkeys to take them, on the second stage of their visit, to the ruins of Segesta. But because it was late afternoon and their hosts were clearly worried, Bommarito and the coachman were loath to make the trip, and the problem was only solved on the appearance at the station of an enterprising young Greek god from nearby Alcamo, who intervened and said: yes, Excellencies, he would do anything they desired (for a consideration of course), yes, Excellencies. So they started off, with Bommarito still accompanying them. After many promises that Calatafimi was just round the corner, they did finally arrive.

> This strange little city, mediaeval to the core, with its winding narrow streets and sense of belonging to another time, was at that moment in the late afternoon receiving back into the safety of its walls all its farmers and workers after their day of labour, leaving the country, as their ancestors had always done, to the bandits and malaria which held sway at sunset.

They checked in at the Albergo Centrale and began their descent towards the river, the donkeys and Segesta.

Clearly, the donkey drivers were not there waiting where they should have been, and Bommarito was considerably put out. The scene is described with great colour by Bazin. From under the wheels of the carriage, he maintains, there emerged the most miserable twenty-year-old youth he had ever seen, who offered to conduct them to the ruins in a deep silence in which not even a bird was to be heard. On the way up to the temple, he explained to the two Frenchmen that 'to sleep there in the valley was to be a dead man'. They saw the ruins in a most romantic fashion under the stars, and in their rush back to the carriage they disturbed the custodian of the ruins quietly smoking his pipe. He informed them that only one other person, an Englishman, had ever visited the temple at that late hour when the moon was up. They had no moon, but they made it back to Calatafimi in time for dinner at the Albergo Centrale. But that was not all. At around ten p.m., to the astonishment of the innkeeper, they decided to visit the town, the architecture of which made a picturesque nocturnal impression on them, as did a mule with a tolling bell round its neck that, taken aback, eyed them drowsily.

It was at this delicious moment, contemplating the dark outlines of the houses of Calatafimi, that surprise overtook them. They heard a pianoforte playing, and a lady singing...what...No, it cannot be! ...Yes, it was!: *GOD SAVE THE QUEEN.*

After a moment of disbelief and even possibly Gallic chagrin, they got the whole story, an 'idylle moderne', from the miserable twenty-year-old who had taken them to Segesta and had never left them thereafter. It was the 'Baronessa Inglese' singing, he informed them. It transpired that a rich, dark-complexioned (but why that should be of importance, I do not know) English lady,[13] a woman who had seen the whole world from the Himalayas to the Rocky Mountains, had been travelling in these parts – like all English women, dauntless and carrying just a pocket handkerchief, a guide-book and a notepad – only to arrive at Calatafimi and be completely overwhelmed.

Since it was a very poor town, any rich foreign woman was of course promoted Baronessa, and this she became. She rented a large apartment and looked around to buy sagaciously the sort of things that would render her life even more romantic than it already was. She bought time on a balcony, that is to say it became hers when festivals and processions were taking place, so that from it she could look down at them. Then a particular rocky bit of land with a startling view. Then a windy promontory (although it seems to have earned an asterisk in Baedeker) near Segesta, on which she constructed a pavilion where she could take tea at five o'clock and contemplate the Greek ruins. She thought that ought to have been all she desired, but she failed to account for the intelligence of Sicilian peasants, who have an innate understanding of how to take advantage of poetical natures. One day, one of them presented himself with the usual obsequious excuses and announced that unfortunately, and for compelling reasons, he had to cut down a tree that bordered her land. Horror of horrors, it was a tragedy that had to be avoided at all costs: the tree was wildly beautiful, its absence would cruelly spoil her idyllic panorama – and so it and the land around it were rapidly bought. After that, everybody joined in, and many striking trees together with the land around them were acquired by the Baronessa. Her cash guaranteed her idyllic panorama and no doubt made a number of humble families very happy.

But that was not all. By no means. Her entry into landholding inevitably led to litigation and at one point she had a case going that needed professional advice. Perchance at that very moment the illustrious Professor Commendatore Maruffa, who had been born at Calatafimi but now taught law in the far-off University of Urbino, was back visiting his home town. She heard about this and requested his advice, which was forthcoming. The next morning he received, in an envelope, a five-lira note and he was offended. He sent it back in another envelope with a note saying he would either accept much more money for such things, or nothing at all. The effect was dramatic. A meeting was arranged and an envelope with a suitable amount of money was passed over with the sincere comment: 'Commendatore, you are proud man and I respect proud people.' Other court cases proceeded; she had need of further consultations, with which Maruffa supplied her, and for which she paid him what had been established as the appropriate amount for a proud Commendatore. This became embarrassing even for Maruffa who wrote to her that 'like my medical colleagues, when diverse consultations are needed for a chronic illness I lower my fees'. Her reaction was in character: 'Commendatore, you are not only a proud man, you are also profoundly honest: you are a GENTLEMAN'. Within the hour she had proposed to him. Once again the Commendatore was embarrassed: he was younger than her and had his career to consider, but on the other hand she was rich and the University of Urbino gave status but little money. He asked for time. A month. He accepted.

Apparently all this had only happened three months before Bazin's visit. The Commendatore, however, was now a landowner and proudly held a parasol over his wife's head while she painted sepia pictures of the marvellously romantic ruins of Segesta, framed no doubt by her newly acquired trees.[13]

English ladies, beware of the Calatafimi effect.

7

Some People

Most of the early foreign travellers in Italy were intent on buying up paintings, visiting the right monuments and mixing in 'society' rather than, heavens forbid, becoming involved with the mundanity around them except as a fertile source for take-away conversation pieces for use at home. Which is fair enough. They almost always came with flea-powder and a horror of garlicky breath packed carefully in their valises, which established safe distances from natives other than those of their own class.[1] You will, I'm sure, be relieved to hear that I feel no urge to redress the balance with lengthy descriptions of Sicilians and their exotic way of life either then or now. Anyway you know quite a lot of Sicilians already and you know just how misleading and irritating those weather-beaten signposts of mafia, lethargy, sharp-dealing, dark beauty, passion, jealousy, unreliability and ice-cream are. It's pointless anyway. I have long since given up trying to convince people that numberless Sicilians are blue-eyed blondes (it is usually explained through a vague reference to Norman blood), because people don't want to believe that – or much else that differs from what has been shovelled into their preconditioned minds. How-ever, since I am concerned to tell you about Calatafimi and what I do here, it seems natural to introduce you to a few of my fellow beings, living and dead. If they seem to you a little unusual, it's only because our 'usual' is not Kensington's.

The unusual here would inspire neither Agatha Christie nor P.G. Wodehouse: there are no equivalents to dotty Duchesses, Indian Army Colonels, worthless young men about town, or gentlemen with a shady past in the City; and week-end cottages are few and far be-tween if they exist at all, to say nothing of permanently inhabited stately country houses. That is because, for centuries, wealthy or educated Sicilians have been abandoning the country for the town, the capital, another land – and their periodical or merely occasional return to their origins is confined to the summer or autumn for the harvests (i.e. to make sure they are not being cheated) or to other ad hoc times that are settled by strictly monetary motives. Similarly, in the last century and a half, but with less freedom of choice, the poor and the unschooled have also been consistently leaving their birthplaces to seek work elsewhere, even if from time to time, usually in the summer, they manage to come back to check on how their grandparents, parents and cousins are faring. Calatafimi is no exception to this general picture, although there are many fewer 'wealthy' people around now and therefore fewer of the checking-up sort of return trips, just as there are fewer very poor people and therefore not so many recent emigrants are making visits home from Brooklyn, Frankfurt or Turin, to see their relations and flaunt their 'improvement'.

Nonetheless in the summer some do return. It is a period of the year when most of the townspeople who own any land move sometimes extraordinarily short distances to their country places outside the town for a month of *villeggiatura*: it is the only time in the year when people actually sleep in the countryside. So there is for a short while a different sort of mix and a dash of holiday feeling. There are a few fireworks at the odd festa; lambs are roasted in the open air; young first cousins try to communicate over recently raised language or behavioural barriers; city dwellers reminisce on how they used to live, or try to work out how much an unwanted cottage might fetch on the market; and long queues of visiting housewives form to buy fresh meat and vegetables at a fraction of the price they would have to pay in Düsseldorf or Milan. Some of these temporary immigrants, however far away they hail from and whatever their status, will still have to answer to their local nicknames.

Giving people names is a general practice in rural Sicily and it is particularly well developed in Calatafimi. A great many of her citizens are hardly recognizable from their baptismal names, but answer to absurd nicknames (in dialect *inciurie*; *ingiurie* in Italian) that were bestowed on their ancestors for often unfathomable reasons, and have been meekly inherited out of context by succeeding generations. Often the real names have to all intents and purposes ceased to exist, except on official documents, which in many cases is decidedly beneficial for the interested parties. The other day I saw the official death announcement of Crocefissa Pecora: I don't think you'll need a dictionary to work it out that her parents, whose family name was Sheep, gave Crucified to her as a first name. I asked Giuseppina, who helps here, to make out a list of the *ingiurie* currently in use in

Calatafimi, while she and her family were all together picking olives: they came up with sixty-three before, I presume, they got bored because there are many, many more. They are in casual everyday use and do not seem to offend those who have to answer to them, although how people can live serenely with some of them I find it difficult to understand. I imagine that if someone hailed you on a London street with 'hello there, fresh unsalted sheep-cheese bum' (*culituma*) you would, to say the least, wince and run. But that is an accepted nickname for somebody calmly walking the streets of Calatafimi today.

These names do not usually pinpoint occupations – like 'Jones the Milk' – but were meted out to members of a family for reasons soon forgotten and have been answered to without embarrassment by succeeding generations. I won't take you through all of them, just a few at random. If you walk around the streets of Calatafimi at any time of the day you could, without realizing it, bump into *Cantalanotte* (night singer), *Cinquetreotto* (5+3=8), *Capicchio* (nipple), *Coddulisciu* (smoothe neck), *Pinnamivura* (black feather), *Minnilordi* (dirty tits), *Cannoludoro* (tap of gold), *Babbaluceddu* (small snail), *Vardazucca* (guardian of vines), *Manciacrita* (eater of clay), *Straquamelli* (blackbird shooter), and *Tirazicchi* (tick remover). I could go on and on. And, as I say, the present owners of these names don't seem to bear any grudge; they happily accept their meaningless inheritance, be they tillers of the land or movers in the Town Council, since the *ingiurie* are no respecters of status.

As one of the various layers that make up society here, like in many other small agricultural towns in southern Italy, Calatafimi has always reared a thriving brood of *studiosi*, men of letters with and without nicknames, often connected with the Church but not necessarily so – teaching being one of the other available activities for men with ideas, although notaries have the added advantage of living off the raw material of local history. Their existence is not much heralded: their culture was imbued with the classics, their writings often dealt with local issues, and much attention was paid to poetry. The energy of their debate is sometimes exhausting and they often used pamphlets and periodicals for the forceful declaration of their point of view.

I have already introduced you to one leading example, Biagio Ingroia, Samuel Butler's close friend. He was born in 1836 into a modest country family and, after leaving the priesthood (what else could he do after being hugged by Garibaldi?) and taking up teaching, he published articles and poems in various magazines, and not only in Sicily. There is a fine series of polemical letters between him and the editor of a northern Italian educational magazine, the *Scuola Nazionale* of Turin, which he pugnaciously published in 1890.[2] It so happened that one of the magazine's reviewers had foolishly and ungrammatically lambasted the first edition of a school book written by Ingroia at a time when its seventh edition was already in print, and Ingroia had replied in verse to the foolish review and its illiterate presentation. The editor refused to print his verse reply, and the polemic, with words like *calunnia* (slander) and *villania* (abuse) flying around, was based on the refusal to grant him the right to defend himself. He was also infuriated by the editor's reference to Sicily as being in the 'Paesi Bassi d'Italia', Italy's 'Low Countries'. Strong stuff, and still an invigorating read. But Ingroia wrote many other pieces and poems, dealing with such subjects as the misnaming of the hill where Garibaldi's battle was won – I'll tell you about that later – the 1880 birthday of Queen Margherita and giving support to Butler's theories about the authorship of the *Odyssey*. In 1890 he also wrote a nine-page poem dedicated to his friend and the ex-Garibaldian volunteer, Domenico Sampiere, who had meanwhile become a general and an MP, denouncing workers' strikes that were stirred up, as he judged, by rabble-rousers and that resulted in generalized poverty, and going on to praise the healing properties of capitalism based on Agrippa Menea's theory of the state as a body that needs all its limbs, from head to arms and feet, in working order for the creation of wealth. The general apparently concurred with this analysis because he had the poem printed.[3] Ingroia was the same age as Butler and they became fast friends, as we saw; according to Festing Jones he 'was indefatigable in helping Butler in his Odyssean studies, and his suggestions, unlike Sugameli's [from Trapani, also an ardent helper], never led to any embarrassment.' He also translated a sonnet of Butler's into Italian, and arranged for a recital of Butler and Festing Jones' musical composition *Narcissus* at Palermo: he wrote to Butler on 13th September 1896 that it was 'plaid on violin and piano and the elect auditory did like it very much.' He also, at Butler's request, went to considerable pains to verify whether a gentleman saluting King Ferdinand from a boat as the King visited a tunny fishery at Solunto, in a painting in a Palermo museum, was or was not a portrait of Nelson. From what Ingroia came up with, it seemed unlikely.

A man of varied interests. Festing Jones again: 'In September 1905 Ingroia died at his villa near Calatafimi. He was a man who would have made a considerable mark if his intelligence and his energies had not been confined to such a small place as Calatafimi.' Incidentally a descendant carrying the same surname, a prominent anti-mafia judge, recently decided, like my father-in-law, to spend more of his time in the places of his youth, and has built a small country house across the valley on his great-grandfather's land where he manages to relax occasionally during the weekends, surrounded – sadly, due to his calling – by perimeter searchlights and armed guards.

Biagio Ingroia was no anomaly as a local man of letters: there were and are others like him. Vito Vasile, for example, another poor schoolmaster from Calatafimi, who was one of the original followers of the Fasci Siciliani (socialists, not fascists) in the early 1890s, a movement that militated for agrarian reform and social equality, issues which had not been addressed by the new government of United Italy. He was one of the earliest exponents of socialism in the west of Sicily; and, after the movement's impetus slowed down due to the energetic government reaction, he packed his ideas into more than a hundred volumes of diaries, which are held in the Calatafimi library. They are bursting at the seams with his theories of teaching; how the young were developing; reviews of the books he was reading; the exact workings of the eclipse of the moon and solutions to other scientific problems worked out with painstaking mathematics; curt descriptions of the stupidity of people and institutions; short stories; examples of the iniquity of the *padroni* (the bosses); accounts of rainfall and storms; but, above all in the last volumes, outpourings of his loathing for Fascism. His diaries were later sombrely read by party officials and handfuls of pages were wrenched out, rather unsystematically, before they were returned to the library, still laced with anti-party wrath. He was dedicated to the young in his care and, in times when electric lighting was not commonly available, his classroom was illuminated by a contraption he put up with the aid of his pupils – though in his later years he despaired of his campaign against ignorance. Strangely enough for a dedicated socialist, his later volumes were written in diaries published by a multinational toothpaste manufacturer: he referred to them by year, 'my 1932 Gibbs diary' and so on. He bathed in his *gebbia*, his outdoor water cistern, every day of his life, and he did not like Ingroia for reasons which will be clear if you bother to read the latter's poem against strikes. He was not fond, either, of Simone Agueli who directed the cult of Butler in Calatafimi after Butler's death and replaced him as *direttore didattico* (school inspector) at Vita, the village next to Calatafimi. He became a bit cantankerous in old age, but it is amusing to read about his irrepressible point of view on just about anything.

There was, then, a flourishing, though inconspicuous, body of thinking men in Calatafimi, who continued the tradition of Pellegrino and Longo. Some had wider interests: Cavalier Leonardo Gallo in 1894 published a seventy-five-page description of a trip he made to India, with which is bound (in the British Library copy) an uninteresting nostalgic description of his native Calatafimi that was written while he was serving as a judge at Catania. More recently there were the priests Bonaiuto and Taranto, and the chemist Mazzara, who carried on the tradition of studying the place; and the famous Latinist Francesco Vivona, who translated the standard twentieth-century Italian version of the *Aeneid*, was a native of the town – his first teacher was Ingroia. Then there is Lu Zu Pè (Uncle Pè), less high-flown than the translator of Virgil, if you like, but a poet, painter and storyteller: when he wants his words put into English, he does me the honour of bringing them to me. Neither last nor least is a short book entitled *I Mulini di Calatafimi* dedicated to the study of the sixteen or so water-mills that served the town and the surrounding district until they were brought to a grinding halt by steam and electricity. The authors were Leonardo Accardo, Pietro Boni and Salvatore Palmieri, who took advantage of a special law when they were students in Calatafimi to do the research. The book links the fourteenth century to modern times through an account of the ownership and workings of the mills, and of the technical language used about them and their architecture: it was published in 1996 by the Banca Popolare Cooperativa di Calatafimi, a very local bank. The authors hoped that an understanding of how the mills fitted into Calatafimi life would encourage their restoration and 'the rediscovery of aspects and values typical of our peasant culture'. If you ever come here and park your car distractedly, you may be booked by one of the two authors of this book who are now municipal policemen, and if you infringe the law seriously you may even finish by being locked up by the third of them who is a prison guard in a nearby town – Calatafimi does not boast a prison.

I should have liked to have met a certain Calatafimi priest before he died recently. He had apparently accumulated a most interesting and valuable collection of archaeological finds and objets d'art. I did not manage to – may he rest in peace – but I gather his collection was well worth seeing. As you probably know, there are lots of these collections all over southern Italy, their existence usually being shrouded in fearful silence because all objects with any degree of antiquity belong by law to the state. Italy is so full of 'old' objects that it has absolutely no space to deal with them, not even room to heap them all up higgledy-piggledy and lock the door (which is what happens to a great many of them), because there are not enough funds to keep them safe. I gather there is to be a new law allowing people to keep their more ordinary finds if they declare them. Of course, absolutely no one will do so; and I suppose the collections will be added to surreptitiously as before.

Originally, of course, selling archaeological finds was a way of earning extra money from rich tourists, as it was everywhere where visitors who were richer than the indigenous population were attracted. But gradually the objects began to be appreciated for their own sake, and to be kept and built into collections by such knowledgeable locals, who took a great but secret pride in them, selling only the outstanding pieces.[4] This particular collection had the reputation of being very significant, and it is galling I did not get to see it. Some of the coral pieces were to end up in the magnificent coral collection at the Pepoli museum in Trapani: the Tesoretto there consists mainly of pieces from a 'collezione privata, Calatafimi', which was, in fact, his. Another earlier well-known collection, mainly of coins and 'figulines' or 'handles' from Segesta, formed in the nineteenth century by the lawyer and archaeologist Giuseppe Leonora of Calatafimi, is listed in an MS in the local library.[5] It has now been almost completely lost. The collection was seen by the twenty-seven-year-old Theodor Mommsen on 15th October 1845, when he stayed the night in Calatafimi, noting telegraphically: 'Inscription in the house of the archpriest; Sicilian terracottas from Erice and others. At the house of D. Giuseppe Leonora.' And finds must have been easy enough to unearth at a time when the ruins at Segesta coexisted with farmland. In fact at the site the next day Mommsen noted equally succinctly: 'sheepfold of marble fragments.'[6] There are certainly other less public collections around now, but I haven't yet penetrated the understandable silence that shrouds them, and so far I have only glimpsed the odd item or two, wrapped up in tissue paper.

I also wanted to meet a lady whose name sprang out of the six pages devoted to Calatafimi in the Trapani Province telephone directory (it does not include mobile phones). I made half-hearted attempts to find out about her, but nobody seemed to know anything; so I supposed her to be a private person. Her name was Johanna Liese Hitler. Now, Calatafimi is an unlikely retreat for a relative, and she could hardly be held responsible for sharing his name, I thought. I was going to leave the matter there until I discovered I had in fact already met her. The name in the book is her maiden name, and that was why nobody knew anything about her. She is a delightful German lady, married to a Calatafimaro, who, among other things, organizes and brings a group of people every year to pick our olives. I meet her almost every day in the village. She also speaks perfect dialect, which is rare for a foreigner, and does lacework. Why is she here? I presume it is something to do with emigration, but I have not asked her.

I have known people who will still go to a healer to free themselves of a 'fear' in their stomach (it is done by passing a magical hand over the affected area for a small fee), and other naturally overweight people who will stuff themselves to become obese so that they can qualify for a disability pension. But over 99.9% of Calatafimi's inhabitants are normal, pleasant, law-abiding citizens. There is no street crime and hand-guns are invisible, although shotguns abound and explode repeatedly in season. If the unemployed young get seriously bored, they don't use violence as a therapy, and any pin-striped, mustachioed, slouch-hatted, dark-glassed mafia bosses are confined to large or small screens. There is a muffled, minor mafia in the area, and Calatafimi has the reputation of having provided an important safe haven in the past for characters on the run. But major illegal activity flourishes where there is real money. The backbone of the slender local economy is agriculture, and the small shops that open with bursts of unjustified optimism close fairly regularly. There are always a number of shops 'in-between' that are being altered and fitted out for another head-on attempt at acquiring riches. Shops for seed, fertilizer, tools and machinery, on the other hand, abound and survive. Agricultural administration, the occasional quarrel, wills, the claiming of EU farm subsidies, the division of inherited land, car and tractor insurance and breakdowns, tax-returns, pension management – all these give work to a few lawyers, trade-unionists, accountants and mechanics. Health is taken care of by a scattering of doctors and three chemists, but the hospital is no more. The visit of the Bishop is a major event. The local festivals and processions are taken seriously, and are carefully prepared and thoroughly enjoyed.

There are a few sons of the town who stand out or have done so. My choice of them is entirely arbitrary and those chosen are not so much exceptions to the norm as amplifications of it, not weirdos. Here, for your perusal, are a couple of muleteers, a near saint, a water-diviner, a shepherd who shed light on Segesta, a lawyer who practised nothing but elegance and a priest who brought scorpions into the world via his penis: all right, he *is* an exception. There are many more, but that will do, I think.

I'll start with the muleteers. Looking down from the house onto the road beneath, we can see two of them passing by regularly every day when there is work to do in the fields and the weather allows it. There is the 8.30 mule and the 9.30 one. The 8.30 one turns off the road before getting to us. He once had the reputation for being strict with his family; whether that was true or not I do not know. It is said that until recently he used to ride with his mother and wife following on foot, and his children holding onto the mule's tail so as not to go astray, but that doesn't happen now. I suppose his children have grown up and may be at university or working in Sydney, because he certainly clops along by himself now quite fast on his way to do a full day's work in the fields. He turns to the right before the road climbs up to our house and busies himself somewhere out of sight behind a hill, returning with full panniers as the light fails. He has a lot of bustle about him, and he looks as if he could easily afford a car but prefers the mule, no doubt disagreeing with the adage that holds cars to be more economical than beasts because they don't eat when not working.

The 9.30 rider I know a little more about. Comfortably slouched on his mount, he slowly undulates past the house every morning on his way to his fields, and it was he who stopped to see if he could help me when, as I told you earlier on, I was walking into town one day. It is on the dot of 9.30 (curiously late for around here) that he passes leisurely by, the mule knowing exactly where to go while he reclines on the saddle, contemplating perhaps, as the 'Baronessa Inglese' might romantically have hoped, the Greater Things of Life, although I suspect he is just half asleep as he puffs very intermittently at a cigarette. There are two things said about him which might interest you. The first is that he enjoys the reputation of being a faith-healer. It is said that once, not too long ago, an apparently dead man lay by the roadside, ignored by passers-by – that seems very unlikely, but it is what they say – until our Samaritan muleteer arrived, dismounted and began to pray. At this point the dead man came to, and saw the man praying next to his mule, and to this day he maintains publicly that his life was saved by those prayers. That is what they say and what many believe. The other incident concerning him which could be of interest is far less biblical in tone. Rumour has it that he was complaining one day to his wife about their exorbitant electric light bills, and her instinctive counter-attack was simply: 'Well, why do you leave the windows open all the time, then, and let all the light out: what can you expect, if that's what you do?' Though this will mean little to you and anyway is quite irrelevant, he also has a supremely contented-looking face.

I met him some time back near his work-hut in the hills, in the middle of a considerable area of well cultivated land, and after inviting me up for a talk he gave me a melon and a sheaf of oregano, which were much appreciated. Steering our conversation, he elicited the fact that I 'normally' lived in Rome, which seemed to interest him enormously: so much so that he called over a son, who had previously arrived by car and was working the land with a hired labourer, and explained to them that, if they ever needed anything arranged in the capital, I could help them because I lived there. Doubly useless, because they would not need anything and I would not have been able to do anything. But he felt he had gained a strategic arm-hold in the battle of life.

His mule died a short while ago. After a stint of walking and hitching rides to his land, he acquired a horse which seemed much less cooperative than the mule as it did not, as a matter of course, convey his master to the farm but had to be coaxed. Soon after he had acquired it, it proved to be a she and produced a foal, and until recently the three of them passed by every morning at 9.30 sharp. Unfortunately he stabled his animals in an old rat-infested house in the abandoned Borgo Vecchio area of the town, and they died the other day after munching packets of rat poison. I wonder what he will come up with next. We have become quite friendly, so I shall certainly be in the know. He gave us a cheese he had made for Christmas.

There are not many mules left and even fewer donkeys, but there is still a mule that trudges round and round blindfold for a week or so every autumn crushing the grapes of those whose harvest is not plentiful enough to make it worthwhile taking to one of the local wine co-operatives, in an antiquated iron press. In a field across the valley from the house there is also a mule that stands there day after day, motionless, doing absolutely nothing. Just occasionally he lowers his head and takes a bite of whatever happens to be beneath him. I don't know how he drinks. There is a small hut nearby, but I have never seen him move from the field during the hours of daylight: he is there from early in the morning until the evening closes in, and is a living symbol of deathly boredom.

There are even a few painted Sicilian donkey- or mule-carts with scenes of the 'Paladini di Francia' on the side panels that are brought out on a Sunday. But gone are the days when all workaday Sicilian carts were carved and painted like this, though I can remember the last of them; so it wasn't all that long ago. And increasingly a few people use horses and pony-traps for pleasure, even if, generally speaking, quadrupeds have given way to four-wheel drives. There is also a combination stage: a four-wheel drive regularly exercises a fully grown horse up and down the road in the valley below the house, the driver's hand languidly holding the reins from the driving seat window. The pace is civilized and the horse looks sleek and well.

Enough of dumb animals. I think it is now my solemn duty to let you know about our near-saint, the Blessed (Beato) Arcangelo Placenza, who, I am sure you will be put off to know, was related to Caterina's family, at least according to Pellegrino.[7] There is nothing triumphant in this revelation. Everybody has been related to everybody else for centuries around here, and the families have remained the same down the centuries. So he probably has many living relatives.

Our local historian Longo wrote the Beato's biography on the basis of, as he says, what little written material had survived and from such traditions as had been handed down to his time. Arcangelo Placenza was born in about 1380 into a well-off family which, he says, kept slaves (though this was not very unusual[8]), but he soon opted for the life of a voluntary minor Franciscan friar without formal submission to the Rule, which during the first part of his life consisted in poverty, praying and flagellation: in his case in a cave under the present church of the Madonna di Giubino at Calatafimi. Longo describes him as having 'great austerity with regard to life, being of the greatest humility and praying continuously; he was a great lover of poverty and a true observer of the Rule.' While he was there he had visions of the Madonna and Child who appeared to him at night on top of a cypress tree. Another somewhat earlier chronicler, Mancuso,[9] describes her appearing to him every evening 'as the Lord did to Moses in the burning bush, above a cypress tree, which is still green and growing, and from here the Gran Signora passed the time with him in sweet and celestial debate.' A painting done of his vision, prints of which are still to be found today in the town and in the occasional book, show the round flat top of the tree where the Madonna and Child used to rest during these celestial debates. Tradition has it that this same cypress tree was struck by lightning in 1786 or 1789 and thereafter, to the immense distress of the whole of Calatafimi, slowly died. It was still standing, though dead, in 1804 when, according to Longo, it was sadly decided that the wood was not up to supporting the image of the town's patron saint, the Madonna di Giubino, in procession. I will take you through the Madonna di Giubino and her procession anon. Blessed Arcangelo's life as a voluntary minor friar was changed by order of Pope Martin V, who required all the voluntary friars to submit to the established Rule. He did so and went to the monastery of Santa Maria in Gesù in nearby Alcamo, where he was wont to lie on a form of nail-bed, fasting and holding a lily in his hand. It wasn't actually a nail-bed, but made of woven stalks that 'could be described more justly as a bed of pain than one of rest.' He would not hear confession because, as he said, he would not be able to understand the sins that might be described to him; but he was worldly enough to become Vicar Provincial of the Order in Sicily. His soul went to heaven in about the year 1460 when he must have been about eighty, and thereafter his body was subjected to a hectic life[10] when compared with what it had been used to up till then.

The first episode took place after his burial in a common grave in Alcamo. He was in fact exhumed by public request, probably around 1500. In Longo's words:

> At the moment the Friars raised the sacred body from the common grave they were presented with a portent which filled them with marvel and stupor. Since those vine stalks, which are commonly put under the bodies of the dead and which the Friars had also put under our Blessed Arcangelo's, had not only sprouted leaves but were also bearing fruit.

Various, mostly medical, miracles followed, which are dutifully noted in Longo's biography, and the fame of his sanctity grew. His ribs were widely distributed. One was given to the Countess of Modica in Alcamo and authenticated by Fra Pietro d'Alcamo in 1649; another, authenticated in 1736, was in the church of San Michele in Calatafimi but was mysteriously stolen in 1949 (nobody has ever discovered what happened to it); and another relic – I don't know whether it was a rib or another part of his anatomy – is with relics of Sicilian saints in the convent of Santa Teresa in Palermo. His body was dug up again in 1961. It was formally recognized, brought to Calatafimi for a fortnight of celebrations with the participation of the Cardinal Archbishop of Palermo (10th-24th September), and then re-buried. During this process his right shoulder-blade was consecrated and the year after it was formally bestowed on the church of San Michele in Calatafimi, which would have given his biographer Longo immense satisfaction, as he devotes rumbustious energy to refuting that despicable sixteenth-century Alcamese poet Bagolino's claim that the Beato Arcangelo Placenza was actually from Alcamo rather than Calatafimi.[11]

Sad to say, Caterina's father now does his football pools in a bar on the Piazzetta Beato Arcangelo Placenza near the bank, hardly an appropriate way of remembering an ancestor and, much more important, still a revered figure in Calatafimi's history. A week of minor festivities in Calatafimi is devoted to his memory at the end of every July.

Less saintly is the water-diviner, a small, well-dressed man of some reserve and a recognized professional. First, however, a little background. Francesco, Caterina's younger brother whom you know, recently bought a small piece of land almost adjoining where all of us live. It is beautiful and fertile (a sapling from a fig-tree there, much appreciated by our friend Andrew, is, as you know, even now pushing out perplexed Sicilian leaves into the London air on the banks of the Thames near Richmond), but the land was apparently bereft of water, although there is water all around. That explains the diviner. He was about seventy years old and bow-legged, with a piece of grass permanently in his mouth which he never seemed to chew. He was asked to make an assessment, and the order of the day was silence as he slowly wandered around and around with his fork of olive wood: he assured us it could be made of any kind of wood. This stalking of the water took about half an hour. Then came the *pronouncement*.

> There is water. I do not know how much (it could be as thin as a human hair) or how deep down it is. But it is here, in at least three places. You just need to dig where I tell you, but I need to be here because I can tell you if you cut the thread.

(The cut 'thread' or vein of water was for some reason defined as 'morta la mula', a female mule being dead.) He went on to say that he would not accept payment unless the outcome was satisfactory, but that he had already found about fifty wells, one of which produced 1,000 litres of water a minute. The point to make about him is that he exercised a normal, honourable profession, and, if he was in any way out of the ordinary, it was because he was reputed to be rather better than his rivals. The next step was to decide when the excavation should take place.

Act Two: a Sunday morning. After the arrival of the diviner and a mechanical excavator with two drivers who knew him and had absolute trust in him, the whole family and the dogs gathered, and great were our expectations. I have to tell you straightaway that no water was discovered, although we all knew it was there: the old man had said so and we believed him. The excavator's first raucous grappling with the ground went down four metres, with difficulty, through the rocky surface, leaving an untidy wound. The diviner decided it might be better to try another site as the machine could not get down much further than that. At the next site the machine growled rapidly down to three and a half metres because there was no rock. No water either at that level, but our faith was still intact. It wasn't the man but the machine that was at fault. He had said quite plainly he did not know how deep down the water was and clearly another machine that could get down further was needed. By which time it was the moment for Sunday lunch and that took precedence. I was sorry that my sister was not there. As you know, she has graduated from water-divining to civilization-divining which much embarrasses me when she is using her rods in Rome, as they get visibly out of control among all that civilization. Though I would never admit it to her, I did sheepishly try some rods that the diviner had brought to the site (they worked, damn it!).

Another day, and another machine did duly arrive. The large yellow drill-on-wheels accompanied by an equally yellow compressor and a lorry full of pipes were parked in the field which was yellow itself with the *cavuliceddi* flowers. We watched decadently from green chairs under the olive trees as the mechanical finger pierced the earth to a depth of seventy metres, washing up the slurry from the successive layers of earth, clay, rock and gravel that flowed across the field in distinctive waves of red-brown, black, white and grey, with a glittering of foam in the water and chemical that had been pumped down to bring it all up. The first notable vein of water was struck at around thirty-five metres but it was followed by layers of gravel which would have allowed it to seep away; so the drill was allowed to probe on past more rock and clay, more water and gravel, until a substantial layer of clay was found just below a good vein of water. Clay is of course impervious and forms a natural seal for the pipe to rest on, and so here the probing came to rest. There was no diviner this time, but he had been instrumental in the summoning of these machines which were, if you will excuse me, *machinae ex deo*. His successor, the owner of all the yellow machinery, was an immensely calm man from far away who had become well off by specializing in much-needed wells. The whole operation took two days, punctuated by breakdowns and lunches of sausages and pork chops roasted on the cinders of olive-prunings. During that time the plopping eruption of the different coloured muds gradually became runnier, clearer and more watery and, after a final clean-out of the drill-hole which sent up a brown geyser about twelve metres into the sky, the water capacity was judged to be about 25-30 litres a minute. Even though it was not mine, I felt that the land under our feet harboured a friendly benefactor – it was a romantic, reassuring feeling. I was somewhat dashed when I learnt that you had to make an application to the state to drill a well, and, if it is successful and the borehole goes beyond a certain depth, you also need a complicated series of formal permits to use the water at a fixed maximum volume per day.

I don't know the water diviner's name nor that of the drill owner, but the shepherd I want you to meet next was called Antonio Brucculeri, or Nino lu Curatulu in dialect (*curatulu* means factor). While he is no longer alive, his contribution to archaeology at Segesta has been documented by the archaeologist Sebastiano Tusa[12] and I have had the pleasure of talking to his son about it. The story is simple. When the sanctuary of Mango was discovered in 1957, it presented some logistical problems for Tusa, who was in charge of the site at the time: he had established that the sanctuary was an integral part of the main Segesta settlement; but why was it

situated at the bottom of Monte Barbaro, and a considerable distance from the rest of the city which was on the top of the steep hill
and extended down the other side towards the temple; and how did
the population communicate with it? Tusa spent a lot of time at the
new site and was in conversation on many occasions with Nino lu
Curatulu, who had looked after the land and grazed his sheep there
for sixty years, as his own father had done before him. They gradually came to know each other: Nino had to be sure about him, because Tusa was not a local. Finally, the problem came up in their talk
and, after some healthy hesitation, Nino decided to show Tusa the
track around the bottom of the hill from the temple end of the city
to the sanctuary. Some of it had been known already, but not its full
extent; and that went some way towards solving it. After a further
period of assessing the stranger, Nino decided that it would be all
right to show him the steps hewn out of the rock, but hidden by the
scrub, that led right up the mountain to the area of the theatre – and
this was known only to Nino. Problem solved. Nino's son confirmed
it all in conversation with me and told me how his father used to
shelter his sheep from the rain in the remains of the sanctuary before it had been 'discovered'. He also recounted how his father used
to entertain King Gustave of Sweden to home-made cottage cheese
(ricotta) and wine while the king, a famous amateur archaeologist,
was digging at Segesta. I was shown photographs of them at it, and
the king certainly seemed to be enjoying himself.

The next character, far from regal but of a certain 'class', was
someone I never knew and I am using my father-in-law's words,
which conjure up an impression of Calatafimi life between the two
world wars. The man in question was called Cocò. He had a degree
in law and therefore, because of the visceral need of all Italians to
identify people with an appropriate title, was known as the Avvocato, although he never practised. He was a man of elegance. He was
also a cousin of sorts. His land was about six kilometres from the
town, and he rode up every morning at a gentlemanly time and pace,
through a long drive lined with date palms – on his English horse,
clad in jodhpurs, perfect leather riding-boots, black jacket and white
silk scarf, his blond hair and blue eyes crowned not with a Sicilian
coppola but, of course, a flat English riding-cap. Whatever he did on
the land was certainly done with decorum, and at the designated time
in the evening he made his return to Calatafimi. The clattering of his
horse's hooves was gauged to create the right effect and he crossed

the main square of the town in obvious control of his magnificent beast. The townspeople were waiting for him. The evening ritual began.

He started with the barber, a certain 'Ciaschiteddu' (this *ingiuria* translates as 'small round bottle', and was acquired because he was not tall and had a generous belly), who had been to America and had returned with a certain amount of money and two white automatic reclining barber's chairs, the like of which had never been seen previously in Calatafimi. The Avvocato made his entrance; the passing visitors paid their respects; Ciaschiteddu bowed deeply; the incumbent client gave up his chair and the Avvocato settled himself down. His cheeks, jaw and neck were carefully prepared with his own personal shaving-brush and, when at length they were deemed ready, he was ritually shaved. After a few deft clips had ensured that his moustache was as it should be, a towel warmed to exactly the right temperature and sprinkled with his own Parma-violet scent was applied to his face as a sign that the ceremony was about to come to an end. Meanwhile a small crowd had begun to gather outside the barber's shop. It was always the same. The Avvocato had a much-admired tenor voice and a rich repertoire that flowed from operatic arias to the romances of Tosti and tunes in vogue at the time. He was repeatedly asked to sing and a little less repeatedly he refused graciously. Ciaschiteddu was an able violinist and his commercial rival but private friend, another barber called Vito, played the guitar. The evening performance was listened to by a full piazza in reverent silence, interrupted by tumultuous applause at the end of every piece. It all lasted a couple of hours.

The Avvocato signalled the end of the recital with a slight but very distinguished bow. The audience began to walk home, and the Avvocato made his way round the corner to the club, where conversation was indulged in and billiards were played until dinner, which at that time took place at around eleven o'clock in the evening. The billiards would become most intense, especially when *italiana* was played with two very able brothers. One of these brothers was to end his life as the posthumous recipient of the Medaglia d'Oro in the Second World War, the highest Italian medal for bravery. The other was more bizarre. He once rode his horse up to the first floor of his house but could not persuade the animal to come down the marble stairs again, and so it had to be put on a mattress and eased down with ropes. Both were formidable cues and it often happened that they won a bit too much, whereupon the Avvocato developed a mild headache that made it advisable to leave off playing – until the next evening.

Many years later Caterina was born in the surviving of the two brothers' house in Palermo. The evening before, her expectant mother lent him a substantial amount of money for that time, as he was short and was going off to play cards. During what turned out to be a very successful evening, Caterina saw the light of day. On learning later of the birth, he pronounced Caterina to be a bringer of good luck, and (apparently a rare occurrence) immediately repaid the loan, but without any gift for the newly arrived lucky charm.[13]

I hope you will not mind if I end on a whimsical note, far from the sanctity of the Blessed Arcangelo Placenza, though a priest was involved. Antonio Mongitore in his *Della Sicilia Ricercata*[14] quotes a strange incident that he culled from a book by Boccone. It goes like this: 'A priest named Gio. Maria Marcantonio from Calatafimi turned over a stone in the countryside and uncovered a large number of scorpions, and realizing the danger of being bitten by them and being killed, he was in a state of great terror. He was attacked by a fever and suffered from it for forty days. He was advised that before forty days were up he should consult and be cured by a woman healer. On examining him, the woman diagnosed that the priest, through terror, had conceived scorpions and that, before they grew big, he should swallow a quarter [of a litre of liquid, made] of a type of Cantharides called Dilena in Sicilian ['Spanish fly' of illicit schoolboy giggles]. He was convinced by this and, after the treatment, urinated a number of small scorpions accompanied by some blood – and was healed.'

I imagine that would raise the eyebrows of your eminent Harley Street doctor, even if an appropriate fee was almost certainly exacted for the treatment of this unusual complaint.

8

Earth, Fire, Wind, Water

That was very British of you: to ask about the 'elements'. Which I take to mean no more than 'what's the weather like down there?' I had hardly expected it: could it be that you will be deigning to visit us? I suppose you want to know things like: is it too hot in the summer; are there snakes; how far is the nearest beach; will you die if you drink the water; and similar tactical things. But you can find all that out for yourself. Surely what you really want to know about is the basic geophysical conditions that shape life here. Although I can see you shaking your head violently, I shall simply ignore you and plough on with what, deep down, you would actually like to hear about.

In the beginning was Empedocles. He was born around 490 BC at Agrigento, just down the coast from here and it was he who first defined the Elements in his treatise *On Nature*. You are obviously aware that he established that the Universe was composed of four indestructible elements of fire, air, water and earth, and that all change was brought about by the cosmic forces of love and strife mixing with and separating these imperishable elements – a doctrine that was basic to European thought for many centuries. Empedocles himself lasted a much shorter time: while he was born near here, he found death further off, leaping into the fiery crater of Etna in a bid to make a mystery of his death and have himself worshipped as a god.

Although Empedocles considered fire to be the divine element, in any agricultural community the placental earth must surely take centre stage, assisted of course by the other midwife elements. Not surprisingly, the temple at Segesta is dedicated to Demeter, the goddess of agriculture and marriage. Despite a helping hand from the other elements, the earth is basic because it lasts longer than drought, disease, fire, floods, hurricanes or politics, and, battered as it may become, it can always somehow claw itself back again into production.

The earth around Calatafimi is clayey and chalky, which makes it increasingly difficult to walk across after rain because it builds up rubbery wedges under your shoes. In the past, it lent itself well to pottery, not so much the highly coloured and patterned sort, though Segesta did turn out fine pieces: merely the pottery of honest everyday objects, like roof-tiles or the water-jars carried on their shoulders by the women of Calatafimi who were so much admired by Douglas Sladen. The chalk element is responsible for beautiful outcrops of crystalline rock, in the form of gypsum, that delight the eye of the idle beholder and infuriate the farmer because lumps of it cover land he would dearly like to plough up. In the summer the earth is so dry and crumbly that it is hard to imagine anything growing in it at all; but its wrinkled surface is galvanized into fertility by a single drop of water. There is also sulphur here, which manifests itself in the hot-water springs and comes up through the land at times, as for instance during earthquakes. Sometimes the earthquakes produce bitumen, which should whet the appetite of would-be capitalists, but its presence is always kept a carefully guarded secret.

The land around Calatafimi is exceptionally fertile. Mother Earth and her handmaiden elements come up with wheat, oil, wine, vegetables, herbs and innumerable types of fruit, particularly of the citrus variety. In past times, they have produced sumach[1] (that is used in the tanning industry and even used to be exported to Persia as a carpet dye), linen, silk, cotton, pistachio, manna (not the biblical version),[2] soda and sugar-cane. Over the centuries, agriculture has been nudged in different directions by alien forces. The flourishing sugar industry is no longer: the West Indian plantations destroyed cane as a crop in the eighteenth century, although Sicilians were still producing rum in the nineteenth century from cane that had gone wild. And the Persian carpet industry no longer relies on Sicilian sumach. The Sicilian silk industry was strangled by the British development of Bengalese silk towards the end of the eighteenth century, just as the Sicilian sulphur industry, which once almost had a world monopoly, was destroyed by cheap sulphur from America at the end of the nineteenth century. These and other hostile developments had unpredictable effects on the Sicilian economy and in consequence Sicilians have at times emigrated to many places including America, in the same way that Cornish tin-miners (whose raw material was first exploited by Phoenicians from this part of the Mediterranean) went to the Illinois copper mines when their home mining became exhausted, and starved Africans and Asians are landing on Sicilian coasts every day now in their thousands looking for a better future. Not a merry-go-round.

Over the centuries, the big land-management divide has been between the Roman tradition of vast expanses of treeless land allotted to the mass production of wheat, and the more intensive, irrigation-based, Arab tradition of fruit, vegetables and oil. Both these traditions still persist in Calatafimi, but as it is hilly country and blessed with water, the Arab tradition has had the upper hand, and Arabic words have everywhere burrowed into the terminology of agriculture, its buildings and its everyday life, to the extent that few people recognize the words are Arabic in origin.

There is a popular saying, based apparently on a winnowing song which says 'Calatafimi – Dotti e Filosofi: sunnu l'n'virria di autri paesi' (it means that the people of Calatafimi – implicitly those with land – are highly educated and philosophers and are envied by the villages around). This description is less complimentary than it might seem because in essence it just means that nobody who owned land could really be bothered with looking after it; and, as a consequence, renting out land and sharecropping have been the normal methods of working it for the last couple of centuries, except on the few large estates.

Which brings us to sharecropping (*mezzadria*). From the first frustrated attempts at dismantling feudalism at the end of the eighteenth century until the equally fumbling attempts at land reform in the 1950s and to a lesser extent even today, it provided the easiest way for modest landowners to enjoy their land and prosper without having to work it – and for its workers to live and eat without owning it. Instead of trying to explain the system in detail, I think it would be much easier for me to translate a sharecropper contract dated 28th October 1893, but applicable today, as it was then. I shall translate it in full because almost everything in it is a comment on the social conditions of Calatafimi. The contract was shown to me by a friend from another old-established family,[3] and is yet another illustration of how slowly things change in this part of the world.

Conditions Established with the Gardener Leonardo Rimpa

The gardener will provide for the necessary cultivation of the vineyard, pruning it, hoeing it five times a year at the appropriate times, giving it sulphur (half of the said sulphur will be paid for by the Padrone), furnishing the necessary layering of shoots every year (this work being paid for by a 'soldo' every two layerings), and finally harvesting the grapes.

He will also deal with the pruning of the pergola and will carry half of the wood that results from the pruning of the whole vineyard into town.

As recompense for the aforesaid work, he has the right to half of the must and half of the wood.

He will furthermore cultivate the citrus orchard, hoeing it three times and watering it: for this he will receive three 'rotoli'[4] of oil in the summer. He is also required to transport all the fertilizer that the Padrone buys from the town to the land and the cost of the physical work involved in fertilizing the land will be borne half and half by the Gardener and the Padrone.

The cost of pruning the citrus trees will be paid two-thirds by the Padrone and one-third by the Gardener, who will transport into the town two-thirds of the wood that results from the pruning which belongs to the Padrone. For the aforesaid tasks he will receive a part of what the orchard produces, as follows: a third of all the oranges and lemons with the exception of the mandarins and the produce of two Portuguese orange trees which are the property of the Padrone. A third of the peaches and half of the rest of the fruit; however, the strawberries, walnuts and the grapes from the pergola are entirely the property of the Padrone – which must be transported into town by the Gardener, who will also bring all the above-mentioned fruit and such an amount of oranges and lemons as answers to the family needs; [here there is a paragraph concerning fava-beans, which has been cancelled in pen] and the vegetables that are planted will be divided half and half.

This agreement will come into effect after the harvest of the 1893 fruit (which may continue up to March 1894) and will be effective until the harvest of the fruit of 1899 (which may continue up to March 1899 [cancelled] 1900).

Calatafimi, 28th October 1893

(There is a note attached to the contract to the effect that the 'Gardener' had found that the land had not been pruned for three years, and that to deal with this the Padrone would pay for the scaffolding and for a manual worker, while the sharecropper would pay for the work.)

I am sure you don't need any comments on the above. So I shall proceed to give you mine. *Mezzadria* means 'half and halfism' and the owner of this land was in the Orwellian process of establishing that some halves are more 'halfish' than others. After the land reform of the 1950s the balance was redressed in favour of the sharecropper (i.e. his half came to be legally considered the more halfish), and that was another nail in the coffin of sharecropping, the role of which has been drastically reduced as a method of land management. The ex-sharecroppers have usually bought their own land or work land they have rented by now, and in these new circumstances have to deal themselves with the eternal hazards of wind, water and fire, as well as the taxman, who is perhaps a fifth 'imperishable' element – certainly so in the mind of the ever diffident worker of the land.

'Tyger! Tyger! burning bright in the forests of the night.' Sorry, sorry...but I have just been re-reading Blake and thinking how he would have reacted to Sicily: I imagine he would have been fascinated by eruptions of Etna and would have felt deep sympathy for the plight of the sulphur miners in the mountains to the south-east of here. Be that as it might have been. Even to us mortals fires are mystical at night, like necklaces around the high woods or aboriginal freedom-fighters cracking their rifles off in a struggle to wrest land back from farmers. But for us to be in a position to indulge in minor visions like these, clearly the fires will have got out of control. And then everybody will turn up to help, often with beating instruments made out of rubber strips cut from the inner tubes of tyres, which are highly effective for beating out flames. They do not often get out of control and directed fire is an essential process of country life. It serves to clean the land and feed nitrogen back into it; to summon up fresh, young green grass-shoots (which is why shepherds have a bad reputation for starting fires); to regenerate the growing process by a sort of incendiary pruning; and, more mundanely, to get rid of cuttings, rubbish and weeds. Plumes of smoke from such small fires are a reassuring sign that unseen people are hard at work over a large area where nothing otherwise seems to be happening.

When fires do get out of control, we have even had a helicopter scooping water out of our very small artificial pool further up the hill, where Francesco is trying to breed carp, and also from Nicola the shepherd's pool, just down the road. Nicola was away with his sheep and was most put out when he brought them back in the evening and saw the water level, but he gets water from one of our springs and he was gradually persuaded it wasn't too much of a problem. But when fires become dangerous, the helicopters don't ask permission. Motiveless arson, if not common, has certainly been known to occur and it is said there have been cases locally of cats being given a special *imbraccatura*, a harness with inflammable strings attached: they are supposed to be let loose in the undergrowth to spread the flames. The main motives for causing fires are said to be the creation of new pasturage and building speculation. The latter motive is more likely nearer the coast. If, in the course of normal administration, a fire becomes too big and control proves difficult, crowds of helpers materialize from nowhere, as I have said, since fires are very unpredictable and threaten everybody. Mostly fires are a premeditated operation of the first kind, and there are always a few people around who make sure that the conflagration is confined. But they can be used occasionally in private conflicts that tend to remain private, however much damage is done. It is something of an art steering a fire, with wind as an enemy, but the country people know what they are doing and their fires are quite quickly contained and put out, leaving the earth clean-shaven, with flecks of black shaving-cream sticking to its brown skin.

And fire creates food: you will find no one in Calatafimi who is not expert with wood fires, either in an outdoor oven or a stone-fringed barbecue or on the *tannura*, the traditional grill-hob. Among amateurs, few will concede that anybody else knows how to make a fire better. The ovens were principally designed for making bread once a week, if fewer and fewer families bake their own now, despite loudly blaming themselves for their laziness. Their heirs, the professional bakers, whose varying abilities are enthusiastically debated, use wood-fired ovens. Caterina has a slight dislike of her father's favourite, because in her opinion his bread tastes a little too much of the olive prunings he favours as fuel. Bread-making used to be a family affair that started early in the morning, with sleepy children waiting for the first loaves to be shovelled out of the oven, broken open, dowsed with olive oil, sprinkled with oregano and wolfed down with moans of pleasure. But when private ovens are used today, it is always for an occasion, and it takes a long time to get them to the right temperature for bread – or a kid or a lamb. There is an almost religious element in the use of the oven, because it creates bread, the god of foods, and because sacrificed sheep are also burnt inside it. It is not surprising that by tradition bread is never cooked on Good Friday.

At night you can smell the warming fires that give off that delicious dragging-you-back-to-what-you-will-never-completely-recall sort of smell; you can enjoy it walking around anywhere in rural southern

Italy in the winter. The earlier form of communal warming, the round brass brazier or *braciera* under the table or a communal blanket, is little used now – and it burnt charcoal not wood, for obvious reasons.

Fire to 'winnnd'

I wish I could put that sound into words but I am not even going to try. However, merely to recite the Italian names of the winds is like a line of poetry: there are the *libeccio, grecale, tramontana, maestrale, levante, ponente, mezzogiorno* and, of course, the *sirocco*. In dialect, they sound even more elemental: *libbici, gricali, tramuntana, maistru, livanti, punenti, menzuiornu* and *sciloccu*. In either form they sound as if they are winds with stories to tell, and they are, but I shall just leave them to roar and sigh.[5] The whine of the wind in the blazing heat of an otherwise silent, pungent countryside I find most unnerving. It makes it easy to believe in gods – the naughty kind that get entangled in your everyday life, whom you can safely blame for almost anything that goes wrong.

Stop wagging your rational finger and I'll tell you what winds have to do with my life here. We are high enough up and near enough to the coast to get a lot of them, and they have their negative side. For instance, if you are trying to read in the sun and drinking a glass of wine at the same time, wind can make keeping your place in the book fairly irritating. And, again, trying to train a climbing plant, tendril by tendril, to where you want it to go is not made easier by wind. You might with some justification question the validity of doing either of these things, but I don't because I enjoy doing them both. What I do not enjoy is the efficiency of the wind in distributing dust and sand everywhere, and making necessary the interminable brushing and washing of floors. But there are positive aspects. Wind, they all say, puts suffocating heat to flight; and so we are much envied here. The heat doesn't bother me, but it does just about everybody else, so that extensive experiments are continually being made to find out where the coolest breeze is at any given time; and the company will shift around as conditions change (I imagine you would be of their number).

Wind may seem the least useful of the elements to the earth, but one must never forget that, in conjunction with birds and feet, it persuades seeds and pollen to leave their parent and it conveys them to their new homes. It is also the boon companion of rain, which needs no introduction as earth's good friend. Everybody here knows everything about the local winds and exactly what weather they will bring. But obviously, opinions differ considerably and give vent to turbulent conversations, bent on understanding what the winds have in mind. Early morning conversations are wind-based. Lunchtime is often taken up with debating if they will change. Evening conversations are still about the wind, though orientated towards the following day. Despite their fiercely individual characteristics, the winds have one thing in common: when they reach a certain force they bring down the electricity system and we are left in darkness: it matters not whether it is the *maistru* or the *gricali* that is blowing.

A couple of words about the *sirocco*, the most notorious of the winds. It is, as you know, the insufferably hot, moist south wind that blows Saharan sand up into the heart of Europe. It has not changed over time, Swinburne (our Swinburne, not the poet) describing it at Segesta on Christmas Day 1777 as 'the pestilential suffocating blasts, that rush over the seas from the hot sands of Africa'.[6] The first thing that comes to mind is that it is the only wind that is physically visible: it is a threatening mist of fine sand you can see coming, and you know where it has passed from the sand it leaves behind. The second thing is that, for some inexplicable reason, it sometimes arrives cold in Calatafimi. The explanation I have been given is that it grows cold as, poor wretch, it crosses the sea coming up from North Africa. I have never been able to understand how it heats up so quickly after that short sea voyage. And hot it does get. Jacobi, Stollberg's companion in Sicily on his *Travels* (London, 1796), talks of ladies of fashion lying down naked on marble tables while servant girls sprayed them with water during the *sirocco*, and of water being poured on the floors of tightly shuttered rooms. So much more picturesque than fans or air-conditioning. The Duke of Buckingham and Chandos, plodding up to Segesta on a mule in 1827, was less picturesque, although he expressed himself authoritatively.[7]

The day was a true sirocco – the sky clear, but the vapour over the earth thick, hazy, and lead-colour; the air at that height strong, so as elsewhere to be called a strong breeze, but the wind felt as though it came out of the mouth of an oven; and if you stood opposite to it, and held your mouth open to receive the freshness of the breeze, you inhaled heat instead of coolness, and the lips and face were dried and caked as if over a fire. Liquor passed down the throat and gave a momentary coolness as it passed, but it did not quench an incipient thirst, and produced no refreshment. Those who walked lay down and panted like dogs, and, I, who rode, could scarce sit upon my mule. We had some water in a bottle which we brought from the last spring, but it was hot and frothy ere it reached the temple: I hung up my thermometer under the broad shade of the vast columns, in the strongest influence of the breeze, and perfectly independent of the heated stone, and I never could get it less than 90° of Fahrenheit.

We still suffer, but a fraction less dramatically.

Wind to water

Water shyly hides itself from view in Sicily. Most of the rivers on the island are *fiumari* or seasonal torrents which, after short-lived boisterous activity in the winter, slink underground and can only be enticed to the surface by the sinking of wells, the delicate art of which I have told you a little about. When the retiring liquid has been located and persuaded to reveal itself, its place of confluence and confinement is the *gebbia*, an Arab name for a cistern that collects spring water, as we have seen. These are usually square, cool and deep, and a few people even use them as elementary swimming pools when the weather is particularly hot. Ours is protected by two venerable palm trees which have never had their dead leaves barbered, and the resultant long brown stubble under the higher green leaves forms a resonant metropolis for hundreds of birds in the evening. When you pass by, there is an explosion of plops as the frogs dive in fright for safety in the depths, hardly disturbing the myriad dragonflies that patrol the surface. Most of them still contain varieties of fresh-water crustaceans that seek them out. Recently, I saw a very defensive crab trying to get to a tiny pool where our ducks live; so one has to assume that fresh-water crustaceans are to an extent amphibious and have an acute olfactory sense, at least for fresh water. But why on earth do they move? Talking of crabs, Mongitore[8] says that around the town of Corleone (which is quite near Calatafimi), 'there is a type of crab that does not have a shell; for which they are known as "soft crabs"; and which everyone catches whole and eats with pleasure; being of good taste.' He does not mention whether they need cooking, and I have not had the fortune to come across them in our *gebbia*, which does, however, contain crabs with hard shells.

In an island so dry but so fertile that if you drop water on the land you barely have the time to get out of the way before a blade of grass shoots up, Calatafimi is fortunate in having an abundance of water. One of the reasons why most Sicilian agriculture was and is based on corn is that the seeds can be sown before the winter rains, and have time to erupt into green fertility and ripen for harvesting before the late spring heat and drought makes growing impossible, except for vines or irrigated crops. The fact that Calatafimi has water means that it can go Arab rather than Roman and produce fruit, wine and oil.

I have already mentioned that a number of people come to our land for the drinking water because they enjoy its taste. Just near us there used to be a major spring called Pantano. It is now part of the municipal waterworks I have told you about, which has dried up the small river that ran through the valley below us. I have made a copy of a legal document relating to this spring: it has no date but I should think it is mid-eighteenth century, and it illustrates nicely the interest this water roused.[9] It starts with a legal preamble detailing ownership, and going back to documents dating from 1573, and is written in a mixture of bad Italian, difficult dialect and appalling bureaucratic late Latin. It is long and really tricky to sort out, so I shall merely try to give you its essence. It begins, after obeisance to various notables, by saying that

> it is now nine years since the legal pronouncement involving all those with rights to enter the area of the river and wood of Pantano was established...But certain esteemed gentlemen, their vassals and certain citizens take this water without any order or measure, to such an extent that...they could come to blows and be the total ruin of the owner's house.

That should hardly surprise us now, with widely predicted water wars just over the horizon. After long lists of those who had the right of entry and use, the document establishes that:

> From Sunday midnight till midday on Monday it is common land. From midday on Monday till midnight on Tuesday it is for the Scianna family. From midnight on Tuesday till midnight on Wednesday it is for the Triolo, now called the Lena, family...

and so on for the rest of the week. Most of the family names still exist in Calatafimi: I presume they paid for the water. Old legal documents in Italy, as indeed in England, are often folded neatly up with an explanation of the contents written on the outside. This one has:

Division of the Waters of Pantano
Between
The Gardeners of Passo di Cola
And Margi, in Calatafimi

Margi, which I described to you some time back, means 'full of water' in Arabic/dialect and was where Caterina's grandmother was born. We live between Passo di Cola and Margi.

Such is the importance of water that the search for it is continuous, and when found it is jealously guarded, as you can see. But it is also bought and sold. I have another small document headed 'Sale of Pantano Water n°456 before Notary Bonanno in the year 1774'. In it the rights to twenty-four hours of Pantano water, which had been sold to the Archpriest Antonio Brandis by Giovanni Aloisio De Ballis on 1st February 1605, and then by Brandis to Stefano Vivona on 10th January 1609 (in both cases the name of the notary is given), were sold in 1774 to Vito Sicomo, son of Franco before Notary Bonanno. Since the 1609 notary was also called Bonanno, I presume they were from the same family as professions were normally passed on from father to son.

Those twenty-four hours were probably used for watering sheep or cattle. Normally, though, where there is water, it is sold with the land; and when the land is divided up, so are the detailed water rights; and this is a situation we recently found ourselves having to sort out in the same Pantano area. Caterina's great-grandfather had all the land around here and produced two legitimate sons. Her great-uncle's family moved away from Calatafimi and sold their interests in San Giovanni to a third party together with the water rights. This third party does not cultivate the land directly any more now and has let off the farming to a family, the younger generation of which are try-ing to develop a more intensive form of agriculture that requires a lot of water. They said they needed a *gebbia* of water a week, but it takes a full week to fill up the *gebbia*, and what does anybody do in the meantime? How much water were they entitled to? The situation could have led to endless arguments if it had not been sorted out, and that was really quite simple: we just had to go back to the legal agreements in order to establish the exact division between Caterina's father, uncle and aunt and the third party. But it was an important matter, as we do not have any municipal water here and water for drinking, cooking, washing and growing for all parties comes from the same *gebbia*.

Over the centuries the lack of water inside the town compared with its abundance outside has been remarked upon. I have mentioned King Roger's Arab geographer in the twelfth century and Longo in the late eighteenth, both of whom commented on the fact, and I quoted Sladen in the nineteenth describing the women carrying pitchers of water into the town on their shoulders. The imbalance has now been resolved. An early attempt to municipalize the water of Pantano was described by Nicotra in his *Dizionario dei Comuni Siciliani* (1910): 'The Municipal Council is trying to conduct these abundant waters, but the expense and the quantity of the water to be transported do not allow for such an opportune and highly important work.' They did, however, manage to surmount the problems in the end, no doubt after gargantuan arguments, and Pantano water is now pumped into the town, a fact proclaimed by iron plaques on the walls of the houses that read: *Acquedotto di Calatafimi; rubinetto idrometrico* (Calatafimi Aqueduct; water-gauge tap). But regulations to ensure that it is hygienic beyond a shadow of a doubt must have been put into effect, because it does not taste as good as our water, which is untreated and comes from the same source. That's why they come up here to get their drinking water sometimes.

Empedocles must have miscalculated when he laid down that all change is brought about by the cosmic forces of love and strife, mixing with and separating the basic elements. There is no lack of love and strife in Calatafimi, yet change is barely perceptible.

9

Festas and Processions

A little thanksgiving now, after that brush with the elements?

Festas and processions in Calatafimi, I will persuade you, still rouse simple and spontaneous emotions. I am not claiming that her citizens are more religious or morally superior – nor the reverse, for that matter. They just let themselves be carried along by the natural impetus of their celebrations, and thoroughly enjoy these bends in the flow of life. People all over the Mediterranean have their own distinct ways of giving thanks, doing penance, or seeking favours, but many I think are losing their feeling of consensus, which dwindles into the sectarian, or metamorphoses into tourism, or both. That is a towering generalization, but the trend is there, even if I can't lay the statistics out on the table. What is certain is that tourists are not drawn to Calatafimi's celebrations, with one exception, of which more anon. They tend to be quiet local affairs, expressions of thanks for a past on which their present feeds. So you will not need much historical background to appreciate what they are celebrating. You should come to see some of them one day. They do act like a tepid shower on our sometimes ardent sophistication.

In 1655, Calatafimi, like Egypt before it, was visited by a plague of locusts, from which it was saved by the Madonna di Giubino. Giubino is the hill behind Calatafimi where Arcangelo Placenza initiated his progress towards the state of Beatitude I have already told you about. The Madonna who takes her name from the Giubino was promoted to Patron Saint of Calatafimi as a result of her sweeping victory over the locusts, a triumph which has been described by various local and ecclesiastical historians, and most recently by Father Nicolò Bonaiuto in his excellent concise account of her festa, which I am about to loot for your edification.[1]

In that fateful year the Giurati[2] of Calatafimi (they were unpaid local magistrates) wrote to their bishop in Mazzara del Vallo, in that same beautiful mixture of bad Italian, dialect and worse late Latin, to say that there had been a visitation of:

...such a quantity of grasshoppers, that eat all the seedlings, the farmlands, the trees and other things creating great damage to the *università populu*.[3]

The situation was clearly extreme and another contemporary account used even stronger terms. The voracious insects devoured the plants and herbs and 'filled the air with a stinking odour' ('e l'aria di puzzolentissimo odor riempivano').[4] In what was genuine panic, it was urgently decided that the names of the saints of all the churches in the town should be gathered together in an urn and whirled around, and an innocent young boy should be chosen to extract the predestined name of the saint who would save the town from the locusts, it being understood that the winner would be embraced by a united community, and do what he or she had to do to free the town of the scourge.

The name of the Madonna of Giubino was picked from the urn. But for some reason she did not convince the jury: officially, she was rejected because her image was too firmly 'installed' in the wall of her church, and therefore she was less endowed with the mobility necessary for processions. I am quite sure, however, that there must have been some parochial politics involved because, even at the second successful lottery she was not adopted, and it was only the third time round that it finally became evident even to the halt and blind that she was the saint to save Calatafimi from this and all subsequent plagues and disasters. She was adopted, carried in procession – and the locusts...disappeared. As the procession with her image, which had been torn from the wall of the Giubino church, entered the town

> a great murmuring sound arose, and at that very instant a whirlwind came, and drove out from the whole town, the countryside and the appurtenances of Calatafimi the innumerable swarms of those locusts, leaving the land free, the air serene and all the watching people astounded [subito sentesi levarsi nell'aria un gran mormorio, ed all'isstesso istante un turbine di vento valido spinge, e discaccia dalla Città tutta, dalle Campagne, e pertinanze di Calatafimi la innumerabile turba di quei cavalletti, restando libero il terreno, sereno l'aere, e stordito tutto il Popolo spettatore].[5]

Such faith is placed in the Madonna that at many critical times in Calatafimi's history she has been brought out and has saved the town. She became recognized as the Patron Saint of Calatafimi and her procession takes place on the last Sunday of September every year. Hers is the oldest surviving public ceremony here and she was, is and will continue to be loved by the people of Calatafimi. When she is not being processed, she is prayed to and talked about, and she has never failed the town. It goes without saying that there has never been another plague of locusts: as you certainly know, in southern Italy patron saints are taken seriously and those that fail to perform lose their jobs without much ado.

I must take you back in time to explain how her image came to be here in Calatafimi in the first place. Tradition has it that the marble bas-relief of the Madonna of Giubino was found in bad condition in the wood of Angimbè near the Giubino hill behind Calatafimi. It was unearthed by peasants ploughing, and the word spread like wildfire: citizens from Calatafimi, in whose territory Angimbè stood, assembled as well as those from nearby Alcamo and a dispute quickly broke out as to where she should be taken, to Calatafimi or to Alcamo. The Madonna herself resolved the issue because, after being placed in a driverless ox-cart, she elected to stop at the small Angimbè church in Calatafimi territory, or so the tradition goes. She was transferred to the Giubino church at a later date.[6] Her first miracles, even before the locusts flew in, had occurred in 1644 when she restored life not only to the priest of the church of Giubino who had been attacked by a 'blackguard' with a musket and knife, but also to a child who had been violently run over by horses on a public occasion. The very attractive image with the Madonna leaning her cheek on the Child's, while he plays with the collar of her shift, was originally the centrepiece of a triptych which got broken, possibly when it was wrenched from the wall for the original anti-locust procession; and the side parts of the triptych and the base ended up in private hands.[7] They were only re-discovered in 1931 and they finally rejoined the central panel in 1947, thanks to the dedication of two local historians: Bonaiuto himself and Mazzara. The polychrome white marble bas-relief is most beautiful and may have been done by Laurana[8] or his school, though that is far from certain. White and gold, the predominant colours, often combine badly as far as I am concerned, but if austerely painted they can also be beautiful. She is beautiful. When not being processed or visiting her original church on the Giubino hill, which she does every year, she is visible in the church of Santa Caterina, near the library. People know where she is at any point in time and you ought not to be surprised to hear that 'è tornata la Madonna' or 'non è tornata la Madonna' (meaning the statue has or has not returned to Santa Caterina from the Giubino church) is actually a comment on the time of the year.

She even received a Papal coronation in 1778. It began with the suppression of the Jesuits in 1767, as a result of which Calatafimi was, in Pellegrino's words, 'penalized by the expulsion of Father Catalano Baldassare S-J', who ended up in the Vatican as the Chaplain to the Papal Palfreniers. He did not forget his native Calatafimi, however, for by 1778 he had managed to obtain from the Vatican Chapter the concession of the special Papal Golden Crown for the Madonna di Giubino, a crown only bestowed on the holiest images of the Virgin Mary in Christendom. Bonaiuto ascribes this initiative to Monsignor Ugo Papè, then Bishop of Mazzara, but the actual decree names both Catalano and Papè. The crowns were paid for by the clergy and people of Calatafimi, and Catalano brought them down in person from Rome. The official crowning, a ceremony which lasted five days, was conducted by Monsignor Francesco Sanseverino, the Archbishop of Palermo, beginning on 4th May 1779 and it is not difficult to imagine the excitement in this small out-of-the-way town at having the great man in their generally forgotten midst. His inconveniencing himself by leaving the capital Palermo without concern for the 'disastrous' journey distinguished and honoured the city, which was full not only of its native sons but of strangers, too, from all over Sicily.[9] And he was not alone: also present was the Illustrious Signor Don Giovanni Emmanuele Rigano, Chevalier of the Holy Order of Jerusalem, General Procurator of the Duke of Alba, Count of Modica, at present at the Court at Madrid, Master of the City of Calatafimi and the celebrated County of Modica; and, as if that were not enough, the Viceroy had in addition sent along a troop of cavalry to protect and be of service to the high prelate. No wonder the insignificant town felt distinguished and honoured.

Much later on, in 1802, Pope Pius VII confirmed the Madonna di Giubino as the Patron Saint of Calatafimi and conceded a solemn particular office to be held in all the Diocese of Mazzara every 4th May for the 'Misericordia di Giubino'. Less ceremoniously, the other day Father Diego Taranto, another local historian and parish priest of San Michele and Santa Caterina, showed me the back of the image where holes had been bored for the coronation: the crowns, one for the Madonna and one for the Child, are held on with brass wire. Father Taranto has a photograph of her and the Child without their heavy crowns, and I agree with him that they look much lovelier like that. The original polychrome marble has one simple gold crown held up above them both by angels. While I was looking at the back of the marble, the postman came into the church with the mail. He did not see us, but I noticed that he spent significant minutes praying to the Madonna before getting back to his business of delivering the rest of the mail.

The people of Calatafimi have held their festas and processions over the centuries, and these have acquired encrustations that give them extra zest without detracting from their sincerity. Not least of these novelties is the use of the festa as an excuse to come together and eat, and the *tavulidda* (dialect for 'small table') has become customary either before or after events. They would probably have only had a modest feast after the first election of the Madonna di Giubino, because the locusts would have eaten up whatever was left during the bad agricultural year of 1655, nor would they have had much available towards the end of the nineteenth and the beginning of the twentieth centuries when conditions were so harsh that emigration was almost a *sine qua non* if you wanted to eat at all. The habit grew up in more prosperous times and, these being prosperous times, the *tavulidda* is an essential part of festivities now – it is usually at night and is mostly based on roast meat. Parallel secular feasting, if you like.

A new arrival on the festa scene in December is the Presepio Vivente, a tableau vivant of the Nativity. It is not exclusive to Calatafimi, but they do produce a fine version. It takes place in the oldest part of the town, the abandoned Terravecchia or Borgo quarter below the castle. After the 1968 earthquake, compensation money for damaged housing eventually became available, the new dormitory town of Sasi was built and the residents of Terravecchia were shunted off there, leaving a lot of abandoned houses that lent themselves to becoming a sort of film-set for the story of Christ's birth: film-set, because mostly just the walls had been left standing. It is very well done and everybody takes part. An Arab-like village is created where protagonists in Arab dress (striped curtain material) demonstrate Sicilian arts and crafts in a biblical ambience. There is also a tavern with clients. Suitable background music is provided by Perry Como singing *Jingle Bells* and there are a great number of very patient animals: pigs, donkeys, cows, rabbits, geese and even peacocks. My niece Elenuccia went wild about the rabbits. The crowning scene is a baby playing with its mother's face while Joseph and the animals (including real placid oxen) look on. The passers-by have interesting dialect conversations with Mother on how little 'Jesus' is standing up to the ordeal. He seemed to be thoroughly enjoying it, like everybody else.

The Immacolatella, a much older, nocturnal event, takes place on 8th December at 4 am. I got there rather too early and ended up in a *tavulidda* in a pizzeria: it had closed and the staff were having a small private feast, but they took pity on me. When the time was right, the procession started at the church of San Michele: traditionally, at least up till the last war, people were allowed to drink wine in the church because of the cold early December mornings, but I did not see anybody doing so this time. It was clear, though, that other early morning feasts had taken place as everybody was warm, contented and happy. The Madonna, bedecked with flowers, emerged from the church preceded by the traffic police, a drummer and a man whose job was to extinguish fires, followed by the clergy and a surprisingly large number of teenagers who roared a series of fifteen traditional question and answer slogans in favour of the Madonna that began merely loud and ended up cataclysmically loud – to the applause of the crowds carrying lighted reeds that lined both sides of the streets or followed the procession – which explains the fire-extinguisher official. There were hordes of small children carrying their small bundles of burning reeds, which lit up their faces. It is a popular procession with children and they push their parents hard to participate at this inconvenient time. It was raining, but the reeds kept on burning. They are gathered in the country and are tightly lashed together, which is why they don't go out. Unfortunately, there was an ecclesiastical loudspeaker, but it did make for a more audible broadcast of prayers to the Madonna and of the singing of a nun with a surprisingly good voice. The main focus, however, was on the teenagers and how loud they could shout the Madonna slogans, a sort of public contest accompanied by laughing and clapping, as I have said. It was all good fun, and I left at about 6 am, by which time the confused birds in the palm trees had long since given up trying to get to sleep.

Although the tradition of sculpting bread is really more developed in nearby Salemi, it is also at home in Calatafimi. For the day of San

Giuseppe (19th March), the Guild of the Borgisi di San Giuseppe
prepare a beautiful altar of sculptured bread in the sixteenth-century
Chiesetta (little church) in via Garibaldi, just in front of the old
carabinieri barracks – when people got in trouble with the law here
it was said that they had 'gone to the Chiesetta' – with bread in all
shapes and forms and etiolated wheat plants grown in the dark
(which is a continuation of the Middle Eastern 'Adonis gardens'
tradition and an integral part of the ritual of Nurouz, the Persian
New Year). Fish are a part of this ceremony, but, because they think
live fish might die, they make them out of bread and place them
before the altar. As far as I can see, it is the only time the Chiesetta
is used, because, even though it is prominently situated in the un-
clerically named via Garibaldi, it seems to be permanently closed
otherwise.

Throughout the rest of the year there are a host of other celebrations. By far the most impressive is the Festa of the SS Crocifisso,
the only occasion on which tourists actually flock to this 'insignificant' little town. It is a festa well worth seeing. Traditionally held
every year at the beginning of May, the prohibitive cost of the full-
scale festivities, which the willing citizens meet by digging deep into
their collective pocket, has meant that it is now held only every five
or seven years, an interval necessary for them to catch their financial
breath. A less ambitious version is celebrated in-between. Although
the municipality and the provincial government make contributions,
ninety percent of the cost is borne by the citizens themselves through
the ancient guilds which still play an active part in town life. Even the
Church has been a beneficiary rather than a contributor since the
much lamented confiscation and sale of the manor of Giumarella in
1866, the revenues from which had been set aside since 1728 for the
benefit of the church of the SS Crocifisso.

It all began in 1657, two years after the plague of locusts. In June
that year, on the 23rd, 24th and 25th to be exact, an ancient and
somewhat worm-eaten black crucifix which was lodged in the sac-
risty of the church of Santa Caterina Virgin and Martyr, performed
a series of miracles. A lay brother was cured of hernia, the wife of
another lay brother had spirits cast out of her, a ten-year-old boy was
cured of paralysis, and the people of the town quickly came to ven-
erate the crucifix with such devotion that the authorities were moved
to petition the Bishop of Mazzara del Vallo for the concession of a
special cult in favour of it. It was granted. At the beginning of May

ever since, the crucifix has been processed round the town by the guilds (or *ceti*) and its church has received homage from them and thanksgiving gifts of gold and silver (*prisenti* in dialect). The presents are rather more mundane now, more in the line of cassocks, candelabra and cash, and the church is a different one: the burgeoning cult required a larger building, and so the present church of the SS Crocifisso was begun in 1741 – it is the one so much admired by Houel, as I told you. The latest version of the original procession was organized again this year by the *ceti* in a jealously guarded tradition that has lasted 347 years.

If between 1686 and 1704 thirty-one different *ceti* were involved on and off in the procession, in 2004 only eleven took part. Most of those missing were the victims of progress, like the Cirniturari or 'sifters' (their presents were splendid gold nails in 1766, 1768 and 1769 and a gold diadem the following year), who made their last appearance in 1921, or the Spatuliari, who used to beat linen on the banks of the river Crimiso, now the Kaggera, until the advance of industry at the turn of the nineteenth century made them obsolete. This year, in marching order, a matter of great importance, the eleven were: the Sciabica, the Maestranza, the Borgisi di San Giuseppe, the Ortolani, the Mugnai, the Pecorai e Caprai, the Macellai, the Borgisi, the Cavallari, the Massari and the clergy.

These guilds tax themselves heavily, as well as raising money from non-members, for the great event. Its organization is so elaborate that, even as early as 1728, according to Calcara,[10] there were crowds of visitors from all around flocking to see the magnificent celebrations – 'i forastieri concorrono a godere la magnificanza della festa.' In 1997, it was estimated that a crowd of 120,000 crushed into this small town designed for 7,000 inhabitants; this time the figure is probably nearer 250,000 according to the organizing committee, including around 8,000 emigrants returning, particularly from the north of Italy and America. Special remote parking has had to be arranged and shuttle-buses put on to get the visitors into town. A friend has told me that twelve members of his extended family came from various places for the festa, including a niece who worked in a restaurant in London that was wholly run by Calatafimi emigrants. She and all her colleagues downed pots and pans and closed up the restaurant so they could be here for the festivities. It is the only time the town attracts tourists, but the festa is not in fact for them. It is dreamed of, talked about, worked at, paid for, participated in and lived through by every individual in the town and his relatives abroad: it is *their* festa.

The decision whether to hold the full procession or not is taken in October of the year before, after which months of frantic preparation begin. It is then that the commitment to a personal contribution is made and the fund-raising starts; the emigrants are contacted for donations; the physical work begins; and the rival plans of the *ceti* are studied. Manual workers disappear from the market, and people wander around moaning that there is nobody to prune their olive trees or plough their vineyards. But...*pazienza, c'è la festa*! I managed with some luck to get a pair of trousers altered in early February: it was the last job the seamstress took on before starting full-time work on the costumes for the allegorical procession. Until recently the costumes had been hired at considerable expense from the Teatro Massimo, the Palermo Opera House, but this year all the work was undertaken in the town. Other people were already at work on the caparisons and trappings for the horses, mules and carts. Already by 17th March one of the guilds, the Massari, had fifteen women (they would soon be thirty) at work making *cucciddati*, the circular bread loaves that would later be thrown to the crowds: their aim was to make 130 metric tons of them. As each weighs around 280 grams, I leave it to you to work out how many individual pieces that is. All talk was of the festa and the mere suggestion that one *ceto* was planning something extra immediately set off a domino cascade of meetings to discuss how best the other *ceti* could keep their end up.

Towards the end of that month, Caterina and I helped for just one evening from 5.00 to 11.00 pm together with twenty or so other people from one of the guilds, filling up little bags with confetti and nuts. There had been many other evenings and many other people involved before this, and the various other *ceti* had all their small bags of bread, cheese and nuts ready to fling at the crowds during the procession. Horses, mules and carts began to appear in the country and the town, as people got used to riding again. Rivalry was instinctive, and it was not just between the *ceti*: if a man decided to bring out his horse, his neighbour would feel it necessary for him to do so, too. There have been appeals for moderation for centuries, but this time round, as always, people have got into debt and even sold land to keep their end up or to edge ahead. The Massarioti must not be outdone by the Cavallari, or vice versa: that would spell humiliation. I know of one man who spent five million lire just as his personal contribution to the festivities of his *ceto*; and others surely did the same. I doubt whether the members of the Royal Horticultural Society would do that for the Chelsea Flower Show.

Since at one point on the route the processions have to go up one especially steep hill, rehearsals were the order of the day. They were important because if by some appalling stroke of bad luck the oxen of the Massari could not manage the hill, the horses of the Cavallari would have had the right to supersede them in the processional order, which would break a tradition that has lasted almost 400 years: these two were arguing about precedence as early as 1670. The general rivalry was noted by Calcara in 1728 when he talked of 'innocente superbia collegato con la pieta' ('innocent pride linked to piety'), although I hardly think the 'superbia' was innocent then, any more than it is now. Indeed, I was told that, in the early years of the twentieth century, the steep slope the oxen have to pull their carts up was soaped for reasons of rivalry.

I went to several rehearsals during the nights before the festa. There was no parking space left in the town because people had come from all around to see them. As the carts and the animals began to come up the hill at around 10.30 pm, the crowds scattered to let them pass and applause broke out. The oxen, which had been hired in Sardinia at a cost of 60 million lire, had arrived on 17th April, all six of them. They came with their minders and were slowly made familiar with the people of Calatafimi and the hill. They had achieved this by the 26th when I saw them haul themselves and their carts up it easily enough, even if the more elderly onlookers were muttering that they were not as good as they used to be, which is, I suppose, only to be expected. Gone were the usual clumps of people even at that time of the night: it was a crowd of eager commentators and applauders.

Many days previously the whole town had been decked out in triumphal arches of coloured lights, and there was a large electric cross on the crenellated (i.e. waterworks) part of the castle. Shops had sprung out of nowhere to profit from the crowds when the real festa started, and there were new bars (the 'Zanzibar' was one) and places where local wines and plain satisfying *prosciuto* rolls would be available on the day. All the streets to be used in the procession had been covered with a layer of earth and pebbles so that the animals' hooves could get a good grip. The final rehearsal was held on the night of the 28th, but there had been some rain and it was not thought worth risking the oxen on the slippery surface. Apart from some last-minute details, that marked the end of the three months that had seen the whole town utterly taken up by the preparation of their festa.

The structure of the festivities is quite simple. On the first day (30th April) a series of Masses are said; and, preceded and followed by bands playing for all they are worth, a silver cross that has been transferred from the church of the SS Crocifisso to that of Santa Caterina at Easter, and the image of the Madonna di Giubino which is installed in Santa Caterina, are both separately taken up to the church of SS Crocifisso in a procession. A short while later, the Allegorical Procession gets under way, with eleven floats this time, illustrating biblical themes under the banner of 'Esedra and Neemia', subtitled 'Jerusalem, the Holy City: From Promise to Achievement', all of which is announced to the crowds by an initial float that is drawn by a tractor driven by Lucianone, or 'big' Luciano, the giant who helped build our house – looking almost angelic, dressed in a blue velvet tunic. His tractor is followed by the eleven other floats with their high painted backdrops, each drawn by its own tractor. The various scenes are enacted by the townspeople in biblical costumes; and Christ, King Cyrus of Persia, Governors of Jersusalem, etc., with palm trees, sand, parchments, edicts, wells, sheep, children, city gates, temples, and so on, slowly pass by.

On the second day, 1st May, the *ceti* pay their homage to the crucifix in the church of SS Crocifisso separately and without ever crossing each other's paths; and during their processions they scatter excessive amounts of food to the expectant crowds. This programme is repeated on 2nd May. On the final day, 3rd May, after the Allegorical Procession has paraded once again, the focus is on the Crucifix, and it and the image of the Madonna di Giubino are solemnly processed round the town by the *ceti* which then offer their *prisenti* to the church of SS Crocifisso; after which the Madonna di Giubino is returned to the church of Santa Caterina. Fireworks follow. Every day Masses are said, and drummers drum dramatically. That is the broad outline.

First in the field, on 1st May were the Maestranze. In origin, they were the guild of the barbers, carpenters, blacksmiths, saddlers, masons and other artisans of the town, and they have been taking part in the procession since at least the end of the seventeenth century. Over time they also took on duties as an occasional urban militia, which is why they carry shotguns. A solemn double file of about 150 of them marched slowly up either side of the street: all men, they were young and old and middle-aged, but they all wore black suits, black hats, black ties, white waistcoats with gold chains, white gloves (black if they were officials) and black shoes, and carried double-barrelled shotguns on their shoulders as they marched impassively in time to the band, with their gaze fixed rigidly in front of them. Their banners, symbolic gifts and halberds were carried by black-suited individuals who marched between the two files. When they reached the church they were ordered to present arms in accordance with tradition but, coming down the hill, they did so again just in front of the balcony where we were, as the Bishop was on the next-door balcony.

This *ceto* was followed by four others processing together, the Borgisi di San Giuseppe, the Ortolani, the Caprai e Pecorai and the Mugnai. The Borgisi di San Giuseppe were constituted fairly recently, at the beginning of the twentieth century: they are smallholders who have taken special vows to San Giuseppe and are therefore mystically involved with bread. They were headed by a float with 'San Giuseppe' in person (he was Ivan, the assistant to Mario the electrical mechanic who often performs miracles on my ancient car). This was followed by a double file of their members and officials carrying their symbolic gifts, together with a large umbrella symbol made up of intricate bread sculptures, which was very beautiful and so tall that we could study it in detail from the balcony we were looking from. They threw thousands of small bags containing tiny loaves to the crowd. The Ortolani, or market gardeners, came next: they have been recorded in the festa since at least 1689; and they were followed by the Caprai e Pecorai (the shepherds and goat herders, active in 1733) and the Mugnai (the guild of the millers, recorded at the festa since 1686, as Calatafimi was for a long time an important centre for watermills along the river Crimiso).[11]

The first of these four guilds paraded with a float containing a garden in full cultivation, with running water and various vegetables and fruits, and their marching members showered cascades of cut flowers (gerberas, if you are interested) onto the shouting crowds. The second, the *ceto* of the shepherds in which Nicola from just down our road was conspicuous, had a float with live sheep and goats, including young suckled by their mothers: their followers pelted the bystanders with pieces of cheese. The third guild paraded a revolving millstone, and the millers flung pieces of bread in all directions. All the costumes were beautifully made locally, and the crowd responded frantically to the showering of gifts, struggling to collect as much as possible in plastic bags. Each of the *ceti* had back-up transport containing fresh supplies of food bags or flowers, which were continuously relayed to the throwers. The amount pelted at the crowd was excessive. But this is a festa of abundance, and tradition-ally abundance has been taken to mean excess, as witnessed by centuries of appeals to moderation by the Church authorities.

There was then a delay of about two and a half hours before the Cavallari, literally the 'horsemen' but in fact the ancient guild of transporters, rode past. Rumour had it that the delay was no acci-dent, as their rivals the Massari have the honour of being the last to parade, and the Cavallari are not averse to making them wait, especially when people are becoming tired and thinking of going to bed. Whether that was true or not, this *ceto* is well known for its jovial spirits and is a favourite with the crowds. It has been recorded as taking part in the festa since it started, and its disputes with the Massari about precedence in the procession were first heard of in 1670 (the then Bishop making judgement against them).

Most of their parade is taken up with a succession of traditional Sicilian carved and painted carts, pulled by richly caparisoned horses *cap-à-pie* in brightly coloured pennants and feathers, mirror-studded coverings and intricate trappings, red and yellow dominating. The first in line and very warmly applauded was a tiny donkey-cart led by the Mario who cuts my hair, containing his grandchild. There followed normal-sized carts full of people in costume and some of them with bands playing traditional music. A few of the horses were nervous in the crowds, others 'danced' quite happily – they had been taught to shuffle their hooves to a rhythm. They were succeeded by individual horsemen with bulging saddle-bags who, reining frantic-ally in tight circles, pelted the crowds with a hail of small bags filled with nuts, incited by all and sundry for more and yet more. The physical effort of showering the nuts in all directions was evident, and a series of runners kept the horsemen supplied from two decor-ated lorries heaped high with stocks. Shouts of here! here!, children blindly scampering round picking up the bags, old people sheltering themselves from the falling bags, the throwers beaming with pleasure – all contributed to the delirious excitement and a level of noise that hurt the ears.

After another interval came the Borgisi, probably the most numerous of the *ceti* as they represent the tillers of the soil and the smallholders: their animals are mules which are better behaved in crowds than horses. They too have been part of the festa from the beginning and, constituting the backbone of general agriculture, they give a display of its basic activities – the reaping and winnowing of corn, the picking and pressing of grapes, and the gathering and processing of olives, admirably displayed on tractor-drawn slices of moving countryside. Again the crowds were cannonaded with abundance, this time in the form of small loaves of bread, and the same wild scenes were unleashed.

The last procession of the *ceti* was given over to the Massari, the oldest of the guilds with its origins in the overseers of the land that was owned by the aristocrats, the people who actually ran the big landholdings. It has become the *ceto* of the resident rich who finance themselves entirely without any outside fund-raising and it was they who donated the ceremonial mount of silver on which the crucifix is processed. Their animal is the ox, an immense but placid beast. Their procession is introduced by riders on impressive-looking horses, but the crowd is waiting for the oxen drawing the *Torre* or Tower of Abundance, perhaps the symbol of the whole festa, and from the considerable height of which thousands of *cucciddati* or small round crown-like disks of bread are thrown to the people. There were three pairs of yoked oxen this year, the first pulling the tower and the other two large carts of fresh supplies of *cucciddati*. The pelting of the crowds with plenty becomes even more frantic and its effects harder to cope with – the average *cucciddato* is about 280 grams of hard, spiked bread in the form of a discus, as I've said, which, when aimed at friends in the crowd or the balconies above, is dispatched with a flick of the wrist that whistles it through the air at considerable speed and causes fear and confusion among the old, and sore hands among the younger, when it is caught. Not only are there two huge cartloads of supplies following the tower, there are also supply points along the route, so that the quantity of *cucciddati* thrown into the crowd and up to the balconies is truly astonishing. (If you haven't calculated it already, the 130 metric tons of *cucciddati* works out at over 46,000 pieces of sculptured bread.)

All these processions of the *ceti* have one destination, the church of SS Crocifisso where the humans and the animals pay homage to the Crucifix. On the second day of these homage-processions,

I placed myself just inside the entrance to the church. They came right up to the main entrance, the people making the sign of the cross, the animals, sometimes reluctantly, coming up one or two steps – the oxen being made to bow their heads, 'kneeling' in popular language. After homage has been paid and the inside of the church has been pelted with food bags, the processions continue on their way round the town, flinging more abundance at the eager crowd.

The fourth and final day had a different but in no way less impressive character. As it was a Monday, there were fewer outsiders and, the more exhibitionist aspects of the processions being over, things were more spiritual. By the early morning, the streets had been cleaned of the mountains of nutshells and plastic bags, and all that was left of the cattle dung were dark patches in the earth and pebbles that covered the asphalt. I thought I would take a look in the church of Santa Caterina to see the hole left above the altar by the Madonna di Giubino after she had been taken away. The door was ajar, but I couldn't get in for the crush – it was like trying to get onto a London tube in the rush hour, so many people were hearing Mass.

Unfortunately, a forceful *sirocco* wind had got up. The repeat of the allegorical procession had to be cancelled in the afternoon because the backdrops would have become airborne; but in the evening the procession of all the *ceti* (with the addition of the Macellai, the ancient guild of the butchers, and the equally ancient Sciabica, an Arabic word meaning a 'net', hence the *ceto* for those not included in the other *ceti*) solemnly paraded their *prisenti*, their offerings, up to the SS Crocifisso, and returned in triumph to process round the town with the Crucifix and the Madonna di Giubino, guarded by four armed Borgisi each – on their ceremonial silver mounts which raised them to balcony level: they were in strict ceremonial order, headed by the Sciabica and with the Massari bringing up the rear just before the clergy and the authorities. The Crucifix and the Madonna di Giubino were carried on the shoulders of young men who, at the ring of a silver bell, periodically rested their burden. The wind was a problem with the tall standards of the *ceti* and the hooded candles, but the whole thing went off with great dignity and to the deep and proprietary satisfaction of the townspeople, who were radiant. Later on, the Madonna di Giubino was accompanied in procession back to her normal church in a thunderstorm, which did not, however, dampen the enthusiasm of the people of Calatafimi. Around 11.00 pm, a little earlier than usual, there was a magnificent display of fireworks, which we viewed from a distance, back at home.

I started this chapter by saying that I wanted to persuade you that festas and processions are still in essence simple and spontaneous here. You may well say that this festa was far from simple and that it was hardly improvised, but I stand by what I said. The simplicity in this case has more to do with single-mindedness and the spontaneity with spontaneous combustion. But the urge to hold the festa was universal and profound. The 'innocente superbia' is evident in the huge horse's head made for the Cavallari's supply lorry which dwarfs everything around it, and the endless *cucciddati*, the basic food in a poor society, that are flung to the crowds by the Massari. There is excess. The key word is *more*: more than from the other *ceti* as a matter of pride, more than is necessary because it's the festa. Until recently the festa took place in a society of grinding poverty for most people, and abundance, justified by the celebration of thanksgiving, allowed people to forget it for an hour or so. Today, it is conscious indulgence in excess, but it is paid for by widow's mites. And then the 'folla di forestieri' – we had probably about a quarter of a million visitors this time – they are a consequence of, but not the objective of, all the preparations, because the festa is a local event that doesn't obey a general calendar. The people of Calatafimi feel the need for it, they sacrifice themselves for it and they enjoy every minute of it. It is community zeal.

Have I persuaded you?

10

Calatafimi and Garibaldi

Garibaldi, who I know is one of your heroes, provided the only reason why the odd non-Italian on this planet has ever heard of Calatafimi, as I have said. Every Italian schoolchild learns, and therefore exceptional adults remember, that he and his Thousand – almost all of them from the north, incidentally – won his first and decisive victory here in 1860 over the repressive Bourbon Kings of Naples and Sicily, releasing a flood tide that brought about the unification of Italy in the face of all the furtive opposition that the Piedmontese Government could muster against Garibaldi personally. Small provincial skirmish it might have seemed, but it turned out to be a truly important battle. Although the Piedmontese Government was supposed to be on Garibaldi's side, it distrusted him and obstructed him politically, diplomatically and financially throughout the campaign. Count Cavour, the Prime Minister, could not afford to detract from the charisma of the legendary hero openly, but he did manage to substitute the weapons that were collected during the 1859 'Million Rifles Fund' with useless, obsolete rifles just before he sailed. He did give orders for the expedition to be stopped in Sardinia after it had left Genoa for Sicily, and again for Garibaldi to be prevented from crossing the Straits of Messina after he had won the island.[1] He did try to forestall the Garibaldini in Naples and he replaced his troops with the Piedmontese army after Garibaldi had handed southern Italy to King Vittorio Emanuele on a plate after the battle of Volturno. And yet Piedmont graciously accepted his gift of a united Italy. Did you know that on 16th May (the day after the battle of Calatafimi) Cavour managed to engineer a double defeat for Garibaldi in the Piedmontese General Elections?[2] At the same moment the *Piedmontese Gazette* published the following official statement: 'The Government disapproved of the expedition and attempted to prevent its departure with such means as prudence and the laws would permit.'[3] Mazzini put it more accurately:

The men of the Government began by blaming Garibaldi and the *mad* enterprise, and hastened, Pilate-like, to wash their hands before the foreign governments of any complicity in the daring attempt, meanwhile preaching inertia to the Italians. They changed their language, and expressed admiration, though they offered no help, when they heard of Calatafimi. They went to work to get the movement into their own hands when they heard of Palermo.

Cavour may have baulked at what he considered the uncontrollable radical revolution that Garibaldi was fomenting and he may have been prudent to avoid provoking a war with Austria without French backing. So Garibaldi was up against Cavour as well as the King-dom of the Two Sicilies. Far from being a prudent man himself, Garibaldi was quick to grasp what destiny had to offer, beginning with the opportunity that presented itself in the fields a few hundred yards from where we now live.

To give you a bit of background, and because I could not re-member over which plains in South America he and his pregnant wife Anita had galloped against 'tyranny' in all its forms, I opened my 1908 copy of *Chambers' Encyclopaedia*. The entry might do to sketch in something of the personality of the man. He was born in Nice, then a part of Piedmont-Savoy-Sardinia. 'His father was a simple God-fearing fisherman, seldom in prosperous circumstances, but he contrived nevertheless to give the boy a tolerable education, possibly with the object of making him a priest.' This was the man who spent many of his later years trying to topple the political influence of the Papacy in Italy – the famous 'O Roma, O Morte' speech was delivered all over Sicily, including Calatafimi, in 1862, when he was trying unsuccessfully to march on Rome for the second time – though it should not be forgotten that in 1847 he did offer to fight under the banner of the then reformist Pope Pius IX. His early career was as a Che Guevara predecessor in South America. *Chambers* con-tinues:

> ...rebellion against the Emperor of Brazil. He distinguished himself as a guerrilla warrior and privateer, was taken prisoner and suspended for two hours by the wrists for attempting to escape, and eloped with and soon married the beautiful creole Anita Riveira de Silva.

And I cannot deny it: we have a dog called Garibaldi and a hen called Anita.

After some mingled experience as drover, shipbroker, and teacher of mathematics, he offered in 1842 his assistance to the Montevideans, who were at war with Rosas, the tyrant of Buenos Ayres.

The patriotic fervour for stamping out foreign domination and repressive regimes and replacing them with a united, reform-minded system of government, a fervour that was bubbling up all over Italy in the middle years of the nineteenth century, was a clarion call to Garibaldi's personality. He returned from South America already a hero of the fight for liberty, and was quickly involved with Piedmont in the fight against Austria in 1848, where he was firmly sidelined, and in the unsuccessful defence of the Republic of Rome, where he was politically isolated, and from which he escaped with difficulty. There followed a period of relative inactivity before he was taken on again by the Piedmontese in 1859 because they had no option but to do so, and promptly applied himself to the conquest of Italy, to the horror, as we have seen, of Prime Minister Cavour and to the shame of the Kings of Italy who hardly distinguished themselves in the role he created for them.

In 1860, Sicily knew that the famous Garibaldi was coming, but not when or where, and there were anticipatory uprisings: they did not fare well, although they were enough to convince Garibaldi that there was a movement he could harness. While still in the north he had heard of a revolt in Palermo, and it was this that made up his mind to come. But there was activity outside Palermo as well: in a memorandum dictated much later (15th December 1891), Pietro Adamo, Calatafimi's protagonist in dealings with Garibaldi, set down for the record something of what was happening in the town before the Hero's arrival. It is worth quoting parts in full because Adamo maintains that the rebellious state of the town affected both Garibaldi's and the Bourbon army's subsequent decisions, convincing Garibaldi to take full advantage of its rebellious mood, and compelling the Neapolitan general to leave considerable reserves and many field-guns behind in the town when the moment of battle came. And he may be right, given the nervousness of General Landi. This is what he says happened on 7th April.

On receiving news of the uprisings in Palermo on 4th April, which had been brought to Calatafimi on the morning of the 7th by the Baron Mokharta [the brother-in-law of the famous Sant'Anna brothers of

Alcamo] who communicated it to Professor Biagio Ingroia [Samuel
Butler's friend], this latter, who was still a priest, took advantage of the
religious functions of Easter Saturday which were being celebrated that
very morning in the church of the Santa Caterina Monastery to the
singing of the 'Exultet', and gave the sign for the start of the rebellion
by inserting the name of Victor Emanuel into the solemn 'Pro Rege'
oration [instead, of course, of that of the Bourbon King]. As soon as
the service was over and Signor Mariano Sabado, who was among
Baron Mokharta's followers, had arrived from Alcamo and the news
had been divulged, all the patriots gathered together and, to the cry of
'Italia con Vittorio Emanuele', we carried the national flag around in
triumph and hung it on the municipal town hall. It was a day of
enthusiasm which closed with the spontaneous illumination of the
whole town, throughout which patriotic songs echoed. And already
a team of valiant young people was formed to leave the following
morning in aid of Palermo. However, on the morning of the 8th the
post-coach, which had not been to the town since the 5th, brought
the sad news of the failure and the repression of Gancia's rebellion.[4]

On 11th May, the day of Garibaldi's actual landing at Marsala,
Pietro Adamo remembered this: 'Towards midday the sound of firing
could be heard to the north. It was thought to be an uprising at
Trapani and I sent a courier there…to find out what had happened.
It became known that cannon fire had been heard from Marsala and
I sent another courier'.[5] The next day, in the evening, the courier re-
turned and announced to Adamo's secret revolutionary committee
that Garibaldi had landed. A further courier had been sent to San
Vito Lo Capo, a headland to the west of Trapani. The names of
the three couriers were Silvestro Simone, Filippo Santannera and
Vincenzo La Grutta. The telegraph line at Calatafimi was promptly
cut (it was an essential factor in Garibaldi's success because the
Bourbons had virtually no communications throughout and were
thoroughly confused), the urban guards were disarmed, the tricolour
was raised and a demonstration was organized in favour of Italy and
King Vittorio Emanuele. On the night of the 12th, the road from the
town of Alcamo was lit by torches announcing the arrival of the
Bourbon troops under General Landi, and the patriots of Calatafimi
took refuge in Pietro Adamo's country house at Ummari outside
Calatafimi. The next day Pietro Adamo, Antonino Colombo and
Gaetano Cangemi (all relatives, I am afraid) were invited by Giuseppe
Coppola, from the town of Erice above Trapani, to join the other in-

surgents from the province of Trapani at the nearby town of Salemi. Garibaldi was informed at Salemi by Adamo on the 14th of the uprising at Calatafimi and the arrival of General Landi, and he was persuaded to proceed towards Calatafimi, although the strategic importance of the town at the meeting point of the roads from Marsala and Trapani to Palermo must surely have been clear to him.

General Landi, as I have said, had very bad communications (as had everybody: in *The Times* the battle was reported as lost, won or indecisive) and was convinced there were armed bands all around him, a fact that was important in his later decisions. Garibaldi, who was well informed by Adamo and his men, decided to move to high ground just outside Calatafimi, and Adamo and Colombo were sent to collect men and arms and to inform the population. The people came out to watch, giving Landi the impression that his actual opponents were much more numerous than they really were, another local, if not exactly aggressive, contribution to the successful outcome of the battle. Landi sent out a force of about 2,000 under Major Sforza with orders to reconnoitre only, keeping a reserve of 1,172 and two mountain guns in Calatafimi; while Garibaldi by now had something less than 2,000 men. Adamo informed Garibaldi that the troops were coming out of Calatafimi, which pleased him, and since he (Adamo) knew the terrain well he was at Garibaldi's side during the battle, although on foot as he had given up his horse to Sirtori, a leading light in the Thousand, who had it shot from under him during the fray.

Landi was considering falling back on Palermo even before the battle began because he was convinced he had the whole countryside against him, but against his orders Sforza engaged and the die was cast. The reality is that, with overwhelming defensive odds in his favour and against an undisciplined attacking force consisting mainly of civilians, Landi clearly had the upper hand though he did not know it. Even the vigorous Nino Bixio, the number two of the Redshirts, considered retreat during the battle, but this was promptly quashed by Garibaldi, who pronounced in Genoese dialect: 'Here we make Italy or die.' If the battle was touch and go, the patriots knew they could not afford to lose it. Garibaldi met with stiff resistance and was rebuffed on several occasions, losing the personal flag that had been worked up for him by the ladies of Montevideo; but Sforza (who may have run out of ammunition) was called off and General

Landi, convinced all along that he had little chance and that, anyway, withdrawal to Palermo was the better strategy, retreated in disarray to Alcamo, rather comically leaving behind both the regimental coffers and his own personal luggage in Calatafimi. He then did fall back to Palermo – with some considerable difficulty – through country by then controlled to a large extent by rebellious Sicilians who had been unleashed by the success at Calatafimi.

In the aftermath of the battle, Garibaldi asked a local volunteer what the name was of the hill where the victory had been won. The answer came back in dialect, 'Chiantu Rumanu'. The General asked what that meant and, off the cuff, an italianized version was offered, 'Pianto Romano'. Intrigued, he asked why, and, in the heat of the moment, his informer concocted a story he thought would gratify the General. He said it was it was on this hill that, centuries before, the Segestans and their Carthaginian allies had bloodily defeated a Roman army and made them suffer, hence the name 'Pianto Romano' or 'Roman Tears'. Garibaldi was delighted with the information and even suggested it should be called 'Pianto dei Romani'. And so it has remained in history books, acts of parliament, maps and literature. The battle of Calatafimi was therefore fought on the site of a Roman defeat that never took place. But the name appealed to the victor and to his contemporaries, too, no doubt with Pope Pio IX's Rome in mind. As the false name gained national credence, the embarrassed locals let it stand, and it was not until September 1894 that Biagio Ingroia, Garibaldi's ecclesiastical ally and later Samuel Butler's friend, tried to put the record straight.[6] However the myth was not to be dislodged; it was too convenient. It had appeared in Garibaldi's *Memoirs* and in 1901 it was consecrated by D'Annunzio in his *Canzone di Garibaldi*:

> Ecco irto d'armi il colle di sì grande
> Nome, nomato Pianto dei Romani
>
> [There bristling with arms the hill of such great
> Name, called the Tears of the Romans]

Further attempts were made by local learned societies to correct the mistake and a leaflet was printed in 1910 at Palermo by Salvatore Romano, a Trapanese writer,[7] explaining that (as Ingroia had already pointed out) there had been no Roman defeat in the area, *chiantu* means 'plant' (*pianta* in Italian, not 'tears' which is *pianto*), the correct name in dialect 'Chiantu Rumanu' means 'the vineyard of the Romano family', and there were notarial records going back to 1601 proving that the land belonged to the Romano family. But the enthusiastic fib invented in the heat of the moment by that citizen of Calatafimi to gratify Garibaldi did not go away. The hill *is* called Pianto Romano or Pianto dei Romani.

It has been suggested that the famous victory at Calatafimi – the site of the battle is recorded today by a solitary obelisk, lit up at night and visible from our windows – may have been bought, and that the Neapolitan General Landi received a bribe. Garibaldi denied this publicly and always said the Neapolitans had fought gallantly. In England, there had been public subscriptions in Garibaldi's favour, which were much debated in the House of Commons, with the opposition (and Queen Victoria) maintaining it was illegal to collect money for the downfall of an allied king, and anyway it was iniquitous to be supporting the 'notorious' republican and atheist Riccardi and the 'priest-slaughterer Zambianchini'. The Solicitor-General, however, ruled that it was legal and there were many 'hear, hear's' from the House in support of Garibaldi.[8] But there was no talk of the money being used to corrupt Landi.

The mythical Thousand (two thousand according to *The Times'* Malta correspondent) that landed at Marsala on 11th May 1860 and found there the *Intrepid* and the *Argus* (two British ships that had been sent ostensibly to protect the Marsala wine business that was created and managed there by Yorkshiremen[9]) may have been even less than 1,000 strong (though some local riff-raff was picked up when they landed), and was made up of undisciplined civilians from the north of Italy who had no understanding of the southern terrain. But it was driven by an ideal and commanded by a general who would shoot his men if they stole grapes from a vineyard along the way. He was not a man to use corruption as a weapon.

At the end of March 1861, before his death of a heart-attack brought on by a broken heart, it is said that Landi presented a note of credit for 14,000 ducats to the Bank of Sicily. But the figure had been altered and the signature was declared false. The allegation was that it had been given to him by Garibaldi. The Hero denied this explicitly in a letter to Landi's son afterwards, saying he had 50,000 liras for his expenses on that expedition to Sicily and they were used just for that, not to buy generals. But the story was widely believed. Garibaldi had always maintained that the Bourbons had fought well and the correspondent of the *Illustrated London News*, present at the battle, mentioned that a company of Royal sharpshooters, having run short of ammunition, 'used stones instead of balls', as well as the butts of their guns.

The same correspondent added a strange note: 'there were also present [on Garibaldi's side] two Franciscan monks, who fought like heroes. A third friar led to Garibaldi's camp a band of 300 Sicilians armed with excellent English muskets.' I wonder where they got them from? What is more, in the list of billets in Calatafimi for 16th May 1860, there was a 'squadra dei capitani inglesi' (a group of English captains) billeted in the church of San Michele. These may have been the thirty-three Englishmen under the command of Captain Dunne, a veteran of the Crimean War, who had arrived in Genoa in time to embark with Garibaldi.[10] Individual Englishmen and also many other people were enthusiastically on the side of Garibaldi, and contributed generously. Donations were made by the son of the Duke of Wellington, the widow of Byron, Florence Nightingale and Charles Dickens; money was raised in the Athenaeum itself (£300 in one single night); and a certain Reverend Lane Fox even sent from his vicarage in Dorset a hymn he had written asking for God's protection of Garibaldi. I fervently pray, as I'm sure you do too, that the Redshirts and the citizens of Calatafimi sang it manfully as they killed the soldiers of his Sicilian Majesty, although I somehow doubt it. Hymns aside, the exact extent of the international help is not known, but 'it may have been as much as if not more than that subscribed in Italy itself.'[11] To add to the mystery, Lord Henry Lennox got up in the Lords' debate in London on 8th May 1863 to speak against the infamies committed by the Piedmontese regime in Sicily and stated that everybody knew the British had united Italy, not Garibaldi – even if this seems a trifle over-patriotic, British fingers were certainly in the pie and British ships, though technically neutral, were in the offing all through the campaign.

There was also a considerable lack of reliable communication outside the theatre of battle, as I have told you. Take *The Times*. On Monday 21st May 1860 there were two conflicting reports. First:

> Naples May 18th official. The bands of Garibaldi have been attacked at the point of the bayonet by the Royal troops at Calata Fimi [*sic*], and totally routed, leaving on the battle field their flag and a great number of killed and wounded, among whom was one of their chiefs.

This was balanced by the second version (which had first been published in the second edition of the paper the previous Saturday):

> It is asserted that the battle at Calata Fimi was not decisive.
> The Neapolitan troops re-entered Palermo. Two columns of 3,000
> men each have been sent to pursue the insurgents. It is estimated that
> 6,000 Sicilians have joined the Garibaldians.

Even Landi had reported initially to Palermo that Garibaldi had been killed in the battle. Garibaldi and his men had better information.

On the morning after the battle, the 16th, and when the Bourbons had already retreated, Garibaldi was carried in triumph into Calatafimi on a litter from Margi, the house where Caterina's grandmother was born and which can be seen from our terrace. He had lost forty-one dead (not thirty-three) and a hundred and twenty-six wounded.[12] Only six of the dead were Sicilians and none were from Calatafimi; one Calatafimese, Giuseppe Torreggiani, was among the wounded, however. It was a small battle but it was of extreme importance because, had he lost it, his chances of getting any further would have been scant indeed. That he won it reinforced the impression that he was invincible and the rout of the Bourbons became a possibility rather than a dream, which both inflamed the liberators and dejected the oppressors throughout the peninsula. Calatafimi was instrumental in the unification of Italy. Later Garibaldi himself felt that the battle at Calatafimi had been decisive, if others had been more resonant: 'Palermo, Milazzo, il Volturno videro molti feriti e cadaveri, ma secondo me, la battaglia decisiva fu quella di Calatafimi' ('Palermo, Milazzo, Volturno saw more wounded and dead, but, in my view, the decisive battle was the one at Calatafimi'). The next day, the Municipal Council declared Garibaldi 'Dictator of the Provisional Government of King Vittorio Emanuele II', which was set up to annex Calatafimi to the Kingdom of Italy and to express the view that all Sicily should be thus annexed.

It must sadly be said, however, that the principles of liberty and good governance, heralded before the victory, faded with the Piedmontese Government that succeeded it, as Lord Henry, in the speech already mentioned, had expounded in the House of Lords. Heavy taxes were levied on the Sicilians, the most hated being on milled corn, i.e. bread, the revenue from which was invested in the north of Italy; military service was imposed; and the freedom and promised prosperity did not materialize, either for Sicilians in general or for Calatafimi. The people reacted. Even Bixio, Garibaldi's famous trusted right-hand man, was subsequently responsible for the brutal putting down of a peasant uprising at Bronte in the east of the island. It was suggested that this rebellion was quashed because Nelson had been made Duke of Bronte and nobody wanted to offend the English; but I find this hard to swallow. The new government just couldn't, or else wouldn't, fulfil their opportunistic promises and stamped on the consequential reaction. Sicily's acute disappointment with the new regime has been magnificently described in the fictional works of Federico De Roberto and Giuseppe Tomasi di Lampedusa.[13]

I am grateful to Nello Morsellino and his *Garibaldi e i Mille... Guai* for the following emblematic story which derives from personal experience.[14] In 1960, the Italian film director, Roberto Rossellini, was on location at Calatafimi shooting *Viva Italia*, a film commemorating the centenary of Garibaldi's exploits and the unification of Italy. For the 'battle of Calatafimi' scene 'extras' were recruited from the neighbouring towns of Salemi and Vita (the Garibaldi Redshirts) and from Calatafimi (the Bourbon army). They were paid 1,700 lire a day to do battle. But they would have done it for nothing as they took to their job with innate enthusiasm, none of the town needing encouragement to contend with its neighbours. So much so that Rossellini just let the cameras run without even trying to get his actors into the fray for special bits of heroism. However, their enthusiasm created a problem: some of the troops needed first aid treatment, and at a certain point in the proceedings Rossellini decided it was time to stop the Bourbons and Garibaldini fighting – who had become a little too involved in the process of confirming or changing the course of history. The problem was that the 'Bourbons' were winning and did not want to stop, while the 'Redshirts' were damned if they were going to accept this humiliating and unhistorical state of affairs. The production company had to use its loudspeaker to tell them that, if they did not desist, their pay would be withheld forthwith. Only grudgingly were they finally persuaded to lay down their arms. The real unification of Italy has also turned out to be a grudging affair.

Garibaldi never forgot Calatafimi. Indeed, he came back here in 1862 during the build-up to his second unsuccessful attempt to march on Rome, on the occasion when Ingoia lent him his pulpit. Later on, during his self exile on the island of Caprera, he gave his two horses the names of 'Marsala' and 'Calatafimi'.[15] And the impact Garibaldi had on Calatafimi and this part of the island was such that most main streets go under the name of Corso Garibaldi and window shutters are held in place by *garibaldini* – metal stops that, when the shutters are open, show Garibaldi's head, and, when closed, Anita's. We have them, of course, as well as our dog and our chicken.

15th May 1860 was undoubtedly Calatafimi's moment of recognized glory.

11

Charities

Believe it or not, there is a *ruota* in Calatafimi.

The *ruota* plays a significant part in Italian folklore and literature. You may know all about it, but not everybody in the English-speaking world will. It is a bit like the mechanism that is sometimes used when you are buying a railway ticket or exchanging money for some small article and security is important: you place your money in front of you, a wheel swivels it round past a wall or window, the money is taken and you receive back what you paid for with the next turn of the wheel. *Ruota* in fact means a wheel.

The type I am talking about was built into convents and monasteries and was used as a means of conveying things through the wall from the outside to the inner world, and vice-versa. This two-way traffic – turnover I suppose you could call it – kept both sides of the monastic walls supplied spiritually and materially. But the mechanism is mostly remembered in Italian literature as the kindest way of getting rid of unwanted babies which, tradition has it, were lovingly taken care of by the nuns inside after they had been turned in.

So there is a *ruota* in Calatafimi, near the old hospital. I don't know if it was ever used for babies (though, since it is a tightly-knit community where secrecy is difficult, I imagine not), nor how many people are aware it still exists. But somebody has taken the trouble to put a piece of glass over it, so that there has been an attempt to keep its memory alive. When I passed by the other day, however, it was hidden by vegetation because when they glassed it over a seed had been left inside which had burgeoned into a flourishing plant, completely obscuring what the glass was supposed to protect and highlight. I am sure it will be dug out sometime, even though the *ruota* has no 'inside' to turn to now. There must be some sort of parable here – which, you'll be glad to hear, I cannot discern.

That is the passive face of charity: you put your mistakes through the wall and unseen people on the other side take care of them for you, rather like in the confessional, I suppose. Unwanted or unaffordable babies were taken care of in this part of Sicily, and many the last will and testament that provided them with tangible dowries and realistic futures.

Innumerable threads of charity run through this small town: they are difficult to distinguish because they have become woven into the fabric of everyday life. You can see the buildings that have been set aside for charitable purposes, but not so easily how they are kept going – it is an interesting example of not being able to see the trees for the wood. Even today many elderly people unobtrusively bequeath considerable amounts of money to the church or to institutions which keep the wheels turning, metaphorically speaking. Clearly charity played a different role in times before the welfare state came into being, and obviously it was an important ingredient in society right across Italy and elsewhere. But Calatafimi was egregious even by the high Sicilian standards. If manuscript documents describing the town are few, and published ones even fewer, dusty wills and property deeds are legion, often unveiling glimpses of people with a simple vision of community and an innate sense of altruism who quietly busied themselves with doing good, well before governments took over the task and smudged it badly on the wider and much rougher canvas of politics.

The Congrega di Carità (the 'Congregation of Charities'), the organization that still administers what remains of these various foundations and bequests that the people of Calatafimi have chosen to bestow on their fellow citizens over the centuries, has an archive that has been moved recently and hastily installed on the ground floor of what is left of the abandoned hospital I have told you about; and the Congregation kindly allowed me to consult it. It would take a long time to put it into any sort of order and catalogue it, so what little I did there was tantamount to scratching around like the chicken I have described myself as being. What emerges is a community's commitment to itself that ought to shame us all careering through life today. Just to give you some numbers, Nicotra's *Dizionario dei Comuni di Sicilia* has the Congrega still administering twenty-nine pious organizations in 1910, including the Blundo Orphanage that was re-founded at the end of the seventeenth century, which I shall tell you about, and the Civic Hospital which was substantially funded by citizen Giuliano Truglio in 1611. The Congrega is still going strong.

The archive is bulging with huge quantities of document folders, and I have only been able to pick out a few that shed a flicker of candlelight on some aspects of charitable work in the town. The first one I want to bring to your attention is, I'm afraid, rather ambivalent.

It is disloyal of me, in view of the kindness I have been shown, but the paper I want to quote from is fairly recent and might possibly reveal a piece of sharp-dealing, even though it does illustrate how the Congrega worked. It is the notarial record of a land sale that took place on 19th November 1894. What had happened was that a certain Santi Gueci had bequeathed to the Congrega a conglomeration of four pieces of land for charitable purposes, plus a rustic house with several rooms, a well, a drinking-trough and an aqueduct; two of the pieces of land bordered on territory belonging to the Princess Sciara. The Congrega decided to put the bequest up for auction, setting the starting price at 5,000 lire, but, strange to say, nobody turned up for it. This may have been because proprietors with land bordering on property for sale have certain priority rights and word might have got out, or more likely been put around, that the princess was interested. Whatever the case may have been, the document goes on to record that after this abortive auction Giovanni Notarbartolo, Prince Sciara, put in a private bid of 4,000 lire under the name of his wife, Francesca Notarbartolo Tortorici, half to be paid on exchange of contracts and the other half a year later with interest. This was a family with considerable clout, so it is not surprising that the document goes on to state that the Congrega had debated the question and had been in agreement, and that the matter had been put to the Provincial Administrative Committee which had accepted the offer and had exposed it to public scrutiny at the Congrega's secretarial office. So the deal was signed and sealed by Antonio Zuaro (Francesca's procurator) and Domenico Vivona (of whom we shall be hearing[1]), the president of the Congrega. It sounds a pretty cosy deal, even though I suppose the poor did get most of their money in the end.

But I would hate to give you the impression that charitable organizations were willingly or easily manipulated by the powerful. I recently bought, on the Internet of all places, a small cache of pre-philatelic communications between the Provincial General Council for Hospices in Trapani and in nearby Alcamo and the Congrega of Calatafimi that dealt with various administrative matters, one of which, dated 18th February 1840, shows the system standing up to notables with commendable fortitude. It concerns the family of

Antonio Zuaro. A certain Don Giuseppe Zuaro, who owed the hospital and the Monte di Pietà in Calatafimi the sum of 399 ducats 29 grani and 2 cavalli, had asked for the payment to be deferred without setting a time limit. The President of the General Council was far from convinced of the ethics of the petition and wrote:

> Considering [he] is one of the principal landowners in the Comune, that he held the position of Mayor for three years during which time, instead of paying all or part of his debt towards the Charitable Works that he was administering, he used his office to create delay; considering that this substantial debt to the above mentioned Charitable Works means delaying monies destined for the succour of the poor and unfortunate, for all the time required by a debtor who is in any case solvent...

The request was denied and Zuaro was ordered to pay half the debt the following August and the other half within the next twelve months, failing which he would be arrested. Although he did manage to get some time to pay it, he did not get the free hand he might have expected as the Marchese Zuaro. So the poor did have an organization that was able to stand up for their interests. There were six documents in the batch I bought, each of which sheds pinpricks of light on how charitable bodies were organized. Two of them authorized the payment of salaries for the priests running the Truglio and Blundo legacies; one was for the admission of the 'donzella' (damsel) Antonina d'Anna to the Blundo Orphanage; another instructed the mayors of all the towns in the district, which included Calatafimi, to exercise maximum control over the selection of the trustees of charitable organizations and to avoid 'all abuse'; and the last released the sum of thirty ducats for the acquisition of linen to be made up into clothing for the inmates of a Calatafimi orphanage 'in the coming year of 1844'.

Most of the money for charities came from wills. Apart from leaving your property in an incontrovertible manner to offspring and relatives, who would no doubt have instigated internecine family warfare had nothing been written down, the wills often give glimpses of the character of those who made them. Pellegrino's *Calatafimi Scoverto a' Moderni*, in the chapter called 'Calatafimi Fertile for the World', lists a large number of prominent men who left at least some of their money to monastic foundations and churches – and to needy female orphans so that they might marry, or rather so that they could *be* married. Anyway, judging from the number of legacies left for this purpose, there must have been mercifully few unmarried female orphans in Calatafimi.

In his recent book on Calatafimi, Mazzara cites scores of these legacies.[2] He notes that the first orphanage in Calatafimi was set up under the will of Giovanni Antonio Brandis, who was archpriest from 1590 to 1610, and whom I have mentioned in connection with a sale of water. He left a water-mill (that was until recently still known as the Archpriest's Mill) together with other properties to fund the institution. Unfortunately, the finances were to prove insufficient and at his death in 1691 the Abbot Vincenzo Blundo refounded the institution with substantial properties of his own; and his nephew, also Abbot Vincenzo, built near the Chiesa Matrice a large and beautiful building to house the orphanage, with seventeen rooms, a garden and a well. The *Dizionario dei Comuni di Sicilia* reported it was looking after twenty-five girl orphans in 1910, some being descendants of the founder, some not and so chosen by lot. They received a suitable education until they were twenty-five when (or earlier if they got married) they received a legacy of 382.50 lire. The institute is still flourishing to this day in the same imposing though now weather-beaten building.

Another recurring legacy is the leaving of money for Masses to be said, usually in favour of the deceased, but also for other purposes. Of the many of these that have been recorded, there is one I particularly like because it gives you a brief glimpse of agricultural life, so idealized later by the starry-eyed but so tough in reality that it was sometimes described in dialect as 'da stidda a stidda', or 'from star to star' (i.e. hard labour that filled the hours between the morning and the evening star). This particular bequest was made in a will dated 20th October 1775 by Leonardo Grafaci in the presence of the notary Don Tommaso Vivona. He donated 15 ounces[3] for the funding of a daily Mass at the church of the SS Crocifisso 'at dawn, or half an hour before the beginning of the day, for the convenience of the poor country people who need to be off to work'.

The social-security safety net was necessarily private, and over the centuries it sired many charitable institutions that slotted into the town's everyday life. I won't try to list them all, but I want to sketch two of them, both founded in the mid-nineteenth century, which touched on growing public issues and attracted more than their fair share of squabbles: they show us what was being organized on this local charitable basis in Calatafimi, and how different it was from what was paternally devised in England during the same century. You may point out that rural Calatafimi and steam-powered England cannot bear comparison, but I merely wish to underline the stark difference in spirit. England's charitable utopias, such as those at Bourneville and Port Sunlight, were designed to keep the workers hard-working, grateful and sober. Calatafimi had no housing problem, just a lack of coin to convert into food, and drinking was not a problem either, so there was no need to ban taverns or use other forms of moral terrorism. Apart from poverty and all that came with it, Calatafimi was also exposed to other problems. Salvo Amuruso, who built the Capuchin convent at his own expense in 1588, left money on his death for the ransom of Calatafimi citizens who had been enslaved by North African pirates. But that was hardly an everyday bequest.[4] More normal were simple acts of charity that embraced the weaker members of the community – doing good, but, as we have seen with the Blundo Orphanage, not forgetting to look after your own. Manno Catalano was not alone when in 1603 he left part of his fortune in marriage legacies for 'orphaned girls, virgins and widows', although Giuseppe Curatolo was more representative in 1635 when he did the same thing for his relatives. The countless bequests in favour of orphans did often give preference to related orphans.

Before coming to the two nineteenth-century charitable institutions, let me quote another example of charity beginning at home. The other day, I came across a fairly recent example of how these family-orientated charitable bequests have stood the test of time. In the Congrega archive I found a handwriten application from a certain Caterina Fonte to the Illustrious Signor President of the Municipal Assistance Board, which may be translated as follows:

Fonte Caterina, daughter of Giuseppe, spinster, born in this town on 25th January 1912, engaged to be married to Fonte Giuseppe, in her capacity as a direct blood descendant of the pious creator of the charitable last will and testament, Pietro Antonio Adamo, as results from the genealogical tree attached to this document, makes a formal claim to your Illustrious Lordship for the legacy by the abovementioned Testator in favour of his marriageable blood descendents. With due regards. Calatafimi 4th October 1937 (Gaspare Catalano has been deputed).

On the left-hand side of this page, there is a twelve-stage genealogical tree, starting with Pietro Antonio Adamo, who married Caterina Adamo in 1585, and ending up with this Caterina Fonte, the daughter of Giuseppe Fonte who was born on 25th December 1912. An accompanying official note informs the claimant that she has to produce the following documents: a family tree (which she had already done); her birth certificate; a certificate of poverty issued by the Municipal Council; a similar certificate attesting her good conduct; and a final form from the same source proving that she had not previously contracted marriage. I presume the fact that her betrothed had the same surname indicates they were cousins. So there you are, Pietro Antonio Adamo's last will was still being observed after three and a half centuries, and the money he left was being used as he intended.

But now for those two institutions. The first was created by the last will and testament of Pietro Stabile, who was presumably the son of the Vincenzo Stabile who financed the studies of the doctor Macaddino, who left his books to the library of Calatafimi. Don't be put off by the squabbles the charitable institution he founded has been fraught with: a great deal of charitable work has been, and will no doubt in the future be, dispensed by it.

The will is dated 10th January 1828 and left money for the foundation of the Casa Stabile. Pietro Stabile had already provided for the new Monte di Pegno,[5] a sort of pawnbrokerage which, as it gave interest-free loans against collateral, incorporated the original principle of many Italian banks from the middle ages onwards. But this Casa Stabile was to be an organization for looking after female orphans and giving work to those appointed to do the job. Pietro Stabile's heirs were instructed to find a suitable site and to build an appropriate building. Eight highly moral and 'domesticated ladies' were to be chosen (one of whom was to be the 'Superiora'); and then a number of girls were to be chosen by public notice, the number being a function of the money available. They were to be local girls between the ages of eight and twenty-one and their maintenance – food, clothing and other necessities – was fixed at about 2 tari a day. The good women were required to teach the girls to read and write, to weave and embroider, etc. When there were too many applicants, a ballot was to be held (preference being given to children coming from the Stabile family) and the girls had to leave when they reached the age of thirty. If they got married before then they were to receive a dowry of 30 ounces. If one of the good women died, a substitute was to be chosen from one of the unmarried girls under the age of thirty who had to declare her willingness to devote the rest of her life to the institution. It was altogether a noble desire expressed by a man preparing to die. But there was money involved, and therefore everybody wanted to get in on the act.

By pure chance, I found a fascinating document in the Fardelliana library at Trapani called *The Petition of the Commissioners of the Pious Casa Stabile in Calatafimi (Sicily) to HM the King of Italy (via the Council of State)*, published by Paravia in Turin in 1864. It is the petition of the solicitor who had been instructed by the Board of the Pious Casa Stabile in the trial against its detractors, and it sets out his case for the prosecution. What had happened?

In the first place, Pietro's heirs had taken an inordinate amount of time to find a site and build a building: the will was dated 1828, and the Pious House only opened in 1849. But how relevant this was was difficult to assess. The Commissioners said that bureaucratic machinations orchestrated by the Town Council caused the delay, which may or may not be true, but some light is thrown on the in-fighting going on by another wonderful document I found in the archive of the Congrega di Carità.

This is a vitriolic twenty-three-page outburst dated 22nd October 1829, early on in the story, by the Engineer Giuseppe Camerale and addressed to the universal heirs of the defunct Pietro Stabile. In a few words, the problem was this: Camerale had been rapidly commissioned by Stabile's heirs to propose a site and submit a plan for the orphanage, which he did on 21st August 1829. He then discovered that another architect, a certain Palazzotto from Palermo, had been asked by somebody unnamed to comment on his proposals, and this individual's opinion had been seconded by the President of the General Council for Hospices in the Vale of Trapani. The comments had been very negative apparently, and another alternative site to his near the Chiesa Nuova had been proposed. That was why Camerale's reaction was cataclysmic. How can these ignorant people dare to comment on the work of one who had spent three years from 1794 in Rome 'not to follow some Cardinal but to perfect his architectural studies with untiring energy', who had been court architect for thirty years, who had worked personally for King Ferdinand for fifteen years while he was in Sicily, who had created bridges and worked for numerous municipalities, etc, etc. The Sovereign had even recognized his merits to the extent of awarding his son a six-year *bourse* to study architecture at Rome. It is a mounting list, as indeed is his tone of voice.

Had the President of the General Council for Hospices actually got off his chair and come to Calatafimi he would soon have noted that the so-called architect Palazzotto he supported was totally incompetent and that the situation he described was completely invented. Palazzotto's proposed site near the Chiesa Nuova was difficult to get to; it was exposed and high up a hill; it was without water, dangerous for children, a difficult place for female work. The buildings already there were cracked and had been abandoned, and the earth was subject to landslides. Camerale's proposed site at 'Li Cannola' was not, as Palazzotto had claimed, subject to landslides but on solid ground; it was not too cramped – it was, according to Camerale, more than adequate for an orphanage, indeed it could accommodate a full-scale monastery; it was not a trapezoidal area that would lead to 'irregular' buildings being constructed (if Palazzotto had bothered to look at his plans he would not have 'vomited up these ideas'); and the water was not contaminated because the good citizens of Calatafimi had been drinking it, using it for cooking and cleaning and for their animals for centuries. However, the Casa Stabile was built on the Chiesa Nuova site. I don't have an account of Palazzotto's position in the argument, but it should be noted that he had previously been retained to redesign Stabile's home in order to accommodate the new Monte di Pietà, one of Pietro's many other endowments, and it was Palazzotto who was eventually entrusted to build the orphanage on that site.

This was not the only dispute that slowed things up – it apparently took the Town Council five years to approve the proposed site and plans before building could start – but eventually the Casa Pia did finally open in 1849 for twenty-five young girls (deliciously described as *donzelle*, which has the ring of young antelopes, but 'damsels' would be a more accurate translation) and with a staff of seven. In 1853, presumably at the request of the Town Council, the Bourbon government appointed an adjunct Commissioner in the person of Don Domenico Saccaro with the right to countersign payments: effectively he was the Comptroller. In the meantime 'anonymous slanders' began to circulate.

We can now go back to the 1864 petition I mentioned. The solicitor's petition was against the Town Council of Calatafimi and the Deputazione Provinciale of Trapani who had slandered the Commissioners and were trying to impose a statutory reform on the institution, which would fly in the face of the Founder's last will and testament and prove fatal to it. The story is long and the pamphlet analyses a whole series of Town Council meetings between 1862 and 1864, which it says were vitriolic, partisan, factious and slanderous. In essence, as far as I can see it, there had been an attempt to get Town Council people onto the Board of Commissioners. Various deficiencies had been cited, from bad administration to the fact that non-orphan village girls were not admitted to the school (they were later admitted by the Commissioners, even though this was against the provisions of the Founder's will and only necessary because, as the Commissioners stated, the Town Council's 'mohammedan negligence' meant that it was incapable of organizing decent municipal education), from the employment of a marvellously efficient teacher from the mainland who was paid far too much (including her travelling expenses) to an inmate who was teaching but was over thirty years old: they put her on the staff in the end. The level of anger over the accusations and their richness make fascinating reading. The petition was signed on 30th September 1864 by the advocate M. Silvestri in Turin.

I have not been able to discover the outcome of the trial, and even the present Baron Stabile, whom I tracked down in Trapani, did not know the answer. Whatever it was, I am sure there would have been an appeal and a counter appeal, further threats and, in the fullness of time, forgetfulness – because the Casa Stabile is still in existence, although its present state leaves something to be desired. It is at the moment being administered publicly because of various bureaucratic misunderstandings, and there are no orphans in residence, while the building has been magnificently restored recently at the surprisingly large cost of 2.65 billion lire (something like $1.3 million). One of the construction companies went bankrupt at the end of the works, however, and a fire door, which was not included in the original specifications, is being urgently demanded but has not yet been built. So legal problems have been added to the bureaucratic ones and the contractors still have the keys. If festering old disputes give birth to new ones, it must not be forgotten that, between and during them, sterling charitable work has been done. The *donzelle* of Calatafimi have benefited and no doubt they will continue to do so.

The second institution I wanted to tell you about also involves that Don Domenico Saccaro. From the administrative point of view this was a much quieter affair, but politically he was more colourful. His family was immensely rich by Calatafimi standards. How it came by its wealth will be dealt with later.

Domenico Saccaro is still remembered: by local historians as an organizer of charitable institutions as well as a donor of enormous amounts of money to the poor, the worthy and those in need of dowries and as a sponsor for numerous young people's education who also gave food and medicine to the populace in hard times; by the man in the street as the person who founded the old people's home.

He set up and richly endowed the Albergo della Mendicità, a home for thirty old-aged poor people and the physically afflicted in 1869. This Poor House was instituted in a magnificent mansion he had built specially at the enormous cost of 150,000 lire in the grounds of the ex-Capuchin monastery, which he had bought from the government after Church properties were disestablished. In an undated draft appeal to Archbishop Salamone of Palermo, written by an unknown third party (probably the Monsignor Valenti mentioned in the draft) and recently unearthed in a trunk lying around here, I read that after its disestablishment the monastery would have turned into 'a heap of rubble' had not Saccaro intervened with the Town Council to buy it and settle twenty-six unfortunate and disabled poor people in it, together with an ex-Capuchin friar and priest for their spiritual and material well-being. The civil powers were quick to recognize it as a charitable institution, but Saccaro, good Catholic that he was, was not satisfied and asked the Vatican, through Monsignor Valenti, to sanction the ownership by his family of the ex-convent in perpetuity. The Vatican, however, were only prepared to concede the buildings on a temporary basis: they were to be given back to the Capuchins when, as it was hoped, they would be re-established. Hence this appeal to Archbishop Salamone. The petitioner pointed out in the draft that the temporary nature of the concession might mean that they could revert to the public domain or the municipality, either of which 'in a short period of time would cancel the very traces of the buildings' and abandon the poor to their fate. He was convinced of the project's worthiness and noted that Saccaro whose 'hair is growing white, is without heirs and very desirous of donating to his town a grand institution endowed with his considerable patrimony.' He therefore supplicated the Archbishop – 'What Valenti was unable to do Salamone will certainly be able to' – to persuade the Vatican to concede the buildings in perpetuity. Whether it did or did not, the institute is still going strong.

There were also other fights at the time with the ex-friars about demands for extra-payments, about trees being cut down and other petty matters which apparently gave rise to a further petition from Saccaro to the Pope,[6] but these squabbles were overcome and the old people's home was an immediate success. So much so that its fame spread: I have a letter of July 1870 from the prefect of the regional capital Trapani formally asking Saccaro if he would accept poor people from the regional capital Trapani, for which the authorities would pay 50 centimes a day. The Albergo flourishes in the original buildings.[7]

Domenico Saccaro had also been instrumental in founding, funding and administering the Monte Frumentario in 1857. To appreciate this institution, which was a wheat-seed mortgage-bank, you must understand that its clients were the local peasants and farmers who were living a hand-to-mouth existence in very hard times, without ready cash to buy seed for their land. Saccaro's organization, like others elsewhere in Sicily, meant that they could borrow the seed and pay it back (with a small amount of interest) after they had gathered in their harvest. It was a much valued contribution to the local economy.[8] Although the idea was his and the organization too, Saccaro was just one of the original contributors. His own contribution was second only in size to that of the Baronessina Vincenza Stabile. The sole Mollica to give it money was Ignazio, and that was not a lot.

Incidentally, the year the Monte Frumentario was set up, 1867, was a harsh one for the fava-bean harvest, with prices soaring disastrously high. So Saccaro promptly set about organizing a similar Monte di Fave, this time as the sole contributor; and he also founded the Monte del Seme di Lino, a linen-seed-bank, in 1869. The same trunk of papers also produced a copy of the original Town Council minutes of the meeting that officially recognized the Monte di Fave, with a contribution being made by Saccaro of the considerable sum of 1,909 lire and 50 centimes, and, by the Municipality, of the sum of 334 lire and 90 centimes, which it had collected on behalf of the families of soldiers from Calatafimi who had taken part in the 'War against Austria'.[9] Saccaro had in addition bought up large quantities of beans in Calatafimi and the surrounding villages to serve as capital. The minutes and a formal thank-you letter to Saccaro, dated 12th September 1867, were delivered to him in a brown-paper Council envelope beautifully addressed in copperplate hand-writing.

These seed-banks, which granted what were essentially seed mortgages, inevitably metamorphosed into commercial concerns. By the middle 1880s, the Monte Frumentario was dealing with 2,000 agricultural workers and had a capital of more than 100,000 lire. In due course it became first the Banca Saccaro, then the Banca Agricola, and finally the Cassa Comunale di Credito Agrario. Saccaro used his vast wealth, by Calatafimi standards, for continuous charitable work, including subsidized food for the poor,[10] and on his deathbed in 1881 he left money for the education of five young people. I have evidence of this last bequest in the form of various receipts from their parents; and there is a direct receipt from a certain Girolamo, son of Dr Biagio Gallo, acknowledging on 31st August 1892 that he had received for his studies in the years 1886-9 the sum of 765 lira from the widow, in accordance with Don Domenico's last will and testament. This Girolamo was a pharmacist in Calatafimi, and his grandson, another Dr Biagio Gallo, still practises in the town.

Domenico Saccaro was born in 1806 and took an active part in the running of the town for the whole of his life, and Mazzara describes him as 'the last of the many great benefactors of Calatafimi'. In recognition of his charitable activities, he was, in 1877, made a Cavaliere of the Order of the Saints Maurizio and Lazzaro. A note from the Treasury Ministry for Agriculture, Industry and Commerce in Rome, addressed to the local parliamentarian Pietro Nocito, said, no doubt with a dollop of flattery, that his rank would have been higher than Cavaliere had not an 1868 law specifically stated that a new member of the Order could be admitted no higher. Since the note was sent to Pietro Nocito (a lawyer, university professor, member of the National Parliament and eventually Under-Secretary of State for the Ministry of Grace and Justice), I presume it was he who had proposed his fellow townsman for the honour. I could go on about him, but I shall restrict myself to two specific episodes.

The first was an act of 'charity' after a hair-raising episode when he was saved by his reputation as a man of charity. It took place because Saccaro, a Bourbon sympathizer and head of the Guardia Civica, was openly opposed to Garibaldi in 1860, and actually supplied the Neapolitan authorities with a list of rebels before the battle of Calatafimi. After Garibaldi's victory, and possibly at the instigation of jealous relatives who were known to aspire to his wealth, he was denounced to the new authorities and he quite naturally hid himself in the bell-tower of the San Michele convent. He was soon discovered, however, by the 'red-shirts' and arrested, and was about to be shot when the population of the town reacted vociferously and forced Garibaldi to release him on the grounds that he was 'the friend of the poor'. By tradition the crowd shouted 'stannu ammazzannu lu patri di li purreddi' ('they are killing the father of the poor people'). Garibaldi came out onto the balcony nearby, where he had been resting, to see what all the noise was about and was 'persuaded' to let him go. Don Domenico Saccaro subsequently had a change of mind and decided to donate 150 gold ducats and a white horse to Garibaldi's campaign, which caused the general to be very grateful. He also arranged for a friend of the general's son, Menotti, to be taken in one of his carriages from the village of Vita, where he had been wounded, to Alcamo, which brought a letter of thanks from Menotti and another from Garibaldi stating 'Con gli Uomini come voi si fà presto l'Italia' ('With Men like you, Italy will be quickly united'): it was presumably written after the donation had been accepted.

More significantly, as far as the economy of Calatafimi was concerned, in 1862 and 1864 Saccaro made a magnificent gesture of thanks towards the people of Calatafimi who had spontaneously saved him from the firing-squad. In the family records, one can watch him parcelling up and giving away – with family comments – the manors of Bernardo, Morfino, Giummarella and Amburgio and also that of San Giorgio in the area of Vita and Salemi. This was done by issuing deeds of *emphyteusis* (a legal term for land concessions in perpetuity, or for a given period, with the obligation to make improvements and pay rent) at purely nominal rents. He was, in fact, ploughing back his immense riches into the humus of the community. A great number of landless citizens were helped to a better standard of living. The numerous heavy volumes recording these *emphyteuses*, some of which are in my possession, were destined to dwindle, since time surreptitiously bestowed ownership on the beneficiaries.

The second episode only involves Saccaro indirectly because he was already dead, but contributes a sober balancing note to the infighting involved in the Casa Stabile affair I have told you about. It celebrates the introduction of modern accountancy to the Monte Frumentario, the wheat-seed-bank he founded, through the person of Luigi Paladino, the author of *Il Nuovo Impianto Amministrativo-*

Contabile del Monte Frumentario di Calatafimi (The New Adminis-
trative-Accountancy Regime in Calatafimi's Monte Frumentario), a
pamphlet which outlined a new approach for the book-keeping of
the seed-bank in 1884.

The author of this treatise, Luigi Paladino, was a *ragioniere*
(accountant) and the work was published that year at Trapani. I must
resist quoting extensively from it, in spite of its delightful language
and his irrepressible enthusiasm for what he sees as new developments in scientific accountancy. Paladino had been asked to give a
consultancy on the running of the seed-bank and he begins by setting
out what he thought was wrong with the administration. '...The
small and formless register that has been used so far for the
accountancy of the Monte is not sufficient for the task nor does it
measure up completely to current regulatory requirements...' and
there is also some confusion about who is paid how. He describes
the administrative requirements. A balance sheet must be available at
the beginning of each financial year (1st September), mortgages have
to be drawn up in October, and each farmer must have a guarantor.
Seed has to be distributed in that same month (being given out by the
storeman in the presence of the administrators and correctly documented); it must be given back after the harvest in July and August
(with all the necessary documentation). The Monte's capital needed
to be increased in that period, because the returned seed came with
interest, and also because it was returned dry and gained in weight
and volume for climatic reasons (a financial reckoning of this had
also to be made). During the whole year administrative expenses had
to be paid. For budgetary reasons corn had to be sold from time to
time (he here specifies the necessary documentation). And he then
sails into how to solve the whole complex administrative tangle in
the most modern of ways, citing as his professional holy bible *Primi
Saggi di Logismografia*, written by a certain Giuseppe Cerboni and
approved by a Council of Experts in Rome. I am no accountant but
it simply appears to be a question of balancing the books, which
apparently was not a method that was over-practised at that time.

He goes on to describe in almost sensual terms the various printed
forms that were needed in modern administration, but he is sadly
brought down to reality at the end, having to face the fact that, as
far as Calatafimi's Monte Frumentario was concerned, a simpler
approach would probably have to be adopted because there were so
few accountants in Sicily – despite the fact that many were available

in the north of Italy: the same north-south divide, even then. He concludes thus: 'The younger members of well-off families come back to Calatafimi with their degrees as doctors, pharmacists, lawyers and notaries public; finding a capable accountant outside Calatafimi would cost too much and he would only be needed anyway in the months of July, August and October.' He therefore decrees the following: a simpler system 'without the scientific luxury of the complete *Cerboniana* scripture, but which contains its principle in simpler and severer form'. He makes accountancy sound like poetry.

From some of these home-grown acts of practical benevolence, relatively sophisticated modern structures have grown up over the years. But in case I have given you the impression that acts of spontaneous practical charity belong to the past, let me offer you a synopsis of the last will and testament of the widow Luigia Scimeni: a copy of the hand-written will, dated 19th March 1953 when she was in her seventy-third year, is to be found in the local library. Her Universal Heir was her house and outbuildings in via 15 Maggio, where she was already giving free board and lodging to twenty-one poor women and girls deprived of maternal love or suitable parents ('prive di protezione materne o di decorosi genitori') and some Franciscan nuns. The will made provision for executors to be appointed, and it was their task to create a charitable trust, the Casa della Carità Luigia Scimeni, which was to be funded by the various farms she bequeathed to it. Future inmates were to be found among females between the ages of two and twenty from poor families living in Calatafimi or nearby villages – poor males were customarily dealt with by being apprenticed – who were to lead a modest, sober life in the house without doing outside domestic work or being taken into adoption. With the help of the nuns they were to do all the housework, learn sewing and weaving (the will states that her house contained spinning-wheels and other equipment: unusual, I should have thought, in 1953), go to the elementary school, be enrolled as secular sisters of the third Franciscan Order and generally work to prepare themselves to be responsible mothers ('per poter riuscire a divenire buone e brave madre di famiglia'), and, if a suitable sober Christian presented himself, the lucky girl was to be given a very modest dowry in the form of clothes and linen.

Luigia Scimeni was an authoritarian lady – those who remember her recall that she required her hand to be kissed in greeting – and she expected her charges to behave with restraint: riotous individuals were conceded a brief period in which to buckle under, after which they were dismissed from the house with a meagre month's allowance. The uniform they had to wear during their time as inmates of the house was precisely ordained: simple brown- or coffee-coloured cotton or woollen garments, depending on the season, the will specifying the exact number and type. Her various farms were to be cultivated by sharecroppers and all surplus (chickens, rabbits, pigs, fruit, wood, vegetables, olives, corn and must) was to be sold off to cover general expenses and the preparation of a poor seminarist from Calatafimi with aspirations for the priesthood, who was to go to the Diocesan Seminary at Marsala, and would eventually look after the spiritual needs of the establishment. Although there must have been eggs and the odd chicken from the farms, the will stoutly decrees that the poor maids were to have bread and fruit in the morning; pasta with oil and either vegetable, bean or tomato sauce (alternately) for lunch; and bread with fruit or vegetable soup, greens or potatoes in the evening. A rather Spartan life, you may think. But it was just after the war and times were hard. Although only a short span of time has passed since the will was drawn up, those few years have brought about a salutary decline in the numbers of poor young females who are deprived of maternal love, and Luigia's last wishes have had to be adapted. The establishment in via 15 Maggio now solely houses Franciscan nuns, and further up the street there is a new parochial social centre for young people, the Centro Giovanile Luigia Scimeni.

1 Print of an old painting of Calatafimi. It was published in Longo's local history (1810), but no trace of the original painting has been found

2 Calatafimi photographed by Samuel Butler in May 1896. The castle was much more dominant, but not much else has changed

3 Caterina's great-great-grandfather, Vincenzo Mollica, and his family, photographed by Samuel Butler on 11th May 1898

4 Pietro Adamo (with his family here) was Garibaldi's liaison with Calatafimi before the battle. Butler took this photo in May 1896

5 Biagio Ingroia (with his wife here) was an aide to Garibaldi and assisted Butler. Butler photographed him in Calatafimi in May 1896

6 Donna Maria and Don Paolo, who looked after Butler's accommodation arrangements when he stayed in Calatafimi. Butler took the photograph in May 1896

7 Print of the results of the Duke of Serradifalco's excavation of the Theatre at Segesta (1822-33), Naples, 1835. The high-backed seats in the foreground were unearthed in the orchestra

8 You get this glimpse of the Temple of Segesta on the road from our house going into Calatafimi

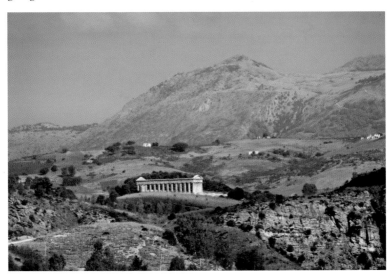

9 Calatafimi in the distance, seen from below our house. There is a small *gebbia* in the bottom right of the picture

10 Calatafimi. The ruins of the castle appear at the top. Underneath on the left is the church of the SS Crocifisso and, further up on the right, is the Chiesa Matrice

11 Looking back towards our house, on the road into town

12 Another view of the town on the way in, at the end of the concrete section of the road

13 Basile's Monument to the Battle of Calatafimi: although a key military engagement in the history of Italy, it is seldom visited

14 This imposing slab of rock commemorates the town's change of name to Calatafimi-Segesta

15 Our very own
Obelisk, with the
bank behind it

16 Not a firing
squad: pacific
members of the Guild
of the Maestranze,
at the festa of the
SS Crocifisso. In
the past they did
occasional duty as
an urban militia:
hence the guns

17 A member of the Guild of the Borgisi distributing gifts, at the festa of the SS Crocifisso

18 Members of the Guild of the Cavallari, a great favourite with the crowd, during the festa of the SS Crocifisso

19 The 'Tower of Abundance' of the Guild of the Massari, from which the customary *cucciddati* are hurled at the crowd, at the festa of the SS Crocifisso

20 Another view of the tower being drawn through the crowds by placid oxen

12

Underground Activity

In a puff of smoke I am going to whisk you away from pleasant charitable doings to dark subterranean goings-on. You will hardly be surprised to learn that the slumbering gods, lurking in the bowels of the earth under Calatafimi, occasionally turn over, sweat, scratch themselves and cough. These fidgets and wheezes are not confined to Calatafimi, but when they happen they are just under your feet. The turning over and coughing usually takes the form of tremors and earthquakes; the sweating and scratching give rise to more stable geological sores like sulphur emissions, the appearance of bitumen, or even petroleum, and permanent vents in the form of hot springs. In troubled sleep, the ancient world twitches away endlessly under its thin blanket of earth.

I will first take you through some of its more pacific manifestations. Give me your civilized urban arm and be not afraid.

Bitumen has been observed here over the centuries. When the earth opens during earthquakes, bitumen often oozes out, accompanied by a strong smell of sulphur. Descriptions of this happening in the 1693 earthquake are mentioned by our local historians. Permanent traces of bitumen still lie about in the Calatafimi area[1] (there is even some on a bit of our land), and there are also wells with traces of petroleum on the surface of the water: petroleum was often mentioned in the past long before the invention of the internal combustion engine, and was even used in medicine.[2] Many of the early writers touched on it, but I'll just quote you Count von Riedesel writing about the phenomenon in 1767, in nearby Agrigento:[3] 'The water of this spring contained such a quantity of oily matter that it collected on the surface of the pool, so that that one can skim it off and make it into lamp oil that burns quite as well as olive oil.'

In this day and age, you might have thought that it would fuel greedy dreams of a new Mediterranean Texas, but on no account must a word be spoken about it here. Silence. I suppose this attitude may partly come from reflection on the mess that the state oil company has made of Gela and Agusta elsewhere on the island. But it is much more atavistic than that: the pervading thought is that, if something valuable comes to light in your fields, *they* will come and take it away. So keep quiet, and you'll be left in peace. Silence, both the passive and the active kind, is used as a weapon on this island, and respect for it is innate. It is also endemic and comes under the heading of *omertà*. It stands in the way of any sort of investigation, and how it works is beautifully illustrated by the saying: 'Nenti saccio – e su stessi nenti porta priggiudizziu, 'un saccio nenti di nenti' ('I know nothing – and if that nothing brings prejudice against me, I know nothing about nothing'). While such a stance drives the judiciary to impotent fury, it is judged politic if petroleum is found on your land, as in many other circumstances.

Another harmless, and indeed salutary, manifestation of underground sweating is the presence of hot springs around Calatafimi. References to the sulphurous hot springs near Segesta go back through the steams of time. Diodorus Siculus has it that the nymphs prepared these springs to refresh Hercules after certain of his many fatigues in 1184 BC. Alberti writing in 1561,[4] talks of the much celebrated baths being near 'Calattasimi' (sic), and Longo cites Strabo, who maintains that, unlike other sulphurous springs which give out brackish water, the Segestan waters, though sulphurous, are not salty and can even be drunk when cool. The Romans used them, as did the Arabs: they built a castle there originally called Calatha–Jamet or the 'castle of the baths', the remains of which are on the hill above a disused quarry, now used to pen cattle and sheep at night. And so did the Normans, who built on the site as well: the great Count Roger I when establishing the See of Mazzara in 1093 made these waters and the castle part of its foundation. If you want to visit the ruins, however, you must remember to wear boots in the summer: the librarian tells me that two grazing horses were killed by viper bites there last year. Ibn Jubayr passed there on 29th December 1184 on his way back to Spain after his Hadj and wrote:[5]

> we passed not far from the castle of Hisn al-Hammah [the Castle of the Baths]. It is a large place with many thermal springs which God throws up from the ground charged with special elements, and so hot that the body can hardly bear them. We passed one on our road and, dismounting from our animals, refreshed our bodies by bathing in it.

My favourite quotation about the hot waters, cited in Longo's book, comes from Savonarola's (that is Michele Savonarola, not the great mad monk) *De balneis e thermis naturalibus omnibus Italiae*.[6] It goes like this: 'there are three springs ['balnei mansiones']; one warm, one warmer and one very warm in which it is easy to cook eggs' ['ut in ea facile coquantur ova']. The idea of boiling an egg in Latin, even if it is late Latin, has a strange appeal for me. As always, Longo loves an argument and he says there are six not three springs, which he describes in some detail. Incidentally, the fourth was the 'women's bath', and in the sixth you can boil meat if you leave it in overnight. In his thoroughness, Longo quotes Diodorus Siculus as saying that many foreigners came to Sicily for the waters. Do you think there was a Season and an Assembly Room? William Young, travelling in Sicily in 1772, says:

> a few hundred Yards westward of these Ruins [of Segesta: the distance is more likely to be two kilometres], we found the famous Baths *Segeste*, still frequented, and in some repute. They have therapeutic effects that have been recognized over the centuries, and to this day they are prescribed for skin complaints.[7]

Mongitore, again quoted by Longo, said that when Etna erupted in May 1669 the waters of the sixth spring, which was a sort of lake, rose by more than half and another sulphur spring opened up, which led him to concoct theories about a network of underground passages connected with Etna, distributing healing properties throughout the island. What a godsend to any politician in a general-election era: Citizens, vote for me and I'll deliver you ecological health and heating at zero cost; our party can give you all this because we know just where to dig.[8] He might have got his votes.

The modern buildings at the Segestan baths sit on one of the six springs Longo mentions: which I do not know, though it feels as if it might be the sixth, the one in which meat could be boiled over night. Although it is less romantic than you might have hoped for, the establishment is efficient enough: there are medical facilities, a swimming pool, a paddling pool for children, deck-chairs and even a minute bar. The water is very hot, and my immediate thoughts on getting in for the first time were that the infernal cauldron was close underneath. This unnerving thought was not long lasting, nor was the impact of the sulphurous smell, and I often go there for a swim.

I find swimming there on a windy, rainy winter's night an experience, particularly if there is thunder and lightning: the hammering of cold rain on your head while the rest of your body is simmering in warm liquid is unusual, and when the steam blows sideways off the water it can look like the lashing of spray in an Atlantic storm, if you put your mind to it. As the pool is kept open late at night, it is also satisfying in less tempestuous weather to swim lazily on your back in the hot water, contemplating the stars and wondering why other human beings are not as wise as you think you are.

I went there recently with Andrew and Christine who were on holiday, not to the modern establishment but to the river below it. You turn off just before the pool, and after fording the stream you come to the first smallish shallow round pond with bubbling warm water. It looks dirty because it is chalk-coloured – the whole area is chalky – but it is clean. There are signs that people have been here, though there was nobody then. If you push on, and that means actually pushing through a wall of reeds to the right and then turning left, there is a much bigger oblong pool, which is quite deep. The water is clear and hot, and it is overhung by cliffs with stalactites beginning to form at the top. The rock-face overhead is visited by pigeons, rooks and swallows, and there are the usual fig trees, capers and other types of vegetation sprouting out of it. The pool is fringed by reeds and skirted on the left by a narrow path cut into the rock, which leads to a second and even more beautiful pool with the same vegetation and bird life, and a small rock island sticking up in the middle. The stream between the two pools runs fast, but the water in both of them is warm, calm, swimmable, and it is busily patrolled by myriads of flashing multicoloured dragonflies. I believe you can go on further, but it looks rather difficult and anyway where you are is just too beautiful for you to wish to do any further scrambling. You have a feeling that your noisy arrival may have disturbed a minor god who was dallying with a nymph in the warm water, and is cursing you from somewhere near at hand.

That is a glimpse of the pacific side to what goes on under your feet here. But when the gods below start turning over and coughing, the situation is nearly always tragic. Together with the rest of Sicily, Calatafimi has suffered on many occasions. Not much written testimony has come down to us on the human dimension of far-off earthquakes. They are usually remembered for their physical effects. Here are a few examples for you.

The 1693 earthquake was a particularly cruel one. The epicentre was on the other side of the island and it destroyed Noto as a town and as a political power, its mantle being taken by Syracuse – and much the same thing happened after the 1908 Messina earthquake, when Catania was the inheritor. On the other hand, it did allow the stricken town to be rebuilt on another site which is, arguably, the most perfect baroque town in the whole Italian peninsula. Things were much less dramatic in Calatafimi. Pellegrino says that 'our Calatafimi suffered an aperture two miles long and two or three "palms" wide', which, after the quake, closed up to 'four geometric ounces' (whatever that may mean), giving off a foul stench of sulphur and bitumen. The earthquake took place on 11th January and you may be surprised to learn that, barely more than a month after, Evelyn wrote in his diary for 19th February

> ...the dreadful and astonishing *Earthquake* swallowing up Catanea
> and other famous and ancient cities, with more than 100,000 persons
> in Sicily, on 11 Jan. last, came now to be reported among us.

That was really quick. Strangely enough, in the placid English country-side in the summer of 1783, Gilbert White in letter LXV of the *Natural History of Selborne* was linking the peculiar weather in Selborne and other parts of the country with natural catastrophes in other parts of Europe, including an earthquake that 'convulsed' parts of Sicily. But I have no record of how Calatafimi fared in that one. How news of natural calamities did travel! But who on earth carried news of a Sicilian earthquake up the lanes of eighteenth-century Hampshire?

Pellegrino also notes that on the occasion of the earthquake in 1726 the citizens of Calatafimi solemnly swore to celebrate the Procession of the SS Crocifisso, which I have told you about, on 14th September every year, in addition to the main celebrations at the beginning of May.

There have, of course, been many other earthquakes, as the area is seismically unsound. But I want now to tell you about the most re-cent one in January 1968, some of the effects of which we have seen. It is a much more tangible event because we have not yet been in-sulated from it by the passage of time. While it left many a mark on Calatafimi, it should be emphasized that the town got off much better than other places around here. None of us was present when it happened.

Some bare unbearable facts.[9] The first two major quakes (8.75 and 9.0 on the Mercalli scale) occurred very early in the morning of Monday 15th January, and were followed by two other major ones on the 15th and the 25th. There were forty tremors of more than 4 on the Mercalli scale in twelve days, and 345 altogether between 14th January and 10th June. The epicentre was at Gibellina, about ten kilometres from Calatafimi. Officially, six towns and villages were destroyed completely: they were Gibellina, Montevago, Poggioreale, Salaparuta, Santa Margherita di Belice and Santa Ninfa. Two were almost destroyed (Menfi and Partanna) and six were damaged 'between 30% and 50%' (Sambuca, Calatafimi, Salemi, Vita, Camporeale and Contessa Entellina). The official death toll was 231 dead and 623 injured, but on a conservative estimate it is said that those figures should have read 400 and 1,000. The official estimate for emigration from Sicily as a result of this disaster was 25,000, but the figure was certainly much higher. Out of its total of 3,288 houses, Calatafimi had 198 that were 'gravely damaged', and 61% of the total were 'lesioned' (i.e. it was thought they could be repaired). No house 'collapsed'. Nobody died at Calatafimi. Those are the bare facts.

I have serenely slept through various tremors over the years and occasionally seen a ceiling light waver a bit, but I have never experienced a real earthquake. When one strikes, I am told, people are controlled by their instinct: they rush out of their houses into the open, and they are too terrified to go back inside for a period of time.[10] The month was January, so that the countryside was filled with groups of people trying to keep warm round fires, or wandering about dazed with shock, all of this in deep mud everywhere. That was the beginning. As always, it was very difficult getting the right aid quickly to the right places, and so tensions began to develop: where were the blankets, where was the food, why wasn't anybody doing anything, what was going to happen to everybody? Bureaucracy was heavy-handed as usual, and co-ordination was conspicuously lacking, piles of bread rotting in one place while people were crying out for it elsewhere. There was a stench. There were people and dogs wandering round lost. But the blankets and tents did eventually arrive – followed much later by the huts – there were government representatives and private individuals bravely trying to help, there were even foreigners who came. Much appreciated were the Russians, the British and the French. Of course, there were not enough coffins, and milk for the children was hard to track down. Of course.

Because of the relatively small amount of damage done in Calatafimi, newspaper reports rightly tended to concentrate on other, worse-hit areas. But here is one about the town in the *Giornale di Sicilia* for Friday 19th January.

> At Calatafimi the situation is not getting any better at all. The few families remaining, appalled at the devastation in the town, have left it and fled to the surrounding country. A high percentage of these refugees, especially children and old people, have been hit by an acute form of influenza, and doctors are often forced to travel to far-away corners of the countryside to give medical assistance. Medicines are scarce and there is no milk for the children or other types of prime necessities, tents above all.

After the bad tremor of Friday 26th January, the same newspaper's journalist reported a further exodus of people from the town, leaving abandoned prams, clothes and food, and 'in front of the Town Hall [there were] 200 people waiting in the cold for pasta'. Another article on 28th January speaks of 100% evacuation, 300 citizens in goods-wagons at the station, and thousands out in the country.

One short-sighted, immediate, tactical solution had serious long-term effects: because the easiest commodities to come by in the tent cities were instant passport photographs that were offered by policemen from Palermo, and travel passes with free rail travel to the Italian frontier and 10,000 lire for help after that, the social services went round looking for candidates and practical assistance was dealt out in the emigration tent. Too many people took advantage of this thoughtless attempt at exporting the disaster.

If the huts arrived late, they overstayed their welcome by many years. Indeed some are still with us, although they are used for other purposes now. It was the impression of many that concrete help actually in the form of concrete was diverted to the new motorway instead of being used for patching up the damage to houses, or re-building them. I really cannot comment on that. However, it was and is accepted that many things were done for reasons that were not as clear as daylight. It is said that Calatafimi was the last of the benighted towns to undertake permanent re-building work. Nothing had been done by March 1973, a good five years after the event, though other towns had already begun utilizing the available funds.[11]

While it is debatable whether it was really needed, the new town of Sasi was eventually built at some distance from the old town despite bureaucratic muddles and spectacular logistical mysteries: the taps had to come from the north of Italy and the tiles, of all things, from far away Rovigo. But, after considerable delay,[12] it did get built, and hordes of people were moved there from the old Borgo Vecchio quarter of the town, which has remained tumbledown and practically empty. Although it is still a dormitory centre without, as far as I can see, a heart, many Calatafimi people now live in modern housing. Oddly enough, in spite of there being few services and no shops, a considerable number of 'university' buildings were put up that, it is said, occasionally house students for a 'university diploma' of no known value or official status. Earthquake-resistant housing, however, is an advance, ugly though it may be, and just how ugly can be gauged by looking down on the magnificent Belice valley from old Calatafimi above.

With even greater delay, government compensation did become available for individual houses that had been damaged by the earthquake, too. The old house in what is now the hamlet where we live was given compensation, and the two brothers and sister who inherited it have new houses in sight of what has survived of the old. While the damage the earthquake wrought is still visible, all around it there is life and activity once again. Compensation money continues to be paid out after all this time, and at least the local building fraternity have sufficient work to do in the town and neighbouring areas.

There has been a tangible benefit for Caterina's family. Before the earthquake the old house had been divided between her father, her uncle, her aunt and a third party that had bought land from the relative that sold (ownership of land on a property carries proportional rights to the water and the buildings on it), as they do here: e.g. this room is mine, you have the corridor and the bathroom, and she has the two small bedrooms, etc. Everything is done to precise rules and with a measuring tape. The process of dividing up inheritances has caused the abandonment and decay of countless houses and farms here, which are fragmented further by every death. That the earthquake made the old house impracticable and that compensation was received means that, in place of one house that was incapable of housing the divided families and therefore destined to be abandoned, there are now four smaller houses which are lived in most of the time. We have added another smaller one, which has been built over the place where the stables had been in the old house – it has room for guests, were you to condescend.

13

Emigration and Immigration

Calatafimi has husbanded social stability for a long time, as you will have gathered from the notarial documents I have quoted from. Both the notaries and their clients bear surnames that crop up with absolute regularity over the centuries. Not just that of the Mollicas which I monotonously keep bringing up. Take the surname Vivona, for instance, although other family names would equally apply. Here are some home-made statistics: there are thirty-six entries for this very common name in Calatafimi's telephone directory, but only fourteen in Trapani's – the provincial capital less than forty kilometres away with a population more than sixty times larger than that of Calatafimi – and only twenty-six in Palermo's which has a population of about 700,000 and is not even a hundred kilometres away. There are quite a number of Vivonas living in Alcamo and Castellamare del Golfo, the neighbouring towns, but as a percentage of the population they are fewer than at Calatafimi; and the further you travel from this area, the more rapidly they dwindle into being merely another name one occasionally comes across. But, despite its long-term stability, immigration and emigration have left their mark on Calatafimi, as on many other small towns in Sicily.

Immigration is, of course, the earlier of the two phenomena and I have already dealt with it elsewhere, if superficially: the Elymians, Sicans, Phoenicians, Greeks, Arabs and the Normans blended into the loam of this part of Sicily, while the Byzantines, French and Spaniards only left pebbles on the topsoil. Plants also immigrated with such success that you would swear they were autochthonous. However, immigration is now a *fait accompli* in its human and vegetable forms. On the other hand, emigration is still much alive even if it has lost the lemming-like urgency it had around a century ago: some of its effects can be gauged from the remittances and foreign correspondence at the banks and the post office, the dusty, boarded-up broken windows of some of the houses and the average age of the elderly drivers that crawl through the narrow streets in their ancient cars. Incidentally, if you are interested, there are seven Vivonas in the Brooklyn telephone directory.

Those waves of immigrants have been so neatly assimilated that some sleuthing is required to pinpoint the marks they have left. As far as Calatafimi is concerned, the Arabs probably left the most. Apart from the *qal'at* in the town's name, the collapsed remains of the mosque, the traces of Arab burials and the so-called Arab quarter, the local dialect is full of Arabic words – the terminology of agriculture is largely Arabic – water is revered and there are Arabic place-names all around. My favourite is a small village just down the road towards Trapani called Ummari (not 'Yummahri', but 'Oommahri': if it is pronounced slowly in a low voice, it sounds very African), where not a soul is to be seen. What they do there is a mystery. Oooommmahri: what *are* you up to? Perhaps the men are out in the fields digging *vattali* (an Arab word for an irrigation furrow) or cleaning out the *ganzaria* (the pigsty). I don't know if the deep sense of fatalism that reigns here is an Arab trait or, more likely, a useful virtue in a harsh environment.

The waves of incomers have now dried up, though there are a few 'migrants' left. I have a vague impression that in the early years of the twentieth century the beaches of Europe were trudged by itinerant Chinese selling sunshades and gadgets. They disappeared for a time in this country together with the station monkey and bathing-machines, and were replaced by North African peddlers of mats and sunglasses on even relatively isolated beaches – or umbrellas in the towns when it rains (*Vu Comprà?* or 'you buy?' has been coined as the Italian expression for black immigrants). But the Chinese peddler has returned both on and off the beaches with his tray of gadgets: a 'migrant' because he or she just moves on with the goods, which include everything from extraordinarily good compact tools to amazingly kitsch lighters. We bought a lighter in Calatafimi in the form of a small dark-red plastic bedside lamp, such as you might see in a Wild West bawdy house in an old film: you pull the cord, it lights up and gives you a flame from the top of its heavy red shade. A strange thing to be offered by a serenely smiling Chinese girl on the street in Calatafimi, which one would have thought well out of the reach of the tentacles of international commerce. Yet the movement is putting down roots. Recently a Chinese shop, clothing mostly, was opened in the town, with red lanterns hanging outside and a smiling Chinese couple running it. Yes, very strange.

Apart from the Chinese couple who run the shop, I have only ever met one real human immigrant, and even his story dovetails into emigration. He was a Sardinian from Nuoro. We met him in the local supermarket and he seized on this opportunity to tell us about his life. He had emigrated to Stuttgart in 1960 where he had met and married a girl from Calatafimi. He was talking to us while the American war against the Taliban in Afghanistan was taking place and the conversation began with him announcing that he had just seen that Kandahar had been surrounded, on German satellite television. This led us indirectly to the Arabs: he said that when he had first gone to Germany there were 800,000 Italians working there. Then came the Turks, followed by the Arabs. He did not like the Arabs (neither did the Germans, according to him): they were always at war – why, didn't even Jesus Christ have to leave Egypt for Palestine because the Arabs pushed him out? Some years previously, his Calatafimese wife had died (he showed us the black button he wore *per rispetto*) and he decided to leave Germany and come to Calatafimi where his wife had had some interests. Despite what appear to have been family misunderstandings, he now lives between a place in the country – rather lonely with dogs and chickens – and a place in the town which he has modernized. We were given his whole family history in an Italian spoken with a heavy German-Sardinian accent. As I say, he is the only proper immigrant I have come across so far, apart from a few German wives who have come back with the few husbands that return.

The vegetable immigrants are legion: they arrived hundreds of years ago and made themselves so much at home that they have now, most of them, become symbols of Sicily. Needless to say, Calatafimi abounds in them. The prickly pear, the agave, the aloe – those plants you think of as quintessentially Sicilian – all of them came from the Americas (the prickly pear as late as the seventeenth century). The wood sorrel (*Oxalis pescaprae*), which paints the countryside brilliant yellow in spring, apparently comes from South Africa. The cypresses come from Persia, the tomato from Peru, the aubergine from the East Indies, the oranges, lemons and palm trees from nearby North Africa, and so on. The original citrus immigrants were lemons and oranges of the bitter 'Seville' type. It was only much later, in the sixteenth century, that sweet oranges were introduced from

Portugal, and there are still types referred to as *portoghesi* and *portogalli*, and also *brasiliani* and *thomas*. That famous Sicilian dish, the *caponata*,[1] comes from Asia (its aubergines), South America (its tomatoes) and Africa (its sugar) – and the word itself is of Spanish origin. Incidentally, I must remind you that sugar-cane was grown for a long time in Sicily until competition from the West Indian plantations killed it off and, even after it had ceased to be a commercially viable crop, it grew wild for a time; and visitors in the late eighteenth and even the early nineteenth centuries wrote of a passable rum being made from it. Perhaps the only indigenous crops were wheat, olives and figs – Homer talks of Sicily rich in figs and olives – because the grape was probably imported by the Phoenicians. Wheat for bread, olives for oil and grapes for wine. A piece of bread soaked in oil and accompanied by a glass of wine has been the peasants' sustenance down the centuries, and to some extent still is. Oil and wine were the *cumpanaticum* of late Latin, to be eaten with bread as the basic meal.

Peacocks came in with the Arabs presumably, although they originated in southern India. They are still quite widely kept and are not a luxury – you often see them in dirty farmyards. I was told at one of the local agricultural co-operatives that, if I wanted to keep them, I should get a young couple because single birds and adults tend to fly away; but I am not going to take them on, even though they shed their dramatic feathers generously, as their elegant necks produce really unbeautiful sounds. Since birds have come up, my favourite temporary immigrant is *Merops apiaster*, the bee-eater. They arrive in the spring and their relatively slow undulating flight and monotone cry are not very attractive either; but if you manage to get a good look at them, you will see a veritable eruption of colour – rusty brown, yellow, green-blue, white, light blue and red. There is a large colony that lives in holes in a sandstone cliff about three kilometres across the valley in front of the house. Their habits are regular: in the morning they fly over the house to the hills just behind, where they spend the day swooping on and munching bees and wasps – they are immune to stings – as well as dragonflies and the like; in the late afternoon they fly lazily back and float around above the house, presumably because of the bee-hives near by, although they never venture anywhere near the actual hives; and towards evening they retire languidly, slipping their kaleidoscopic bodies into the small dirty holes in the cliff-side across the valley.

Human immigrants or 'economic migrants' (a bad term, for some reason) do not seek out Calatafimi as a haven, despite the tragic shiploads of them that manage by the skin of their teeth to gain Sicilian shores on their desperate way to other parts. The very few of them that do reach here must do so out of confusion, and, while the locals fully understand their predicament and give kindly, they move on because there is no work. Economic migrants don't come to Calatafimi but head for the big towns where they are stamped 'illegal immigrants'. But the young of Calatafimi are also economic migrants as droves of them leave to look for work, and they are looked on almost as suspiciously as their immigrant counterparts the further north they go. On achieving their degree the well-educated young citizen of Calatafimi – and the number of them is growing – needs to open up their atlas. Even those without the boost of higher education are finding it harder to get work, as expert machines manufactured far from here are gnawing away at the few opportunities there are. The south is the Third World of the Italian peninsula and Calatafimi is a poor part of it; but the modest cost of labour that results is not low enough to seduce industry here and governments have never been over-concerned with questions of socio-economic balance. So the north hugs the money and the south has become accustomed to lying back and hoping, with the result that qualified young brains and hands have no option but to pack up and move to where they can hope to find gainful employment.

Emigration on a grand scale began around the middle of the nine-teenth century and gathered momentum steadily up until the First World War. It is estimated that Sicily lost a million people in the period 1871-1914. The reasons were many, but they can be boiled down to poverty caused by the corn-tax, army service, general re-pression and land-management that brooked no improvements, the trade war with France, ineffectual government, the wholesale di-version of southern revenue to the north, the collapse of the sulphur industry through cheap American competition, the unrealized dreams that had been ignited by Garibaldi's oratory and the Sicilian equiva-lent of the potato famine, the outbreak of *phylloxera* or vine pest. They explain those cries of 'Muoio di fame' ('I'm dying of hunger'), registered with such distaste by the American Paton and others when they visited Calatafimi at the end of the nineteenth century and the beginning of twentieth.[2]

This period of emigration from western Sicily looked first to North

Africa, particularly Tunis, before concentrating on the United States. It was the time of the popular song 'Mamma Give Me 100 Lire 'Cause to America I Have to Go' and Mamma who says 'I'll Give You the 100 Lire, but to America, No, No, No'. The idea was to go to America, make money and come back home rich. Many did: English-speaking tourists in the 1920s and 1930s were plagued with natives wishing to keep up their English, and quite a number of relatively well-off citizens in today's Calatafimi owe their standing to their great-grandfathers. But not all of them succeeded and, since it took time to make money even in America, they dreamt of home. There is a typical plaque in the church of Santa Caterina in Calatafimi, just inside the main door, on the left. It says:

> The paving in the *marmetti* [slabs of composite marble], the iron chain, the galvanized iron gutter, the threshold of the main door, the wooden spiral staircase and the other staircase which give access to the bell-tower, were executed by the committee and with money collected by the citizens of Calatafimi who emigrated to Brooklyn and New York, America.

And Americans of Calatafimese origin still send back contributions towards the major festas, particularly the SS Crocifisso, which they return specially to see, as I have told you. The traffic went the other way as well: Bonaiuto[3] reports that in 1922 a certain Cavaliere Civiletti was commissioned to sculpt a copy of the bas-relief of the Madonna di Giubino, which was shipped to the church of St Joseph in Brooklyn, for the comfort of the Calatafimesi exiles living there[4] – it was the church of San Giuseppe to them.

After the Second World War, between about 1951 and 1971, there was another major outbreak of emigration during which Calatafimi lost an estimated 26% of its population, according to official statistics. While the flow of people to America had never really stopped, most emigration was now taking place towards the industrial north of Italy where Sicilians were treated like cattle – in Turin signs saying that 'Sicilians need not apply' were commonplace outside houses with rooms to let – to other parts of Europe, including Belgium, England, France and Germany, to South America ('America scarsa' or poor America, as opposed to 'America ricca'), Canada and Australia.[5] (I have mentioned the park benches donated by Calatafimi emigrants to Australia.) Just as the confiscation of ecclesiastical lands in the nineteenth century gave rise to speculation rather than equitable re-distribution, even occasional government moves to redress the situation in more recent times, such as the attempt at land reform in the 1950s, have backfired to a large extent. That was designed to break up the big estates in Sicily and to cut down on sharecropping by allowing the peasants and others to buy smallholdings cheaply. Almost 250,000 hectares changed hands – being acquired by labourers, peasants and artisans, and also shopkeepers, salaried office-workers, professional people. Many of the smallholdings were a failure because the parcels of land were too small to be profitable, and many of the new owners sold out and emigrated. Their dream had been to own land. It now was to earn a decent living. At the same time, the dismembered large estates became less profitable because wheat farming in particular needs large tracts of land, a fact that the Romans were well aware of. Big estates were getting smaller and smallholdings were getting bigger, through selling and buying. There was less work around and more machinery. Then the 1968 earthquake took place, and the authorities, as we have seen, hid their total inability to deal with the wider social issues under the carpet of subsidized emigration.

Almost everyone who leaves now goes for good. A man who patiently works the land near our house has a son who travels the world as a cook. He was recently in Mauritius, but he then moved to Dubai with his Malaysian wife and is currently in the Philippines. He will probably never come back except for short visits because he wouldn't fit in any more. He has, moreover, bought a house in Malaysia. His ageing father, with his Sicilian cap and no linguistic weapon apart from the local dialect flew off with his wife to the Philippines recently for a holiday with their son's new family, travelling so much further than the mere mileage involved. Luciano, who built our house, was for many years in Germany with his wife and children, and is one of the few who have come back: the money he made there served to establish his family in the new town of Sasi outside Calatafimi, and to set him up in business on his own. But he and his wife still have many relatives with young children back in Germany, and their daughter who is studying English and Arabic at the University of Palermo is already half way to going because there is precious little she can do in Calatafimi with English and Arabic. There is a bar in the town owned by a man who spent a number of years in Manchester. I have conversations with him in English, usually about Manchester United football club. As you know, I am no football fan, but I hear the results on BBC newscasts and haltingly discuss them with him in English, which greatly impresses bystanders.

Fewer and fewer people are coming back now. In the late 1960s a survey was carried out in Australia among Sicilian immigrants and showed that only a very small percentage of them said they would return home, even if they won the lottery: they were there to stay.[6] While it is true that Calatafimi and her sister towns in Sicily have benefited from remittances, this second phase of emigration is fundamentally different from the first. Today's emigrant no longer plans to come back except for a holiday in the summer to see his parents and the family. Many small houses are abandoned and for sale: nobody will buy them in the circumstances that prevail. Another consequence is that the average age of the inhabitants of Calatafimi is soaring. I do not know what the actual figure is, but if you are foolish enough to try to get into the post office on pension days you will see that payments have had to be staggered by people's initials: A to F one day, G to M another, and so on. By the way, the majority of non-business correspondence going through the post office is either from or to North Italy, Germany and America, and parcels abound. But the elderly, queuing up to get their pensions, and sometimes not understanding the bewildering bureaucracy, or else wrestling with the intricacies of sending a parcel, have all the help they need from other people queuing up with them, as well as from those behind the counter. I was held up for about half an hour this morning by an elderly lady in black who wanted to send a parcel off to Sr Domingo Mazara in Mendosa, Argentina. Mazara is a common surname in these parts, rather like Vivona, but Domenico has already become Domingo and I don't suppose he will be coming back to see his relatives. Judging by the old lady's black attire, his grandfather, presumably Domenico, had already departed this life.

Minds emigrate as well. It is inevitable in a small agricultural centre where there were only elementary schools until quite recently and where, even now, pupils of fouteen and over have to go elsewhere to continue their studies. As has always been the case, anyone who wants to pursue his education beyond the minimum must go to Alcamo, Trapani, Palermo or the 'continent' (the mainland). So that the first steps beyond the town are taken early on – in the past by the better-off or those who showed exceptional talent and were helped by individuals or the Church; now it is by a larger swathe of the population. I have told you about Natale Maria Macaddino, who was quickly noted by the community and financed by a local dignitary at the beginning of the nineteenth century, became a distinguished physician in Palermo and on his death there left his books to form the basis of the Calatafimi library. The Church was good at picking out bright pupils and sending them to seminaries in Mazzara, the head of the diocese, Trapani or Alcamo. The sons of the wealthier did not need charity or the help of Church organizations, but sought education elsewhere for the benefit of themselves and their families. Only a few returned as lawyers, notaries, doctors, elementary schoolmasters and pharmacists, all the rest following their careers further afield, although they would until recently have maintained a link with the town since they would have had financial ties here.

That is what most of the men in Caterina's family did, like others of their kind. You can see this pattern with Francesco Vivona, who was to become a renowned Latinist, and Nicolò Zuaro (his mother was yet another Mollica): they were both enrolled at the Ximenes Lyceum in Trapani in 1876 and boarded there in a student hostel. Vivona began as a schoolmaster in Sicily and on the mainland and ended up teaching Latin at Rome University, but much of his holiday time was spent in the town. His companion Zuaro came back to Calatafimi to look after his considerable property here. Today, many fewer ex-students will spend their holidays here, and few will have enough land to make it worth their while coming back to live off it. Now, after their degrees have been taken, work is sought wherever graduates might be able to find profitable occupation, certainly not in Calatafimi. The town is an exporter of people.

The other day, I went to a small restaurant for lunch while Caterina was on a shopping spree in Palermo. A restaurant offering lunch in Calatafimi is something of an anomaly, as no local would understand why anybody should want to have lunch anywhere except at home. Apart from the three or four small pizzerias that have sprung up here, into which the young squeeze in the evenings to chat and eat the spongy Sicilian pizza called the *sfincione*, and the local *rianata* variety, the few restaurants that exist in small Sicilian towns usually cater for outsiders. In fact, at this establishment one table was taken up by the bank manager (who does not live here) with two visiting inspector-like officials, who talked soberly among themselves. At a second table, three male agricultural workers proceeded to get drunk, in no way a tradition here, and decided finally – though not too loudly – that they could not drive. They might have driven here to do a job, which would explain why they were in the restaurant. A third table was much sadder with a well-dressed family of three: the father was reading a newspaper and the daughter a computer magazine all through the meal, while the mother took a well-known pharmaceutical sedative and other medicines and contemplated her phone book without making a single call, although her mobile phone was in front of her. Not a single word was spoken throughout the meal. It was the antithesis of a normal Sicilian family lunch and I have no idea why they were there. The fourth table was occupied by a very loud, blond-haired woman speaking in a heavy Milanese accent with two young locals. At first I thought she was a Milanese con-woman trying to clinch some sort of tricky business with people she considered ignorant and exploitable. I was happily wrong. Her blondness was typically Sicilian and she was rather publicly going through the break-up of her marriage – her husband phoned her on her mobile from Milan during the meal – and the two much quieter-speaking locals were relations trying to give her support at a difficult moment. Whether they managed to or not, or what happened to her marriage, I do not know. What struck me was that this distressed, second-generation Milanese daughter of Calatafimi had come back home for comfort at a time of stress, which says something about the underlying stability of Calatafimi.

However, whatever stability is left is slowly eroded. For every Luciano or Manchester United supporter who returns, there are the scores who do not. As time and distance work their will, 'Calatafimi' gradually turns into a word that crops up in parents' conversation to describe a place that is hazily connected with a previous life. If you look up common Calatafimi surnames on the Internet you will find pages of second- and third-generation Americans, Argentinians and Australians groping for their disappearing origins, which will elude them because it's too late. Whether it's a pity or it's progress, the pattern of living that survives will be firmly rooted in the basic common values that have been nurtured over time in Calatafimi, as it has always has been. Calatafimi will imperceptibly adapt.

14

Some Injustices

The succession of foreign invaders that have settled in Sicily have often had ulterior motives. The Greeks, Arabs and Normans intended to remain and brought things with them of lasting value, as we have seen, but others – the Romans, French, Germans, Spanish, Bourbons, Piedmontese and Italians – behaved like migrating vampires: they had cavernous habitats elsewhere and flapped away after they had sucked what they could from the island. Their taxes were generally clumsy and short-sighted, while the browbeaten victims only occasionally found the energy to retaliate in bloody uprisings. For the most part, these foreigners ruled a subject people, who sullenly complied with a system that pauperized them and the island it was designed to exploit.

I have put on my high black hat, broad white collar and quadrangular buckles: I intend to preach to you. The iniquities were legion and unrelenting; initiative was sapped, and apathy pervaded everything until a run of bad harvests, a series of particularly objectionable administrative misjudgements, or both, rendered life that little bit more intolerable, and blood flowed. Calatafimi was no worse than anywhere else in this respect. So there are only a few specific chapters and verses that I can lift from a general text. You should bear it in mind that, unless you were an aristocrat, rural life and most urban life as well was passive, dull and annihilating for most people most of the time. I shall spare you a general homily and pick out just three Calatafimi examples of injustice that, *mutatis mutandis*, might still pass as parables for today. The first of them was in Roman times.

Back then to Roman government in Sicily after the Punic Wars under the infamous governor Verres. You probably remember him from school. The thieving, bullying, corrupt administration of Verres led to his being brought to trial in 70 BC, a rare occurrence for a Roman governor, since Rome like all colonial powers usually exonerated its own for political reasons. When the home authorities finally decided they had to act against him, Verres found he had to face a formidable public prosecutor in the person of Cicero and right at the beginning of the trial he realized that he hadn't a chance, and that the wisest thing was to take to his heels. Which he did. This left Cicero with his adrenalin pumping, no outlet in a public court and therefore none of the public applause he found pleasing. Happily for us, he decided that the best he could do was to publish his harangues in book form – the *Verrine Orations* which, though they may be biased as he was the prosecuting attorney, give us a great deal of valuable information on the state of Sicily at the time. Our Segesta comes into the story on various occasions, but I shall confine you to a theft and a piece of illegal taxation.[1]

The theft was of a statue, that of the goddess Diana, the central cult symbol at the temple of Segesta. Cicero describes how the Carthaginians had looted the island during the Punic Wars and after sacking Segesta had borne off their revered bronze statue of Diana. Many years later, after the Third Punic War, the Roman general Publius Scipio Africanus, a soldier of noble disposition who had crushed the Carthaginians definitively, called the Sicilians together and asked them to list the works of art they had lost to the Carthaginians. He promised them he would make a search for them in North Africa and repatriate whatever he managed to find. As well as many treasures belonging to other places, he managed to trace the statue of Diana and was able to restore it to Segesta. The citizens rejoiced at having it back, carved Scipio's name on it and enshrined it again in its public place. It was reported to be very beautiful, and it should not be forgotten that Cicero himself had actually seen it. Verres, the Roman governor, also thought it was beautiful and threatened the magistrates, the elected civic leaders, in an attempt to persuade them to give it to him. Scipio Africanus' name being carved on it, the Segestans argued that it belonged to the Roman nation; but Verres was not to be put off and applied heavy pressure to Segesta by requisitioning large numbers of citizens as sailors and oarsmen as well as making demands for quantities of corn the city could not afford. Faced with this pressure, the citizens had no alternative but to give way in the end and

amid the grief and lamentation of the whole community, with tears and cries of grief from every man and every woman in it, a contract was authorized for the removal of the image of Diana.

Because of the religious feelings involved, nobody could be found in Segesta to move it and foreign labourers had to be sought out in Lilybaeum, present-day Marsala. Unaware of them, they carried it away for a fee through the grief-stricken Segestan crowds. It never came back, and indeed was lost. Verres showed little *iustizia* while in Sicily: cash was the driving force behind most of his actions, ostensibly on behalf of the Roman government.

But Verres was not only an art thief; he also officiated over the brutal exaction of taxes. First some bureaucratic background. Although the Sicilians were subject to a large number of differing taxes under the Romans, over and above the local Sicilian ones, the backbone of the Roman tax system was the Decima tribute, a tax of one tenth in kind on all wheat and barley grown, which was sent directly to Rome. However, Segesta, as an ally of Rome's in the Punic Wars together with seven other cities, had been legally exempted from this tax. Cicero takes the matter up:

> To deal with Segesta, another community exempt from the tithe, there was sent another of these temple slaves as collector, by name Symmachus. This man brought with him a letter from Verres which authorized him – in defiance, alike of all our Senate's decrees, of all the inhabitants' advice, and of the Rupilian law[2] – to cite farmers outside the limits of their district. Listen to this letter that was written to the people of Segesta [the letter was read out]. The sort of game that this temple slave played with these farmers you may appreciate by knowing how he settled things in one case with one esteemed and reputable man: the rest of his doings are of the same type. There is a well known gentleman of Panhormus [Palermo], named Diocles Phimes, who was working a farm in the Segestan area; a leasehold farm, for none but Segestans may hold a freehold in their district; for this farm he was paying a rent of £60. After being knocked about sufficiently by that temple slave, he agreed to pay the man as tithe £160 as well as 654 bushels of wheat. This is confirmed, as you shall hear, by his own books. [The account was read.]

So, after being beaten up by a slave, Phimes paid an exorbitant sum (more than four times his annual rent in sesterces) when he should have been legally exempt from any payment. This piece of injustice was imposed on the man who, as I have told you, probably bequeathed his Roman surname to the second part of Qa'lat al Fimi.

That was Roman injustice. But now I am going to take you forward more than one and a half thousand years: from the over-weaning arrogance of Verres, through centuries of other injustices quietly endured, to the subtler but equally iniquitous, slower-moving machinations of feudal superiority, and the so-called *terraggiolo*, an illegal tithe that reared its ugly head in the Calatafimi area around the middle of the sixteenth century and was not finally guillotined until 1846.[3]

Under the Normans Calatafimi had been part of the royal demesne for more than 250 years. This was a condition that suited the towns-people who always aspired to live under the crown, even after the town became feudalized in 1336. That was because townspeople were generally far less exploited under the crown than under feudal lords; but they rarely succeeded in obtaining crown patronage, except for very short periods during royal/baronial spats. The big break for Calatafimi occurred in the year 1336, when Frederick the Second of Aragon bequeathed the town as an apanage to his third son William with the title of Duke and its feudal history began.

It passed to William's sister and then to his daughter as a dowry on her marriage to William Peralta, the Count of Modica, after which Calatafimi became a part of the great County of Modica. These were critical times, both for Calatafimi's aspirations to regain status as a royal demesne and also for the barons' desire to assert their strength against the crown. To cut a long story short, Calatafimi rebelled against the Peraltas in 1392 and surrendered to the sovereign. King Martin took it under his wing for a few dubious months before giv-ing it back to the then Count of Modica, Nicolò Peralta, who, to calm the waters, but with little intention of being held to his word, conceded the town a Diploma of Privileges in 1393 recognizing, among other things, that the *mandrie*, or middle-sized landholdings freely rented from the lord, had always been 'allodial', which means that no further taxes would be due to the County of Modica; that the *parecchiate*, or lands conceded to individuals on a leasehold basis and paying rent, were also subject to *compascolo* (i.e. the Count had the right to graze his flocks on their land), which was not liked but was accepted; and that the *chiuse*, or small tracts of land for sowing and pasturage, were subject to a set rent and nothing more. Peralta was involved, however, in conspiracies against the crown and, on his death in 1398, King Martin again confiscated Calatafimi and restored it to the demesne. The following year he granted that the town should remain 'irrevocably' under the crown by a privilege dated 1st September 1399. Even that did not last long, and in 1407 Calatafimi was granted to a relative of the royal family, Giacomo de Prades, although with dubious legitimacy, with a fresh settlement that stated that all tributary matters should revert to the *status quo ante* Prades and Peralta, to the position under the demesne: i.e. to relative freedom from taxation, and merely to the payment of rents. The *terraggiolo*, the illegal tax that we are considering, was not contemplated in this agreement.[4]

The *terraggiolo* was a tithe of one *salma* (220 kg) and 4 *tumoli* (one *tumolo* was 10 kg) of wheat or barley for every *salma* (3.3490 hectares) of sown land, which was to be paid to the Count of Modica who lived in Spain, over and above rents and other recognized taxes. Exaction became the norm around the middle of the sixteenth century. But tradition has it that in origin it was a spontaneous donation by the citizens of Calatafimi in aid to the Enriquez family, who were the Counts of Modica, when they bought back the lordship after a period of financial difficulty had forced them to sell it. The Enriquez family had had a debt of 500 *ounces* that they could not pay, so they sold Calatafimi, with a buy-back clause. In 1551 the Enriquez family bought it back from the Aiutamicristo family, and it is said that the citizens of Calatafimi offered this spontaneous donation of 1,500 *salme* of wheat over five years to help the Enriquez out. *Very* generous of the citizens of Calatafimi.

In the 1554 administrative records of the 'Segreto Baroniale', who was at the time a certain Giovanni Mollica (yet another relative), the first instalment of this spontaneous gift was noted; but in 1560 the notarial records reveal that there were still 278 *salme* outstanding, and a further two years were conceded by the Count. In 1563, a new donation was offered in exchange for forgiveness and freedom from any new *terraggiolo*, by which term these instalments of wheat were now coming to be known. The Count refused: 'non convenit' ('it is not fitting'), was his answer. The generally accepted theory is that the original spontaneous donation had become surreptitiously 'changed' into an accepted practice, which was tamely endured by the ex-donors who had no realistic alternative. The tithe continued to be imposed right up to the nineteenth century. Community indignation began to raise its voice at the end of the eighteenth, encouraged indirectly by Viceroy Caracciolo's brusque attempts at foisting Enlightenment on the Sicilian barons. The basis of the eventual court trial was that the land was traditionally free, as set out in the Privileges of 1393,[5] except for normal documented rents and the like, and that half way through the sixteenth century this exceptional payment to the Spanish Counts of Modica slipped into general use, and the Counts were never able to produce any documentary evidence giving it legal justification, despite frequent demands.

The burden had been borne fatalistically until towards the end of the eighteenth century when the general expectations aroused by Viceroy Caracciolo's reforming zeal created an atmosphere that was conducive to the making of a petition by the citizens of Calatafimi to the Royal Treasury for the abolition of the *terraggiolo*. The current Countess of Modica had died without direct issue and the territory had temporarily reverted to the crown. Although the petition was rejected in 1800, times were changing: in order to survive, the barons were making concessions, and feudalism itself was legally abolished in 1812.

In the meantime our local historian, Longo, had begun the colossal task of collecting, collating and painstakingly analysing all the documents he could lay his hands on that related to buying and selling, and renting and leasing, land in the Calatafimi district since the beginning of the fourteenth century. It was carried out with monastic patience, and published in 1811 under the title *Discoprimento dell'angarico dazio del terraggiolo, che si ricuote la in oggi incamerata Contea di Modica su tutto il territorio di Calatafimi* (Revelation of the oppressive toll called the *terraggiolo* which is levied by the now confiscated County of Modica on the entire territory of Calatafimi), and it was the backbone of the ensuing court cases. He and Don Francesco Avila, Calatafimi's legally trained archpriest, formed a committee of notables who, in the name of the townspeople, dedicated themselves for decades to the abolition of this iniquitous tax. Meanwhile, the new Count of Modica (installed in 1816) was also at work on his defence, signing agreements with various farmers by which they formally recognized the legitimacy of the tax. The next judicial steps took place in 1821 when the Count (then Don Carlo Michele Stuart Fitz-James y Alba y Alvarez y Toledo, Duke of Alba and Berwick) was cited before a court in Trapani: the court was asked to declare the tax illegal and the acts of recognition worthless, and to get the Count to pay back all he had received since the abolition of feudalism in 1812. Calatafimi won the case and the judge ruled that, because of its fundamental importance, the sentence should be published. Incidentally, during the hearing it transpired that the Count had arranged for armed guards, paid for by the farmers themselves, to supervise the harvests and make sure that the tax was paid down to the last centime!

The Count 'appealed by edict', which the Committee considered illegal after the abolition of feudalism. Legal infighting ensued, as was to be expected, and it was a considerable time before another major court case took place in 1835 before the 'Gran Corte' at Palermo: the case was decided in the Count's favour this time and he thereupon tried to sequester goods from the farmers to pay for his costs and the *terraggiolo* he had not received. Enter the King. Ferdinand III happened to be in Sicily, on a hunting trip, and was passing through Calatafimi (it would appear that the Neapolitan Bourbons only set foot in Sicily to avoid invading French armies or to slaughter wild boar). He momentarily lent his royal ear to the citizens and, before he could get back to his hunt, he had been moved to grant public funds for the case to go ahead, and ordered the Supreme Court to settle the matter expeditiously. This it did in 1839 by annulling the 'Gran Corte' decision, despite appeals from Don Carlo Stuart's widow, and referring the matter back to the 'Gran Corte' at Palermo. This court sat again on 3rd April 1846 and ruled in favour of the citizens of Calatafimi on all counts – the 'appeal by edict' was illegal, the ad hoc acts of recognition were null and void, and the *terraggiolo* was '*non dovuto*', that is, not due.

On Palm Sunday, 6th April, the population of Calatafimi rode out on horseback beyond the neighbouring town of Alcamo to greet Don Francesco Avila with palm leaves and olive branches and escort him home in triumph. The legal battle had lasted thirty-three years. Avila, apart from being an archpriest, was also a doctor of law. During the case they had tried to bribe and threaten him; they had shot at him near the town of Partinico on his return from a Palermo hearing; and they had even tried to poison him. If Avila was the spearhead of the campaign, the shaft was the astonishing accumulation of evidence amassed by the labours of Longo. Although he was elected as Calatafimi's ecclesiastical deputy to the Sicilian parliament in 1812, Longo was only a humble parish priest without any land, who died in very modest circumstances in 1825 without even the satisfaction of hearing the final verdict. When I walk into the town, I go past his minute house in a side street, with its small square marble memorial-tablet. The plaque was put up by the Fascists in 1933, which would surely have affronted Longo's balanced view of life, but the Fascist symbol of a sheaf of corn is quaintly relevant. Both the protagonists are re-membered with gratitude in town to this day, as indeed is the whole affair of the *terraggiolo*.

The priestly backbone of the *terraggiolo* crusade was no anomaly. Though the Church did not always epitomize justice, the priesthood in societies like Calatafimi's supplied a framework for the intelligent poor to express their abilities and for richer younger sons to employ themselves usefully; it provided social and geographical mobility in a stable society. Before leaving this point I must commend to your attention a Calatafimi priest – socially, geographically and physically mobile – who used his backside to divert the course of history, in the interests of justice as he saw it. It happened in 1773 at Palermo dur-ing the popular uprising that led to Marchese Fogliani, the Viceroy, being ignominiously ousted from his office, the city and the island. The armed crowd had invaded the Viceregal Palace and the popular Archbishop of Palermo was fighting his way through the mob out-side to rescue Fogliani and escort him out of town. Here is an eye-witness account of what happened.[5]

> While the Archbishop, the Judge of the Monarchia Court and various members of the Nobility were making their way towards the Royal Palace on foot, one of those frenzied rebels suggested to the artilleryman, who stood with a lighted match by the cannon near the Archbishop's Palace [in sight of the Viceroy's], that the best thing he could do would be to fire the cannon and blow up those Prelates and the accompanying Nobles, whom he defined as enemies of the people. The latter was about to execute this infamous piece of advice when the priest Melchiorre di Simone from Calatafimi sat himself on the touch-hole [of the cannon] and began rubbing it with his backside, thus preventing a tragedy. I, who witnessed the fact from one of the balconies of the Archbishop's Palace, cannot forbear from rendering due praise to this Ecclesiastic, worthy of a better fate.

A Calatafimi priest to the rescue once again. I do hope, however, that the last phrase quoted, 'worthy of a better fate' ('meritevole di miglior sorte' in the original), was the author's assessment of di Simone's fine qualities, and did not mean that the poor priest perished in the revolt.

The last instance of outrageous injustice was a few months ago, and is infinitely less important than the preceding two. It concerns a cousin of Caterina's, herself called Caterina, who also has a house in this little hamlet. I don't think you know her. I must explain that our houses are about five kilometres out of town, too far for telephone land-lines, a postal service or rubbish collection by the town's *servizio ecologico*. There are therefore no rubbish bins, and we all carry our own garbage to the nearest public bin in town.

Well, the other month this cousin was, to say the least, surprised to receive a formal tax demand for rubbish collection and, not only that, there was also a fine for late payment, even though she had never received any previous demands. Far from accepting the situation fatalistically, she went in her perplexity to the Municipal Council offices to rectify the mistake. It must have been a hot day or one dogged with numerous other problems, because the tone of the conversation deteriorated rapidly. Positions hardened, superiors were called for, written explanations were demanded, a meeting with the Mayor was insisted upon.

That was some months ago, and nothing more has been heard of the matter. It did not take thirty-three long years, nor was anybody beaten up by a slave; but it was, nonetheless, an attempt at unjustified taxation by the twenty-first-century authorities – even though it was probably the result of papers getting mixed up, or something equally banal. For the moment there is silence. However, you should never lower your guard here if bureaucracy is your opponent. Although unchallenged bureaucracy is unlikely now to change a spontaneous loan into an accepted practice, it seldom accepts defeat in any of its financial demands, because the daunting tangle of bye-laws can usually furnish some unexpectedly useful weapon, and implementation is remorseless. I know of several people living in the town in places where the service is functional who have been severely chastised for not paying their rubbish collection bills on time.

15

Pigs and Climbers

For a change, I am going to tell you about two young Romeo and Juliet pigs crashing through the Sicilian undergrowth in a magnificent run-around love affair: just as it all happened, before our very eyes.

Nothing will convince me that what you are about to hear was not the result of priggish pig-parents trying to prevent a precipitous love affair between their piglets. I know you don't like animals, but I must tell you about the few days they were with us. I trust they will forgive me for revealing their secrets and fervently hope they are now surrounded by hordes of squealing piglets, and reconciled to having grown into adoring grandparents.

It began when Francesco's wife, with the typically Italian name of Desirée, went to pick some late oranges in a reasonably remote part of the country here. She was surprised to be confronted by two young pigs with a sort of military-fatigue-coloured skin (in fact with grey and black blotches rather than khaki and green ones), wandering blissfully through the orange grove. Defensive forces were called out, the dogs were vociferous, and the innocent young couple was driven to the road. Nicola, the shepherd, was bringing back his sheep at that moment and undertook to look after them. It transpired that they belonged to a cousin of his, who lived a considerable distance away – which reinforced my elopement theory. And so an exciting day came to a close, with everybody satisfied at having been involved. We did harbour thoughts that the shepherd might consider slaughtering the young couple; but the fact that there was a cousin involved diminished that particular worry.

Two uneventful days followed. I shall not deny that a picture came to me of perfect porcine bliss. But on the whole the young couple did not occupy many of our thoughts.

The third day, early in the morning, we were having breakfast on the terrace with some guests when we noticed our two young pig friends trotting up the road. The dogs exploded – to no effect whatsoever – and the couple turned the corner out of sight. We had heard the previous day that damage had been done to the vegetables at Paolo's house across the road, so there we had misgivings. Later we had to leave for a neighbouring town to do some shopping and had our lunch there, without giving the situation further thought.

At about five o'clock that evening, when we had returned and were contemplating the pleasures of life from the terrace, lo and behold, our young lovers could be seen trotting up the road, apparently having again escaped the vigilance of the shepherd and cousin of their owner, and looking forward to more intimacy in the undergrowth.

Remembering that something had been at Paolo's vegetables the day before, I marched down to make sure nothing else took place. But they were simply taking a stroll together and went straight past Paolo's house. It is true that they came back fairly soon afterwards and I stood in front of the entrance in my determination to prevent any further damage to the vegetables. Here a tragedy began. They were diverted into an olive grove which was divided from the road by a concrete wall from which they could not jump down. While they were up there I noticed him licking her face in a way that could only have been a cheer-up-my-girl-we'll-get-out-of-this sort of kiss. They tried to get onto the road again, but without much success, until the young slip of a girl realized that the best way forward was to go back and managed to get down. At that point, a tractor went by and this clearly aroused early memories, as she followed it at some speed down the hill towards the shepherd's, no doubt thinking that this was now her married home. However, this left her ardent lover behind, unable to get out of the olive grove. It took him some time to do this, and he in his turn was favoured with another tractor, which he also followed down the road, though rather less rapidly. I had gone up to the house by then and we were on the terrace trying to resume our interrupted contemplations...

The young male had not followed his tractor all the way down and had got lost. He did not know where he wanted to go. He got onto our land and was discouraged (though not frightened) by our dogs. He went across the road to another piece of land. Apart from being lost, he was clearly anxiously looking for his beloved. He came back to our land. He then decided he would go up the hill again, grunting forlornly, perhaps because that was the last place he had seen her. A jeep belonging to the Forestry Guards saw him and stopped. It turned round and Romeo followed it down the hill, only to get lost at the same place as previously. By this time a man on the

9.30 mule was returning from work and went over to tell the shepherd that he had seen the pig, which the Forestry Guards were already following. Poor Nicola, overwhelmed by events by this time, got on his scooter and, to shouts from us on the terrace, reached the place where the pining male was wandering around forlornly. In the meantime, and you must believe this, Juliet had got loose again, followed the shepherd's scooter and become re-united with her prince. The meeting was genuinely touching, although we could only see it from our terrace. They were very close for some minutes before the shepherd finally found them and unromantically drove them back to their recently acquired marital home.

The next day they came out again and the dogs went berserk once again, but we did not see them ourselves. There was no grunting, so we assumed they were together – a happy thought. A man who works the land next to ours did see them, and he expressed a desire to eat them. In the evening we shouted questions from the terrace to Nicola, down below:

'What happened?'

'They are breaking everything up: I try to fence them in, but they just get out and I've got other things to do without having to deal with them. Everybody thinks I'm responsible, but they don't belong to me at all.'

'What about your cousin: why didn't he come to pick them up?'

'I don't know – he should have come yesterday, but God knows what's happening. I'm just fed up.'

The next morning at 5.30 we were woken up by what sounded like all the dogs in the vicinity, ours certainly and those of the shepherd and the farmer in the valley below – a veritable pack of dogs, all merrily barking at the young couple in the thickets just across the road. The occasional grunts sounded contented. They had probably had a wonderful night.

The day after was a Sunday, the day Nicola makes cottage cheese, if the pasture is fresh enough. We were elsewhere but, since the pasture was right for it, he brought some cheese up for Caterina's father, to a ferocious welcome from the dogs, which is strange because they have known him since they were born. Beaming all over, he announced that the young couple had finally been called for and taken back to their original home in a three-wheeled truck. It turned out they did not belong to his cousin but to a friend of his cousin's who lives at Gibellina about twenty kilometres away.

It is amusing to surmise that the delay in their being collected may have been due to high-level diplomatic bargaining between Montague and Capulet hogs and sows over a proper marriage-settlement, but sad to have to accept that they will no longer delight us with their antics.

Next, the climbers.

The vegetable protagonist I want to tell you about comes not from twenty kilometres up the valley but from far-off Mexico. It is a climbing plant called *Cobea scandens*, and was named after a Spanish Jesuit who lived in the Americas in the seventeenth century. No cousin but we ourselves were responsible for its invasion in the form of seeds we had ordered from a seed-merchant based in Cumbria in the north of England, which were sent to Rome. It did good work for us on our terrace there and produced seeds, which we brought down to Calatafimi. In Rome it contemplated life with some vigour, but when it arrived in Calatafimi it had already been thoroughly indoctrinated by its Imperial Roman upbringing and decided to conquer: *veni, vidi, vici*, it muttered to itself under its green breath.

The plant is described in the *Standard Cyclopedia of Horticulture* (L.H. Bailey, Macmillan, New York, 1947) as: 'a tender plant... [normally] treated as annuals'. Little did Bailey know about the Rome/Calatafimi axis. It turned out to be neither tender nor annual. It began as a small, slender dry seed which we put in near the house to see how it would do. It roared out of the ground and it now extends in many ramifications for well over twenty metres in all directions, much to the astonishment of all confronted with it. The bees from the hives below us are avid visitors to its many blue flowers, and in the morning the whole plant – and it is only one plant – hums with harvesting activity like a great vegetable harp. When it was getting out of control and strangling its weaker competitors, we decided to cut a large part of it back and see if we could create a modest pergola from the rest of it – with a metal framework and solid wires to hold the vegetation up. It has, however, taken control once again. In the space of just three months, we have had to weld on cross-pieces of iron and lateral columns to take the strain of its exuberant vegetation, and I am being continually told that the whole pergola will fall down under its weight at any moment. Our small house is beginning to make me think of South American opera houses being taken over by the jungle.

Despite its rude health and Roman vocation for territorial expansion, this invader does, however, have a dirty background. It was planted, we discovered, over the cesspool of one of Caterina's cousins, and it obviously appreciates the fact. People pray for seeds from us and as High Priests we deliver them. But they do not have their parent's energy, which surely has to have something to do with that cesspool.

16

Segesta

Close your eyes tightly and imagine your butler leading you out to the coach-and-four in the drive, with the trunks already stowed away, and the servants you are taking all appropriately dressed and bowing in attendance. You are lurching out over the muddy, pot-holed road from the village of Kensington towards Dover and the sailing barque that will shake and roll you on the first stage of your leisurely though bumpy journey to Italy and, if your courage lasts, to the temple of Segesta in far-off, savage Sicily. You could just buy an airline ticket to Palermo or Trapani, and I'll be there to meet you, stow your travelling suitcase-on-wheels into a car, and drive you there in the time it takes to have a short talk about what we are going to do after lunch.

Almost without exception, the early visitors were struck by the isolated beauty and total silence of Segesta. Frozen music, to use Schelling's classic phrase. The few intrepid ones who managed to get there, after shipping their Canalettos home from Venice, 'doing' Florence, socializing in Rome and timidly inspecting Naples and Pompeii, would encounter the occasional startled shepherd or hunter who gaped in wonder at these strange aliens while grazing their sheep or stalking partridge through the part of the temple that was still above ground, or up on the hill where there were traces of the theatre. The first reaction of many of them was to bring out their measuring tape and fill up their note-book or – later on perhaps – to whip out their watercolours and brush away energetically.

These first courageous travellers would not have met other visitors and the site itself would have been hardly recognizable to modern eyes. The only thing visible would have been the temple (and some of that would have been slightly buried) because the first excavations were not organized until the early nineteenth century by the Duke of Serradifalco.[1] As the century rolled on, sheep, cattle and partridges dwindled, visitors became more frequent and the silence was noisily strangled. Excavation, increasingly less amateur than Serradifalco's, brought to light more of the actual city, which had been brooding under the ground for centuries, and rid the theatre of some of its accretions. The trickle of visitors turned into a flood, and they now arrive in twenty-first-century motor-coaches and cars with registration numbers from all over Europe. That the silence can no more be heard, can be deduced from the multilingual list of things you are not allowed to do on the notice-board in the car park. At one point the English version reads: 'It is strictly prohibited...to make noise of any sort...' A truly Herculean task.

The thyme, oregano and rosemary; the agaves, cistus, prickly pear, dog roses; the seasonal floral invasions, mostly in yellow or blue; the buzzards and hawks overhead – all are still to be found around the temple and the hill where the great forgotten city had lived noisily before sinking into silence, and is now re-emerging to be looked, clicked and whirred at by the multitude of non-citizens speaking foreign tongues. The whole archaeological zone, now fenced-in, is thankfully lapped by a sea of rippling green vineyards, but it only regains its silence at night. There is a chasm that runs behind the temple and the remains of the town on the hill, which is well worth visiting but seldom seen, so there is silence there. You have to walk down the road past the entrance to the site and turn off to the left, just past a small bridge, to enter a timeless deep, rocky gorge. This runs from behind the temple – you can see it perched on the top of a cliff, whereas it's on a gentle slope on the other side – round past the main hill on which the ancient town stands, and comes out between the cliffs where the 'Mystical Park' was supposed to be, with the sanctuary of Mango opposite. The rocky cliff is stratified, changes colour every few metres, is pock-marked with caves and blotched with patches of vegetation, and there is nobody around. There is a tangible feeling of ancientness: you feel as if you are walking through the fossilized wrinkles of a gigantic elephant's inner leg. I went there for the first time in autumn, and the ground, where there was earth, was scattered with wild iris, anemone and narcissus.

The earlier visitors arrived in litters, on animals or in horse-drawn coaches and they sometimes stayed in Calatafimi or Alcamo. While measuring, sketching, and writing down their impressions, they often commented on the conditions they found in these two towns where they were forced to sleep. I have told you what some of them thought about Calatafimi earlier on: it was a mixed reaction to say the least. As forms of transport progressed, they no longer arrived by litter.

With the arrival of the railway, they tended to chug back to Palermo or on to Trapani rather than risking the night locally. Now the hundreds of thousands of yearly visitors who come in motor-coaches and cars, have no contact with Calatafimi. Only a very few of the most inquisitive of them, with their own cars, ever set foot in the town. The rest either climb back into their transport and move straight on, mostly to the ruins of Selinunte, Segesta's arch-rival in war; or they eat first in the Segestan restaurants before they do so. It depends on the time of day. Some eat in the restaurant at the railway station, others at the nearby Marzuko winery, which offers groups of them Sicilian specialities and local wine. But that is the nearest they get to the town. They must cover as much ground as they can while the light lasts, so they end up sleeping far away. The changing of Calatafimi to Calatafimi-Segesta, and also, to some extent, the 'Mystical Park' idea, was designed to change all that, but it had no effect. The same objective lies behind the putting on of a variety of entertainments in the summer – ancient and modern plays, modern and ancient music and poetry – which brings in new types of transient evening visitors. The initiative is laudable, but nostalgia is a terrible beast, and Caterina and I are unable to forget that, until recently, we could wander in at any time of the day or night, perhaps to sit by ourselves in the theatre at sunset, or to contemplate the black stripes the moon projected onto the white temple floor at midnight. We went to a special dawn event this year, a poetry reading given by a famous, rather vain actor who could not have asked for a better stage; his vanity was dimmed by the arrival of dawn and, try as we could, it was impossible not to think of the mists of time and that sort of thing. As I have mentioned, the early visitors almost unanimously talked of the silent majesty of the temple rising in a kind of desert. Now if I go there from Calatafimi, I have the impression of an island of chattering tongues surrounded by a sea of silent countryside.

It is held that Segesta was founded by a group of tired, elderly Trojan soldier-exiles and their recalcitrant women, who had threatened to burn the boats they came in to make sure Aeneas would register their protest, and were refugees from the disaster created in the name of Helen. After Aeneas' affair with Dido, and the death of his father, these people were left behind at Trapani while this Hero went on to found Rome; whereas they founded Eryx and Segesta. That is the gist of the tradition recounted by Thucydides and Virgil.

It is a fact, however, that archaeological remains can be traced back to the eighth century BC. That the city managed a certain level of greatness and, more important, that it survived, is partly due to the historical fact that the Elymians, its rulers, were past-masters at playing the Greeks off against other Greeks and the Carthaginians, by doing which they achieved a considerable measure of independence. Longo, our local historian, described Segesta's territory as extending from Capo San Vito at the far end of the Gulf of Castellamare to Carini at the other end (near where Palermo airport now stands), the gulf being then called the Sinus Segestanus. Inland to the south, including the Salemi district, it extended down to the mouth of the river Mazzaro and the present Mazzara del Vallo, to the east of which lay the lands of its rival Selinus, now Selinunte. Segesta occupied much of its time fighting Selinus which, with the help of the Carthaginians, it razed in 408 BC, leaving what is still a vast sprawling ruin on the seashore south of here.

There is some controversy about the original name of the city: was it Egesta or Segesta? Tempers rose over the question and a great deal of energy was consumed in the debate: Aeneas, and Acestes, and Thucidides, Strabo and other classical historians were brought into the fray. Although he in no way resolved it, Leandro Alberti, writing in 1561,[2] summed up the various schools of thought and concluded: 'Onde a me pare poca la differenza di questo nome, o' vogliono dire Egesta o' Segesta' ('Thus the difference in this name appears to me slight, whether they want it to be Egesta or Segesta'). While the controversy continued to rage, however, the prevailing theory seems to have been that the original name was Egesta, but that the Romans, fastidious about incredibly small things, added the S to avoid a connection with the Latin word for poverty. Or, as Alberti has it, 'Et accioche non fusse da questo nome pigliato da cattivo augurio, vi fu poi aggiunta la lettera S, e cosi ella fu detta Segesta' ('And so that it was not overtaken by bad omens because of this name, the letter S was later added, and so it was called Segesta').

Currently, 180 hectares have been expropriated for excavation and EU funds have been earmarked, although they were held up for a time by various legal delaying tactics, and time was also lost because of legal manoeuvring by one of the would-be subcontractors which failed in its bid for some of the ancillary work. There is still much to do as most of the city is still buried, but some of the walls, gates and houses have been brought to light. According to the archaeologist

Sebastiano Tusa,[3] Segesta at its zenith produced oil, wine and corn; linen, wool and silk were woven; and the clay soil was used in the production of earthenware. There were two temples and at least one beautiful, venerated statue, which you know about. The lovely sanctuary of Mango was only 'discovered' in 1957 (though it was known to our friend Longo, among others, much earlier), down on the other side of the hill. Despite sackings by the Carthaginians and Vandals, there was a certain continuity of occupation during the ensuing centuries, to which the mosque, the Norman castle (very small: perched on the top of the hill and visible from our house across the valley), a mediaeval church and successive small houses and burial sites bear testimony.

The temple was never finished, its thirty-six columns were never fluted and the *cella*, or altar, was never built. But it is one of the finest examples in existence. The proof that the temple was not partially destroyed in some armed conflict, but was in fact never completed, was revealed for the first time by a Calatafimi lawyer and archaeologist, Giuseppe Leonora, who had been entrusted by the government in 1834 to excavate the stylobate, which was up to that date still underground. (Stylobate is one of those many words I have assumed I knew the meaning of, but didn't: it is the base of a row of columns.) He showed that instead of the rubble of a destroyed *cella*, which would have been expected, the steps were still covered with the original pebbles that had been placed there to roll the blocks of masonry up into position for their assembly into columns. There were only traces left of the foundations for the corners and the portico on which the *cella* was to have been built.[4] Leonora and others have put forward the hypothesis that its unfinished state was the reason why the temple was not destroyed by zealous early Christian iconoclasts or the Saracens – because it had never been consecrated to the worship of a rival god.

The theatre, which had been able to seat 4,000 spectators in its heyday, has an incomparable view over the valley to Mount Inici and the sea in the Gulf of Castellamare beyond, but it was built later, around the second century BC. It was altered by the Romans, when the orchestra and the area in front of it were enlarged so that other sorts of shows – Freeman says the Romans could not do without the 'disgusting' blood contests they were accustomed to see in Rome – as well as plays, could be put on. In the late Roman period it fell into disuse, and during the middle ages some of its material was used for building houses on top of the original structure. By the beginning of the nineteenth century, the theatre was almost completely overgrown; with a mandate from the King in 1822, the Duke of Serradifalco began excavating it and had partially restored it by 1833, not perfectly but at least with the original material that had been used for the mediaeval houses. The Duke is much respected by historians and did sterling work, but his standards would hardly be considered acceptable in this day and age.

The amateur nature of his work, though also his open-mindedness, is illustrated by a short visit that was paid to the site during 'the autumn holiday season' in 1833 by a teacher named Niccolò Maggiore, with the purpose of distracting himself from 'la monotonia delle scuole'.[5] He travelled in company with a monk who taught philosophy at the monastery of San Martino called Father Matteo Naselli and a young friend who showed promise in drawing and architecture, Saverio Cavallari. Maggiore noted with satisfaction how Serradifalco had bared the structure of earth and revealed nineteen rows of simple stone seats. The twentieth row, according to him, was originally made up of more imposing seats, with backrests and room for the feet underneath. Thirty-seven pieces of stone which fitted this description had been left lying in the orchestra awaiting a decision on where they should be placed. Maggiore, on his own initiative, had three of them positioned as the twentieth row. On his return to Palermo (and no doubt the 'monotony of the schools'), he reported to the Fine Arts Commission of which the Duke was President, who agreed with his assessment and ordered the other thirty-four pieces of stone to be placed on the twentieth row of the seats under the direction of the young Cavallari, who had stayed behind to carry out some drawings for the Duke.

Last year in Covent Garden I bought two prints of the theatre, viewed from above and below, which illustrate the results of this restoration: they are dated 1834 and 1835 at the Royal Military Lithographers in Naples and, between *Serradifalco dir.* at the bottom left-hand side and the name of the lithographer (*Wenzel dis.in lit.*), appears *Sav.Cavallari dis.* So they were the result of what he had stayed behind to do. The problem is that I can only count nineteen stone seats in the twentieth row: there must be some explanation for what happened to the other seventeen, but I have not been able to unearth it. Unfortunately, in 1993 modern archaeologists discovered that the theatre had originally been much larger than thought, and that part of the higher area of the site had been used as a Muslim necropolis as well as a place for mediaeval housing.

Even before the good Duke, archaeological work had been carried out by Gabriele Lancellotto Castelli, Prince of Torremuzza, who was also a respected pioneer in the preservation of Sicilian antiquities. His report on the state of ancient monuments in Sicily dated 1778, which has recently been published,[6] established the pressing need to preserve the temple and the theatre at Segesta without suggesting that any attention needed to be paid to the city remains, a policy which continued until not long ago. At his suggestion, King Ferdinand III had two of the temple's columns, which had apparently been knocked down by lightning, set up again in 1788, and commemorated the fact by arranging for a long thin white marble slab to be placed there announcing in large letters: *Ferdinandus Regis Augustissimi Providentia Restituit Anno MDCCLXXXVIII*. This slab, as I shall show you, was the subject of much comment by early visitors to Segesta.

The next person on the scene, in 1809, actually carried out excavations and discovered some burial sites. Roger Fagan[7] was the British Consul at Palermo and was described thus by Longo: 'il Signor Console Inglese Roberto Fagan, virtuoso ricercatore dei pregevoli avanzi dell'antichità Siciliane' ('virtuoso investigator of the important remains of Sicilian antiquity'): his virtuosity, however, had nothing virtuous about it, as he apparently stole all he found and was, strangely enough, used quite recently as a pretext for not letting me, *un inglese*, see a manuscript – an incident which I shall describe to you. If good archaeological work was carried out by the Duke of Serradifalco, as we have seen, the first scientific excavation and serious attempt at the preservation of its results was due to Giovanni Fraccia, who published a series of books about it in the 1850s.[8] He also did sterling work but was dogged by controversy, which I suspect he found stimulating. I came across a pamphlet of his – in a fighting mood, he begins by establishing that he was 'not an Alcamese, but a Palermitano living in Alcamo' – dated 12th November 1859:[9] it was written in reply to article that had been published by a certain Giuseppe Bandiera in the *Gazetta* of Palermo a few days earlier, commenting on a speech made by the Secretary-General of the Trapani Fine Arts Commission, which was complimentary to Fraccia. The trouble was that a large part of the speech had been ignored by Bandiera and Fraccia badly wanted it remembered.

The speech had explained that Fraccia had been entrusted by the central Fine Arts Commission, and hence also the local Calatafimi Commission, to take care of all the excavations at Segesta and of the monuments that could be brought to light, during which he (Fraccia) 'did not omit to publish beautiful illustrations' as well as the detailed results of his labours. Although he was well versed in matters of archaeology, he 'came up against opposition from the local Commission, and the work did not enjoy much progress.' It went on to say that the Secretary-General had asked Fraccia for a report on what was going on, but that in the meantime he (Fraccia) had been informed that excavations were to begin again without his being involved; that the local Commission had also received a further grant of 100 ducats but that Fraccia had not been consulted. This was the passage that had been omitted in Bandiera's article. It seems obvious that the locals were trying to ease him out of the picture.

In the pamphlet Fraccia makes it clear that he had been the first person to propose the excavations in 1854, and that the results had been published by him the following year; that at the beginning of 1856 he had tried to resign from his position for reasons set out in his second book, published by Solli in 1856; that the local Calatafimi Commission would not let him do any work although at the same time it would not accept his resignation; and that, when the Secretary-General had asked the Commission to put him back to work, it had not complied but had entrusted the work to others. Compelled to remain inactive since November 1857, he had been vainly asking the government to assess the situation and make a decision. Meanwhile, the work he had initiated had gone ahead with twice the money he had had at his disposal, as well as a further grant of 100 ducats. Whether the work was badly or well done, he declined all responsibility for it, but demanded the right to study the results for inclusion in the second part of his next book on the Segesta excavations. The first part, *Egesta ed I suoi Monumenti*, had concluded as follows:

> And so, despite everything, we have no satisfaction and we pray for God's help for the completion of the second volume, which we desire to publish as soon as possible, if we continue to enjoy the encouragement and comfort which comes from the compassion of good people and the support of that public opinion which alone gives us satisfaction, whose favour only matters for us, and from whose judgement only do we hope for justice, reparation and – sole recompense – *an honoured name*.

It took me a long time to find the follow up to the first volume of Fraccia's. In the end, I found it on my doorstep in the local Calatafimi library. It is a bit of a let-down. The title is *Preventiva Sposizione di Taluni Monumenti Segestani Inediti e di Talune Nuove Ricerche Archeologiche* (Palermo, Nocera, 1861). The title could be translated as: 'Pre-Emptive Publication of Certain Unpublished Segestan Monuments and Certain New Archaeological Research'. Fraccia puts a leash on the furies of his first volume: he does not even refer to the dispute. What he declares is that he must rush to publish, because

> in the publication of matters concerning monuments and the expression of certain ideas, it is our duty to lay our claim to the originality, the ownership, the right of priority and independence of which we believe we should be rightly jealous and of which we should be careful not to be defrauded.

So he rushes this small book on the numismatics of Segesta into print, promising subsequent volumes on other more important aspects. I presume somebody was trying to put a rival book out. Whatever the case may have been, I cannot trace any subsequent volumes.

The last thing I can find of Fraccia's is a splendidly violent diatribe against the Royal Decree concerning Sicilian Antiquities dated 31st August 1861, i.e. after the establishment of Piedmontese rule in a partially united Italy. It fulminates against the bungling amateurs and swindlers who had been involved in the administration of antiquities – it had led, among other things, to the abandonment and destruction of a mosaic floor he had discovered in Segesta – which had been inherited by the new Piedmontese system. It is an attack on the Decree which was throwing money at non-existent problems (for instance, Segesta was falsely said to be 'threatened with ruin') and suggesting that the money might be being diverted to less cultural ends. It is an impassioned plea for a new administration of Supervision, Inspectors and Custodians, a Museum, an Academy and Publications to be run by professional archaeologists, and indeed – to strike a modern note – for the nationalization of archaeological sites. He notes that the site of Segesta belonged to a Trapanese convent at the time. It ends with a heartfelt outburst pleading that the truth be made public and the system completely reorganized. Exhausted he sinks once again into silence.

While the situation was entirely different, it does remind me of the warmth of the debate about the 'Mystical Park'. Emotions run high where Segesta, and money, is concerned. There was in fact another attempt at developments causing environmental damage near the temple in 1927. On 19th July the Prefect of Trapani wrote to the Superintendent of Mediaeval and Modern Arts at Palermo that a large storehouse was being built on the road to Segesta,[10]

> to be precise near the imposing temple, obstructing the marvellous immediate and distance view...It is to be deplored that the Custodian has not felt the need to denounce this disgrace to the Higher Authorities ...while the genius of the Duce meets sacrifices and expenses to enhance our artistic glories in the eyes of foreigners, there are other ignorant and selfish individuals...

The Prefect added a hand-written note,

> please take energetic action to suspend the construction near the Segesta Temple, a construction which has not been in any way authorized, indeed there has been a court order against it.

Same old story. But in this case the storehouse did not get built. At this very moment, however, the shell of an enormous 'commercial centre' and of a 'chapel' have been erected on the hill opposite the theatre and, although work has been temporarilly 'suspended' while bye-laws and environmental regulations are properly consulted, who knows whether protests by private citizens will equal the Duce's sacrifices or be enough to halt these new 'ignorant and selfish individuals'. *Speriamo*.

A custodian has just been mentioned. There is one such I should have liked to know more about. He is mentioned by G. De Nervo in 1833, intriguingly: 'Le garde-ciceron, J-B Catalano, revêtu de son uniforme à collet rouge, nous y attendant [at the theatre], eppuyé sur sa carabine' ('The guard-guide, J.-B. Catalano, dressed in his red-collared uniform, waited for us, leaning on his rifle').[11] He also talks of an inscription 'still in the guide Catalano's hut'. Apparently he was not a very reliable employee: because the archpriest Cosentino of Calatafimi, who took charge of Segesta after Fraccia's demise, sent a series of letters in 1855 and 1856 to the Fine Arts Commission at Palermo concerning Catalano's dereliction of duty. I wonder what on earth he had got up to. It was when I was trying to find

Cosentino's papers that my attempt was unfortunately brought to a halt by the misdeeds of that English consul at the beginning of the nineteenth century. Of course the memory of Consul Fagan did not actually debar me for long but it was referred to. I have not been able to find the papers – they are in Calatafimi, but the person who holds them stoutly maintains they are lost – and Catalano must remain an intriguing mystery.

After Fraccia, archaeological activity at Segesta was for some time rather undistinguished. More recently the facilities for visitors have been improved. They include a bar and the building of an access road to the theatre and a parking space at the top of the hill. The road managed to cut through two city-wall systems and cover a large number of ancient buildings with tarmac. The clearing of the parking space removed many mediaeval remains, and its site is right in the middle of the monumental area of the city. Both road and parking space will go soon and a return will be made to the original road system, which is currently being excavated.

Although serious excavations did take place after Fraccia, it was not until after the Second World War that the major breakthrough was made. That was when the outlines of the great city began to emerge from the Mediterranean vegetation. Sebastiano Tusa was in charge from 1953 till 1981, and the Scuola Normale di Pisa has been involved since 1986, the work being carried out by their Laboratorio di Topografia Storico-archeologica del Mondo Antico. Their latest report was published in 1995. The object of all these years of work, generously funded by the EU, has been the 'reconstruction of the urban form' of Segesta, which had been consistently neglected since Torremuzza's report at the end of the eighteenth century in favour of the 'Temple and the Theatre at all costs'. The first thing they had to do was to persuade everyone then owning land on the site to sell it to the demesne. With some difficulty they managed to do this, except for a patch of land where the bar stands now. When that was achieved, the whole area had to be fenced in, a cable-duct built around it, and a dirt road round the perimeter – much of it following the Regia Trazzera Tempio,[12] an old royal track where earlier visitors had ridden on their mules, leading to the sanctuary of Mango.

Solutions having been found for these confoundedly difficult legal problems, the work of revealing the city began. The archaic rock-dwellings on the hill – half caves, half houses, with wells, cisterns and food-storage facilities – became visibile, although dating them is difficult because successive centuries used them in different ways. Three defensive systems were revealed. The first, lowest down, was the most spectacular: the *porta di valle* brought to light walls, a magnificent gate (at points six metres tall), ramparts for catapults, storage-rooms for stone projectiles, bunkers for soldiers, and so on. They date from the fifth century BC. Later on in the second half of the third century BC, another defensive wall was built higher up the hill: its existence was discovered in 1993. Further above still, was the Roman wall, dating from the second century: I presume the town must have been decreasing in importance by then. Extensive work was done on the acropolis which, with the theatre, constituted the essential features of an 'international hellenistic metropolis'. The Romans changed all that by radically restructuring everything in the second half of the second century BC so that the city conformed to the ideal of a Roman colony at the time – and possessed luxurious private houses with peristyles and polychrome stucco, and a modernized theatre for the latest shows from town, so making it a small colonial capital in the Roman empire. This was when they changed the name from Egesta to Segesta. The theatre itself, which had not only been modified by the Romans, was subject to a great deal of study, and an almost perfect model was constructed as a guide for future restoration. Work was also done on the mediaeval ruins, and the surprise remains were revealed of an Arab settlement of the first half of the twelfth century: houses, a necropolis and a mosque. There was also work done on the Norman and Swabian remains. The work continues and the city is slowly sloughing off its earthy shroud. The latest discovery is yet another wall, even earlier than the *porta a valle*, which has just been unearthed: it is much further down, and even includes the temple within its bounds, which has disturbed the theories about whether or why it was never completed. It is still too early for an overall picture to emerge, but initial evidence suggests that this wall may have been systematically destroyed; and there are burial remains of North African people in the area. Both of which have led to speculation that the infamous Agathocles may have had a hand in its destruction.

But now is the moment to take you back in time to meet those intrepid travellers. As we saw, the early ones came when there was very little to see, apart from a silent temple overflown by birds of prey and overrun by sheep and cattle, with the odd astonished peasant looking on quizzically. It took them months to get here, but they arrived with their aesthetic, engineering and historical interests intact and they even took part in the polemics about excavation and restoration. It is worthwhile tracing their changing reactions over time. The early visitors in the eighteenth century concentrated more on the accurate drawing, description and measurement of what was above ground for the edification of their peers back home. Then came the sketchers of the ancient remains and, as the nineteenth century progressed, the quiet desolation of the site captured their Romantic thoughts, the measuring stopped and interest in the landscape and the people increased. They usually came by mule or donkey, and were always accompanied, for their personal security but also for guidance, as there were no roads and they did not know how to get there.

I'll start with Count Johan-Herman von Riedesel, an English translation of whose travels in Sicily was published in 1773.[13] He deals with Segesta in one paragraph, which I shall quote in full, since it shows how these early travellers reacted to Segesta: very much with measuring in mind, in this case using palms.

Eight miles from *Alcamo* and two from *Calatafimi*, there appears on a little hill a very perfect temple of the most ancient *Doric* order, such as the temples of *Pesti* are, which you have seen. It is a remaining monument of the ancient town of *Segestus*, but not known to what deity it was consecrated: it has thirty-six columns, thirteen on each side, including those on the corners, and five in the halls, before and behind. There are some peculiarities to be observed in the structure of this temple, which cannot be explained without a drawing; nor are they expressed in my own drawing. The columns have bases, which are two *Neapolitan* palms high, and eight palms broad. The entrance is expressed in the intercolumnia, which are likewise eight palms broad, by a particular excavation on the west side of the temple. Each column has twenty five-palms in circumference, and below the capital they grow narrower, but in a different manner from that of the columns at *Pesti*, *Girgenti* and *Selinunte*, ending with a notch; nor are they fluted, like those of *Pesti* and *Girgenti*. From the manner, I am inclined to believe that the temple at *Segestus* is of later date than the preceding ones. On the same hill, near the temple, are two great round pieces like millstones, of a harder and finer stone than the temple itself; each of these pieces measures six palms and a quarter in diameter, and three palms and a half in height. They seem to be remnants of columns, and not an altar, as I had thought at first, there being none of the characteristics of the latter on them...the same evening I arrived at Trapani (the ancient *Drepanum*) a fine well-built town, in which the salt-works deserve to be visited.

A rapid visit to a 'very perfect' temple, but with all the emphasis on how it was constructed rather than its aesthetics or history. He appears to be unaware that there was a theatre, to say nothing of the remains of the city, although he was not travelling alone: apart from any companions he had, he would have had a guide and he was, in fact, travelling with an escort of soldiers.

Sir Richard Colt Hoare, Bart,[14] left Palermo with a flourish on his tour to Segesta and Girgenti on 1st March 1790, thus:[15]

> I was attended by the following suite: a litter, with two mules; another mule carrying a driver and half a load; and a third with a whole load, namely my bed, kitchen furniture, and many other articles. Also, two other mules, for servants; and two *campieri* as guards. For the litter and six mules I agreed to give two ounces a day, and to the *campieri* twelve carlini.

Before getting down to the serious business of measuring, he notes that the temple

> stands on a gentle eminence, under lofty mountains, and on the brink of a precipice, at the foot of which rushes a narrow torrent. This structure is in a perfect state of preservation; for the damages which it had sustained were repaired, by order of the King of Naples, under the direction of that true lover and protector of antiquities, the Prince of Torremuzza,

and he mentions the commemorative plaque. His opinions, however, were divided on the restoration and the plaque.

Greenhough (*Diario di un Viaggio in Sicilia*, 1803[16]) states categorically: 'this temple must not be considered a picturesque ruin but as a model of architecture on which those who study should form their taste', and starts measuring. There were sturdy debates about whether the site should be excavated and restored or left as it was. Nobody was the winner here, but we are back in the realms of controversy.

The Rev Brian Hill, a few years earlier, in his *A Journey Through Sicily and Calabria in the Year 1791*, states:[17]

All that now remains of Segesta, is one Doric temple, consisting of thirty-six pillars; two rows of fourteen each from the length, and two of six the breadth. Each pillar is composed of several stones, laid like mill-stones upon one another. They are all in their original state of perfection, except three or four, which were repaired in 1781 at the King's expense, as appears by an inscription of white marble placed in front of the building, though in the opinion of most this modern reparation had better have been let alone, as well as what has been done in the same way at Pompeia, near Naples.

Shades of our modern disputes about the correct role of restoration. And the Reverend Traveller was anyway out of sympathy with the royal restorer: 'Next to eating maccaroni, the favourite amusements of the Neapolitan monarch are hunting and shooting...his majesty pursues, or rather murders his game...' etc.

Lt-General Cockburn, who visited Segesta in 1810,[18] was less intellectual in his approach: after suggesting surprisingly that the surrounding country 'would be beautiful cover to draw – here a fox-hunter would be delighted', notes that the King had 'repaired the front, which had been damaged by lightning, and he had the rubbish in the inside cleared away'. This latter fact came in very useful for the general:

> As we determined to breakfast, and rest the mules at Segesta, we brought bread, a kettle, tea, &c. The peasants in the vicinity have a large dairy farm and many cows: they gave me excellent milk and eggs; the muleteer made a fire; my cloth was laid on the pedestal of one of the columns, and with our English appendage to breakfast, viz. a newspaper (of a late date) which lord Valentia[19] had sent me the night before I left Palermo, I made as comfortable a bivouac meal in the ancient temple of Segesta, as if at the best coffee-house in London; and the novelty of it was pleasing.

You can imagine the peasants gawping in disbelief. But there is evidence that they were getting used to this strange rite. Richard Duppa, only a little later towards the end of the 1820s, described a similar surrender to his instincts:[20] 'Under a fig tree, at a distance of half a mile from the temple, we constructed a rude fire-place and a table of loose stones, and enjoyed our breakfast in the English fashion: we then proceeded to Trapani.'

The Duke of Buckingham and Chandos, visiting in 1828, also expressed disdain for the King's poor commemorative plaque and the work of restoration:[21]

> He (*the King*) would have done wiser to have recollected that if the original founder of this stupendous and splendid monument has left no inscription to record his valuable name, his modesty is greater than that of the ostentatious personage who has attempted to hand down to posterity his slight and puerile efforts to stay the hand of Time.

Before the august ducal personage got down to serious sightseeing, there was a musical interlude from early workers in the tourist trade:

> Two wretched blind men, guided by children, came up to scrape a welcome upon two wretched fiddles, which we silenced with a little difficulty and at, indeed, a most trifling expense; which made all parties joyful – us, by what we lost in the shape of music, they by what they gained by a most munificent copper donation...

I bet they were joyful. Although it was quite late in the century serious measuring then took place, including the temperature, the size of the columns, the spaces between them, the floor, the type and size of the rock used, etc. 'I took the measurements exact by rule, and I can answer for their correctness', if you have any doubts. Unfortunately, he had no sextant with him, so the question of the height of the columns was something of a problem. It was soon sorted out.

> One of our party, whose height we measured, stood at the base of a column opposite to where we stood on the extreme opposite side of the temple; another standing where we did, held up a paper perpendicularly opposite to his eye, and upon the edge of it marked first his opposite neighbour's height, and then the height of the whole building, of which, of course, our friend's height stood as a proportional part.

The Duke was well aware that this was not an exact measurement, 'as we could not measure the angle between his head and the top of the building from where we stood', but he was reasonably satisfied that the columns were thirty-five feet high. Against the advice of the local shepherds, the party then decided to go down the ravine behind the temple to find a vast 'unapproachable' cavern where ghosts had been seen to enter. They did not see any ghosts, but two armed men instead, who behaved rather suspiciously and crept out of the cavern. There was alarm at this, but 'I had in my belt the brace of pocket pistols that I always carried with me in Sicily.' By keeping together, the party of five were not only not robbed by the two armed men, but the Duke did not even have to unbelt his pistols. The two armed men must have fled in terror.

Count Auguste de Sayve travelling earlier in 1820 and 1821, was already beginning to get Romantic.[22]

> Now the approach to the temple is defended by masses of thistles, four to five feet high; a single line path leads you to there where formerly sacrifices were performed and where now is the demesne of reptiles and birds of prey.

He also goes on to denounce King Ferdinand's *inscription pompeuse* and says he has never seen 'an antique monument placed in such a savage place as Segesta'. It was actually the first Greek monument he had ever seen. But his profound musings were cut short by a gun shot. It came from a family of nomadic hunters – three men, their wives, a child and three horses – 'Bédouins de Sicile', who according to him wandered round the mountains, shooting their food. They thought he looked hungry and offered him the bird that they had shot, and cooked it on a grill over a wood fire, explaining the cooking technique. An interesting change from English breakfasts, and an unusual account of a French count being given a cooking lesson by Sicilian bedouin.

Even though he did indulge in a few measurements, the tide had turned by the time the Marquis of Ormonde (incidentally his family name was Butler, although Samuel was no relation) wrote in 1850[23] of his first view of the temple as

> ...very striking: It stands in solitary grandeur in the midst of desolate hills. The platform on which it is placed overlooks on one side a precipitous descent...The columns are not fluted, and the spaces between the bases are in many parts not filled up, which injures the general effect by making the pillars look too high. In all respects very complete.

He dismisses 'the remains of a theatre' as being 'in a very dilapidated condition', but, as usual, 'with a fine, commanding view'. Intriguingly, he went on to describe an elderly peasant woman collecting snails:

During the whole of our inspection of the temple and other remains, a custode, gun in hand, was in attendance, apprehensive for the safety of his charge. As we rode home we passed an old lady gathering snails, which are collected and eaten by the people, as they were by the Romans before them; and the descendants of the snails introduced by the latter may still be found about the sites of some of their villas in England. They are not considered as wholesome during the autumn; so, at least, said our host, as we superintended the cooking of our macaroni, to which he made an addition of something which he termed a *galanteria*, and which was an improvement.

The cooking took place at the Locanda di Segesta, an inn at Calatafimi. His interest in snails was shared by many travellers at the time as well as an interest in all sorts of lizards.

There is a different note in later descriptions of Segesta. Following in the tradition of the eighteenth-century Compte de Borch's[24] and Denon's[25] pictorial surveys of Sicily (although they were mainly an attempt to redress the inaccuracies of Brydone), J.F. D'Ostervald in his *Viaggio Pittorico in Sicilia* (published in Italian by Edizioni Giada, 1987, having originally appeared in Paris in 1822[26]) makes comments on his illustrations. He did one of the theatre and two of the temple. Although he gives some measurements and history, his reactions are on the romantic side. When he is talking of the theatre, we hear:

Abandoned for a long time by the Sicilians of today, these ruins, covered with thorns and bushes, have become the haven of snakes and reptiles of all kinds. Wandering hunters in this part of the country often establish temporary camping sites here.

When he is dealing with the temple: 'the temple as it is approached, the effect of which from afar is surprising, does not lose anything in its proportions, and its rough and simple architecture induces one to various considerations which will be dealt with in the next illustration.' That is a close-up view, and his concerns are of a technical and historical nature; but he ends:

from the view which we have given one can judge the picturesque position of the temple and the aridity of the gullies that surround it; in the background one can see part of the city of Calatafimi, dominated by one of those castle-fortresses that the Saracens disseminated throughout the central parts of Sicily.

Gaston Vuillier arrived at full steam by railway at Calatafimi station.[27] Like D'Ostervald, he also drew. Like the American Paton, he also had a bad time at Calatafimi with beggars. This *was* the bad time: his book was published as *La Sicilia* in 1897 at Milan. Like the Marquis of Ormonde, he was interested in crawling life, in his case reptiles. He was conducted to the temple where, in ecstasy – 'in front of us the temple of Segesta, in a severe landscape, appeared as a golden reliquary, with its columns blazing out of the blue sky' – he began to draw. The children who had led him there, began to hunt for lizards, and then, instead of lizards, brought him a young *carabiniere* with his fiancée and their respective families, who wanted to drink a glass of wine with him, knowing he was a foreigner. They all drank marvellous local wine standing up, from the same glass, after which all attention was concentrated on the lizards. A long and fascinating conversation follows, in which perhaps the most interesting part concerns the lizard with the two tails. This animal is extremely rare. When it has been found and put into a bag together with the ninety lottery numbers written on separate pieces of paper, it will come out with the five winning numbers in its mouth, and the world will be yours to command.[28]

This interest of Gaston Vuillier and Lord Ormonde in lizards and snails was shared in the early years of the twentieth century by a young man with a very different background and destiny: a certain Giuseppe Bonanno, better known as Joe Bananas, and a protagonist with Al Capone, Bugsy Siegel, Bugs Moran, Lucky Luciano (also Sicilian) and others in the legendary US gang wars of the 1920s and 1930s. This is what he has to say about Segesta in his autobiography:[29]

> I used to love to ride my pony to the Greek temple at Segesta. This magnificent Doric temple, about ten miles out of town, overlooked my family's farm in the hill country behind Castellamare...The color of the temple would change with the progress of the sun, from soft gold at noon to a bronze at sunset. Swallows nested inside the temple, and green lizards darted in and out of the masonry cracks...On rainy days, I would roam through the temple grounds foraging for snails, which my grandmother fried in garlic.

The future subject of banner headlines in the US press was brought up in his family's home town of Castellamare del Golfo, a few kilometres from Calatafimi, which he must have known quite well before emigrating for the second time to America at the age of nineteen in 1924, to live his well documented existence surrounded by a close network of his relations and fellow townsmen.

There were other interesting animal catches. Quatrefages de Bréau in his *Rambles of a Naturalist*,[30] after complaining about Ferdinand's plaque ('a long slab of not very white marble...like some huge stain'), writes that 'notwithstanding the profound emotions excited by this grand scene, we did not forget that we were naturalists.' One of the party got a *Sytomis phegeenis*, 'the sole European representative of a genus which belongs essentially to Africa': which is more like a large fly than a butterfly. The others: 'after lifting a great number of stones with an immense expenditure of labour, we succeeded in entrapping in our boxes some pretty varieties of lizards and a very fine skink'. This last he goes on to describe at some length and with reference to Pliny. Francis Chenevix-Trench,[31] travelling with friends on horseback towards Segesta, started digging for scorpions, only to be frightened by 'a large and exasperated rat rushing at our faces'. He seemed much more excited by this incident than the sight of Segesta, which he deals with in a matter of fact way, although he did describe the shepherds there as being 'apparelled in garments almost as natural and rude as the very skins and fleeces of their charges'.

Most of these descriptions of the ruins of Segesta come from travellers who were bowled over by the untouched beauty of the temple in the midst of silent desert: the earliest making classical references and taking measurements, and almost all of them with *sic transit gloria mundi* philosophizing and a feeling of unworldliness. The temple's effect on Leonard Woolf was evidently more down to earth, as is revealed in later years when he described first meeting his future wife Virginia and her sister in 1901 in their brother's rooms at Cambridge, when they were all very young:

in white dresses and large hats, with parasols in their hands, their beauty literally took one's breath away, for suddenly seeing them one stopped astonished and everything including one's breathing for one second also stopped as it does when in a picture gallery you suddenly come face to face with a great Rembrandt or Velasquez or in Sicily rounding a bend in the road you see across the fields the lovely temple of Segesta.[32]

Let me end by exposing you to an amusing piece of useless philosophizing by *Anon* (in fact William Young).[33] When he visited the
ruins on 20th August 1772, he writes: 'much the most remarkable
Object there, (and indeed in all Sicily) is a vast Temple of rude Doric
Order, situated on the Summits of a rude rocky Hill.' He then goes
a long way back in time: 'The first Sacrifice was on an Altar shaded
from the profane Eyes by a thick Grove. Man, ever ambitious of
emulating Nature with Art, soon caught the idea of forming the
hallowed Avenue of Stone: The first simple Thought was noble, but
afterwards refined into roof Apartment, and all the Minutiae of
Building, it seemed as if Man, weak, haughty Man, unable to stretch
his Babel Tower to the Heavens, would again attempt to bring the
Almighty to a Level, by confining him within his earthly grovelling
Mansion of Brick and Mortar.' After this eccentric abandonment to
theorizing he did admit that he admired Segesta's temple which was,
anyway, exempt from his moralizing, as neither brick nor mortar had
been employed, and never in all its long history had it had a roof on
it. Despite his cranky theories, Anon was searching for an explanation for Segesta's inexplicable grandeur: for how or why it is so far
from being an 'earthly grovelling Mansion'.

17

Living the Land

I did not come here to slough off city habits and seek regeneration in the fields. I hold nothing fundamental against life in cities. Indeed, I miss many aspects of their social life, and I am sure you will never have noticed any natural aptitude for agriculture lurking in my make-up. So don't imagine me here pruning olive-trees, crashing tractor-gears or indulging in wine-making. While you know that you will not be called on to compliment my wine, you must understand that, although I am not in the throes of amateur agriculture, the working of the land does confront me as I wake up every morning after far from rural dreams – dreams take a long time to adapt and mine still completely involve themes that are alien to my waking life. Bystander I may be. But I am surrounded by what goes on in the fields.

An old saying that lauds the characteristics of various towns in this part of Sicily dubs the citizens of Calatafimi as 'dotti e filosofi' ('educated people and philosophers'), as we saw: this was a diplomatic way of saying that her middle classes could not be bothered with the-day-to day management of their land. Yet, despite this apparent detachment, any wavering of the wind here, any dip in the temperature or any suggestion of a dark cloud is dealt with as a matter of cosmic importance even by people who do not work the land with their own hands. The behaviour of the climate is so much a part of daily life that the *dotti* and *filosofi*, as well as the people who do get their hands dirty, have developed set phrases to deal with any given situation, and conversation can quickly grind to a halt if it comes up against one of these lapidary phrases: they brook no doubts, no debates, no manoeuvres.

There is an appropriate conventional phrase for any given situation; and, as people close to agriculture are not widely known for flouting convention, if one of these phrases is dropped into a conversation it promptly stops. There is nothing deep or philosophical about them, although they sometimes have an elemental ring, as when someone explained to me why hot weather in late autumn is unwelcome: 'nature falls in love again, and when the cold comes there are abortions.' But they are usually basic, simple observations: rain at certain times inflicts *risina* or 'rust' on the corn; at other times *peronospera* on the vine; and when it finally falls after a long drought it 'means bread'. Wind at certain critical stages will damage various blossoms; mist will blight the new growth. March has always been like this; spring isn't what it used to be; the heat is excessive;[1] it's too early/too late; so-and-so has not ploughed yet; the grass is too tender to make ricotta. Such standard agricultural comments are inevitably met with full agreement, and there the conversation ends.

If you enquire about situations or people, the inevitable answer is 'a posto' ('everything in its place, as it should be'); and, if you want to continue talking, you have to change the subject. One man, whom I meet every time I go into the town, is always *a posto* and, since I declare myself to be *a posto* as well, our verbal exchanges end rapidly over a handshake – there is nothing else to say. If conversations on general topics are not quashed immediately by *a posto* or something to do with rain, proverbs are quickly swung into action: there is a proverb for any given situation that nips diversionary dialectic firmly in the bud. One of my favourites, a tombstone on gossip, is 'a verità si dici solu n'ta cunfissionili' ('the truth is told only in the confessional'). What *can* you say after that?

While I am clearly an outsider, it is acknowledged that I just about live here, so I am guaranteed a licence as an accepted semi-native to show off quietly to plain visitors or rank outsiders, which I find very gratifying. Having established that life here is quintessentially rural and that I am passively immersed in it, I'll try to waft up for you the smell of the lost life of Kensington.

There are many Sicilian folk poems and songs that set out the tasks to be done in the fields month by month, and although I know of none that are specific to Calatafimi, the same jobs need to be done here as everywhere, and the centuries-old tradition of ploughing, pruning, manuring, hoeing, burning, cursing, praying, harvesting, giving thanks and complaining has not changed all that much, even if oxen and hoes have given way to tractors. These tasks are dutifully carried out at the appropriate times and everything is *a posto*, except for the weather which is never *a posto* and can only be forecast anyway if you know how to assess the meteorological conditions that appear in the *pirtusu di Vita*, the gap in the hills that screen the village of Vita from Calatafimi: it requires a great deal of native experience but the result is apparently infallible. Interpreting the sky in that quarter does not remove the need to look at the weather-forecast on TV. But it is far more specific to Calatafimi.

To begin with, I must take you back in time because the footprints of several of the invaders I inflicted on you in my potted history have left their mark on the fields here. In Roman times, *latifondi* were the order of the day: these were immense estates given over single-mindedly to the amassing of corn; and the later history of Sicilian agriculture has largely been dominated by vast estates, absentee landlords, private police, heavy taxation and extreme poverty. On the Roman estates, trees were ruthlessly hacked down, slave labour was exploited and every effort was devoted to producing immeasurable quantities of wheat for insatiable, sprawling, ravenous Rome. I have told you about our local gentleman-farmer Phimes, who was mentioned by Cicero in the *Verrine Orations*, and whose name probably accounts for the latter half of the name Calatafimi. He would certainly have worked his land in that way, and what he and his peers on the island grew with sweated labour went straight down the Imperial throat, much to the detriment of this peripheral island's economy. Nothing much was to change over the centuries, and I have offered you one post-Roman case of the Spanish Counts of Modica draining Calatafimi's territory of grain with their *terraggiolo*. Quantities of what they illegally amassed at the expense of their vassals was shipped away via the nearby port of Castellamare del Golfo.

But empires get fat and slovenly, and the Romans were no exception. The hyenas gathered and Sicily succumbed in time to the harrying of the barbarians and the Byzantines, neither of whom contributed much of lasting note to the agricultural development of the island. By the eighth and ninth centuries, however, the Arabs with their reverence for water, were beginning to trickle in, and through them smaller intensive farms began to sprout up. Their influence was particularly strong in this part of Sicily, and their agriculture concentrated more on fruit, vegetables and olives – the big olive trees are still called *saracinu*, or *saraciniscu* to this day. The vocabulary of the fields is peppered with Arabic words, as I have said: one often-recurring example is *gebbia*, the word for the small, deep, cool water-cisterns that are still used to irrigate smallholdings here. While their Norman successors initially took over Arab ways in agriculture, as in almost everything else,[2] the increasing Latinization of the Norman kingdom (that was to be speeded up by the establishment of the feudal system and by their growing, matrimonially-inspired Hohenstaufen Imperial ambitions) favoured a return to the vast estates of previous times. Despite a short-lived attempt by the Aragonese to improve agriculture and to encourage sheep-farming, the endless Roman-style estates continued to hold sway; and successive Spanish governments had little problem luring the major landlords into a life of languor in Palermo, their rambling estates being left to the mercy of tax collectors, agents and enforcers (i.e. the *campieri*, who may have been the origin of the mafia). This made government by remote foreign powers easier to impose, but it did nothing to foster good land-management or achieve a fiscal yield anywhere near the land's potential. The Counts of Modica and other great families held large tracts in the vicinity, mostly on the plain towards Trapani. The County of Modica administered Calatafimi and its territory through a 'Secreto Baronale' (or 'Segreto Barionale') or 'Governatore' who was a local notable and reported to a 'Procuratore' – even more notable – who resided in Palermo and reported to Madrid, where this particular family lived.

The centuries rolled past and changes in Calatafimi's agriculture came and went slowly. As I have mentioned, less emphasis was paid to corn because of the hilliness of the country: silk-farming was practised for a long time (having been introduced to Sicily by the Arabs and much encouraged by the Norman King Roger's monk-admiral George of Antioch[3]); *manna*, a mild purgative, as well as a sweet that is still eaten in the Middle East, was produced by making cuts in the bark of the ash tree (*Fraxinus ornus* and *Fraxinus angustifolia*), as in rubber-tapping, and was much exported; and the best sumach (*Rhus coriaria*) was grown around Calatafimi, Alcamo and Castellamare – it was a valuable crop for the tanning industry and exported in quantity, even, they say, to Persia as a carpet-dye. Linen was, and is, grown, and the local product used to be soaked in the Kaggera river that runs past Segesta. Soda (glasswort) was also grown and pistachio nuts were a flourishing crop, too.

Calatafimi became famous for its *caciocavallo* cheese. In an old folk poem describing things for which Palermo and various western Sicilian towns were famous, Calatafimi was dealt with second (after Palermo, which was famous for its coaches, horses and gardens), and was praised for these cheeses, which are no longer made here. Other local towns were famous for terracotta jars (Sciacca), big sardines

(Mazzara), different sorts of fish (Marsala), beautiful girls (Erice) and red coral (Trapani).[4] It was clearly an oldish poem because Marsala, down the coast, was not yet being mentioned for its fortified wine that had been invented by Yorkshiremen, and was later made famous when Nelson ran out of wine on his way to catch up with Napoleon in Egypt: he had to turn back and stock up with marsala, with which he was apparently impressed because he ordered large quantities of it for his fleet. I only recently came to understand that water was worth far more than alcohol on board ship, which is why alcohol was dished out in daily rations: rum and strong wine sailed well. At the height of their commercial splendour, the Yorkshiremen (the Woodhouses, Inghams and Whitakers) bought grapes in the Calatafimi area, as they also did in the rest of the Val di Mazzara.

By the middle of the second millennium, citrus fruit and olive oil had begun to grow in importance and the vine gradually over-shadowed corn and animal husbandry, at least in the Calatafimi area. Neither the oil nor the wine from Sicily were particularly renowned, the former being widely burnt in oil lamps, and the climate making the latter too strong except for local consumption (although it was exported to France and northern Italy in large amounts to reinforce their weaker products, a fact that is seldom given much prominence). Corn, of course, continued to be grown, if not at Roman levels, be-cause it was a staple food. Sicilian agriculture more or less supported the aristocracy at a level it felt was its due, but it was very much at the expense of the agricultural workers, who did not lead an enviable life. Nothing seemed to change: life in the fields was static, to be borne without complaint. As elsewhere in Europe, we saw that *phylloxera* took its toll at the end of the nineteenth century, and American stock was grafted onto Sicilian vines under government supervision. It happened in Calatafimi, presumably with remittances from the Calatafimesi who had by then emigrated in their hundreds to the USA in search of a better life.

For those who had not left, or could not leave, for Brooklyn, the hours of daylight were exclusively taken up with hard labour. The peasants who worked land for others, or had a bit of their own, would leave their hovels[5] at first light, at the hour of the *Ave Maria*, to stumble home again towards evening when the light began to fade, so as not to be caught out in the fields at dusk, which we know was the time for catching malarial fevers. Those who worked on the big estates slept there and would only return home on Sundays or special days.[6] The two sets of workers had different domestic arrangements and examples of each at Calatafimi are described by Cesare Calcara and Roberto Gambino in their unpublished 1980-1 University of Palermo thesis. I have not been able to get their permission to quote what follows because I could not unfortunately track them down, but they did leave a copy of their thesis in the local public library, and so I assume they wanted their work to be divulged.

The daily labourer, or *jurnataru*, typically lived in a small three-storey house, examples of which can be found all over western Sicily. The one described in the thesis is in via Elia in the Terravecchia, or Borgo Vecchio, quarter, under Calatafimi's castle, and dates from the beginning of the nineteenth century. From the street you enter through a double-door straight into the whitewashed, reed-ceilinged room where food was prepared and eaten. There is an emphasis on bread: in the *maidda*, where the dough was kneaded and left to rise, and the wood-fired oven against the wall, where it was baked. In front of the oven there is the *tannura*, a wood-fired hob – a sort of barbecue, if you like – where other cooking was done. Even now, both the oven and, to a lesser degree, the *tannura* are used, although bread-making at home is rapidly becoming less common. For washing, there was a *pila* or tub and a scrubbing-board, and kitchen utensils were hung on nails in the whitewashed wall together with tools. There is a marble working surface set into the wall – the country around is full of marble, so this was no luxury – and the floor is made of slabs of local gypsum which sparkle in the light. From this room, you go through to a 3.2 x 3-metre stable and storage room: here there were jars of oil, barrels of wine and woven reed-baskets for cereals, as well as the mule or donkey. Under the internal staircase, which leads up to the other floors, there is the lavatory, which has replaced the older *commune*, chamber-pot or close-stool, which was originally placed beside the oven and the *tannura*, its traditional but oddly-chosen position.

Up the stairs, on the first floor, there is a small store-room/cupboard followed by two bedrooms. The first one has no window and little furniture: it was the children's room. The second has a balcony looking over the street and a double bed, the only furniture being a large wardrobe and a chest of drawers. The whitewashed walls have religious pictures nailed on them. Further steps lead up from here to a rather rickety attic where food and other things were stored. Not many people live like this now, but until the 1950s it was quite normal. Although the oven is still much in use on special occasions, the *tannura* has given way to the gas-stove fuelled by cylinders, and there will be a television set, a washing-machine and more furniture than previously. But that description is a fairly recent one. In general, however, the effects of the earthquake and remittances from the emigrants have hauled Calatafimi's citizens well into the twenty-first century. The daily worker still makes for the fields at the break of day and still trails back as the light fails, though without any fear of catching malaria, which was eliminated all over southern Italy after the Second World War through the Marshall Plan – which financed DDT spraying. The fact that it had been done was stencilled on walls and the signs are still visible on some houses. He now travels by car or tractor to the fields. But he will probably still pray with his wife before and after harvesting.

The second form of domestic arrangement described in the thesis is the *baglio*, the *baglio Avila* in this case. Although this particular example was built just outside Calatafimi at the beginning of the twentieth century and was not designed to sleep labourers, it continues a centuries-old tradition, examples of which can still be seen all over western Sicily. The *baglio* (or *bagghiu* in dialect, derived from the Arab word *bahal* meaning courtyard) is a semi-fortified farmhouse built round an internal courtyard that is reached through a main gate in the walls. It was built in the middle of a large estate, and was where sometimes the owners, though more usually their agents and the workers, lived safely and stored their produce while working the land. It was usually the sign of poor, unintensive agriculture, corn cultivation principally and grazing, that was practised over extensive areas of treeless land. Discipline and, theoretically, defence, too, were in the hands of the infamous *campieri*, and the building was usually on high land from which the whole of the estate could be surveyed. There were no permanent peasant buildings outside its walls because nobody lived in the open countryside for fear of bandits or pirates. In recent years, more olives and wine have been cultivated on the land, and the peasants no longer live in. There are around twenty of these *baglios* in the Calatafimi area, though many are in bad repair either from neglect, or due to the effects of the earthquake or, less dramatically but equally sadly and inexorably, because of the inheritance law which destines the house and land to be chopped up into ever tinier utterly useless bits on every death in the owner's family. *Baglios* have recently been declared a type of national heritage and have a measure of legal protection. But their future will probably depend on their being bought up and made into small country hotels, if the various heirs can all be persuaded to sell: usually a Herculean task, particularly if any of them have emigrated.[7]

The *baglio Avila*, small and relatively modern though it is, has the highly functional design of all *baglios*. The central courtyard is about 18 x 18 metres: on one side there is the *macasenu* or storehouse and opposite is the *stada-paghiaru* or stables and hay-barn. These two wings are connected in the middle by the house, and the fourth side is enclosed by a wall and a gate, the archway over which was never completed in this case. In the storage-wing, the wine is kept in barrels and bottles, and there are the silos for the must; and it is here that complicated agricultural work is carried out, produce stored and the larger pieces of machinery are kept. The storage-wing and the stables and hay-barn opposite are exactly the same size, and the stabling section can deal with about half a dozen cows or sheep.

The connecting house has two doors giving onto the paved court-yard. Through the first, there is a big kitchen (about 8.7 x 4.7 metres) with a large oven and a *tannura* cooking surface: this is where the labourers eat. The other door is for the owners or their agents. Through that door there is a small dressing/undressing room, a kitchen, a storeroom and a bedroom (with the inevitable religious prints, but also family photographs) which connects to the larger kitchen. There are two other buildings as you come in at the main entrance: on the right there is a room for storing seeds and cereals, and on the left the room for the man who looks after the machinery and repairs, which is connected to a small store-room with an external door. As it is a recent small *baglio*, there are no sleeping quarters for workers. There are other, much bigger and more com-plicated *baglios* in the vicinity. The original building where we now have our houses was a *baglio*, which used to have a minute chapel until it was taken over by the resident sharecropper's large family – who lived in it until the early 1950s. It is interesting to see that the *baglio* tradition is still being kept alive: recently a fairly large farmer operating in the valley below us needed extensive new outbuildings and he had them built following the same general plan as the old *baglio*, and at least two other neglected ones are being restored in the area and converted into family homes.

Agricultural life has evolved in certain ways, if not as radically as was intended. As a result of the agrarian reforms in the 1950s, a fair amount of Sicilian land (around 250,000 hectares) was redistributed, as we saw, to a wide range of people – labourers, peasants, artisans, shopkeepers, office-workers and professional people – though the original enthusiasm has dwindled somewhat. And it is true that sharecropping is giving way to smallholder cultivation, due both to land reform and also to a regional law which has specified a 60/40 division in favour of the sharecropper (instead of the traditional 50/50 split) under which the owner pays for fertilizers, both of these provisions making things less satisfactory for the landowner.

In the Calatafimi area, vineyards are of increasing importance and some very good wine is being produced: Sicilian wine generally is now being exploited as it should be and not exported as a commodity in tankers. In particular, half-forgotten traditional grapes like Inzollia and Nero d'Avola, to name but two, are being vigorously cultivated in their own right, and they are greatly appreciated around the world. Grapes are being harvested earlier as well, so that the wine is no longer overpoweringly strong. Previously, when it was left longer on the vine, it was capable of reaching 17° without fortification, the strength of a strong sherry, which is a bit high for a run-of-the-mill lunch, unless you are used to it. Plastic greenhouses for forcing early, though locally consumed, produce have made their ugly appearance; mushrooms are cultivated in the darkness of the old railway tunnel; somebody is even toying with ostriches. But backbreaking work in the fields remains the general rule, even if tractors can be hired by the day and brought to your doorstep on a lorry. I think, however, that the toilers today are probably better off than they would care to admit – certainly than they were – and almost everybody has a piece of land. The basic products are wine, oil and grain; and the red-letter days in the agrarian calendar are when these are harvested.

The wine-making process usually gets under way in December. Tractors are brought out into the green fields and set to plough between the vines, churning up broad bands of red-brown earth on either side of rows of golden-brown vines, in the middle of strips of vividly green grass – creating beautiful patterns rather like enormous tiger-skin rugs flung carelessly over the hills. The effect doesn't last long, because the green grows back quickly, in a matter of days. Ploughing, hoeing, pruning, tying and spraying eventually coax green shoots and tendrils out of the gnarled dark-brown stubs that will eventually support the heavy bunches of grapes that were formerly

harvested during an October *vendemmia*. Then school was suspended, whole families moved into the country and everybody enthusiastically got down to the work of picking. Pitrè has a chapter
describing typical *vendemmias* in the nineteenth century.[8] There were
up to a hundred people involved and work was clearly divided between males and females, the latter picking, the former carrying.
Simple food was doled out at 8 am and 12 am in the morning and at
sundown. The grapes were carried to the *palmetto* or treading-floor
where mules or up to five barefoot men trod them. At sundown, after
the food, the fun began. The music of flutes and bagpipes together
with the tambourines of the women accompanied the singing, joking
and flirting of the workers till around 2 am and, according to Pitrè,
this went on every day for two months. Before and just after the last
war, with the involvement of many less than a hundred men, the
grapes here too at San Giovanni were rendered into must and wine;
but the earthquake has eradicated all traces of the *cantina* where this
was done. The sharecroppers had their baskets of picked grapes
recorded with notches cut in a ferule reed. At the end of the picking
process, after all the baskets had been duly recorded, the ferule reed
was split vertically across the notches: one half was kept by the
patron and the other was retained by the sharecropper as a receipt
for his part of the crop. After the evening meal (usually consisting of
pasta with fava-beans and vegetable broth, accompanied by ample
wine), Caterina's father recalls the songs and the rough, simple games
that were played, mostly by the men and boys to the exclusion of the
females – although there was one called the *cutra* or 'tablecloth'
which involved putting a couple, supposedly chosen by chance,
together under a cloth, leaving them for a certain period of time
(usually a generous one), and then slapping them through the cloth
until they gave up and came out sheepishly. That was considered
rather *osé*.

The process has become more prosaic if less harsh now since the
grapes, still picked in family groups, are transported in lorries lined
with plastic sheeting to the local co-operative for pressing and vini-
fication. In September, rather than October. In spite of the plastic
sheeting, some of the premature must does slop out onto the road,
so there is a heady smell of *vendemmia* in the countryside. There is
still a mule at Calatafimi, however, which patiently goes the rounds
on its *palmetto* – he is blindfolded and tied to a central pole, and
trudges ever onwards, pressing the grapes of people who do not

produce enough to make it worthwhile taking their harvest to the co-operative. The badinage lives on in the voices and laughter ricocheting for kilometres around in the normally silent countryside – from coloured dots of people in the distance, slowly picking their way up and down rows of grapes.

Unlike the *vendemmia*, the grain harvest has become fully mechanized. When the wet-green freshness of the early spring corn has given way to the dry yellow expanses of June, enormous combineharvesters, with flashing lights, preceded by cars brandishing flags, block the narrow country roads as they grimly stalk towards the fields, and then gobble up the corn and slowly trundle off on their menacing way to do the same thing somewhere else. It used to be an event like the *vendemmia*, but there is no more cutting with the sickle and tying up of the sheaves, transporting by mule, and practical-joking despite painfully tired limbs. Lunch then was a matter of bread and tomato; then it was back to work because it was a race against time and the danger of fires, or even of an early summer thunder-storm. Dinner was around a long trestle-table on which, without plates or cutlery, *pasta con le fave* was spread out, and everybody scraped towards himself with his hands what he thought he could eat. A demijohn of wine was passed round, each person quaffing and cleaning it before passing it on to his neighbour. And then the games and welcome sleep before the next grinding day.

As in wine-making, the threshing process used to be carried out by blindfolded mules *in situ*: they tramped round and round over the corn, until it was separated from the ears and the winnowing process could take place, hopefully with the help of a little wind. This was dusty work and the straw hats and coloured handkerchiefs, that were used, though attractive, were strictly functional. The incredibly hard work was accepted. Much of its harsh inevitability is revealed in a brief memoir of Caterina's father's when, in 1940, he went to witness the harvest on his land in Acqua Salata, on the other side of Calata-fimi. His overseer had just been called up into the army, but his wife was working as usual. As there were no roads there at the time, he rode up to the only tree on his land, a fig tree, when his horse suddenly made an unexpectedly abrupt movement. The reaction of the overseer's wife was instantaneous:

Careful, be careful! There's a baby there. Born last night. He's just there, under the tree.[9]

The woman's name was Gna Ciccia; within a few hours of giving birth and without her husband's support, asking no questions, and making no complaints, she just got on with the unavoidable job of earning a piece of bread for her and what were now her seven children. That sort of thing doesn't happen any more, but it was not all that long ago. Thank God for the combine-harvester.

The olive harvest is the third pivotal event in the agricultural and social year. The trees begin yielding their best after ten years or so and carry on giving it for at least a hundred. Ploughing around the trees and anti-parasite spraying are regular necessities, the ploughing, to keep the humidity from evaporating from the earth, taking place fairly often, and the spraying seldom more than twice a year. Pruning goes on until May when blossoming takes place, although it will inhibit the yield for a year. The fruit forms in June and it is disastrous if it rains then. The goodness of the harvest can be assessed in September or October. Table olives are picked and prepared half way through October; but the main picking takes place in November. In Sicily, they do not beat the olives off the trees with a pole as they do in Calabria, and they look down on Calabrian oil that is harvested in this way. They place a net under the tree and pick the olives off, only shaking the branches if the olives cannot be got at by hand, although modern pruning techniques keep the tree low and wide, so that most of the fruit can easily be reached. In the past, the olives traditionally had to lie in a dark covered place for some time, because the water content was somehow supposed to exude from them, before they were taken to the press. Now they are taken to the press immediately, and the sooner the better because they begin to ferment very quickly.

Olive-picking is also a happy time, but perhaps not as jolly as the *vendemmia*. There is the singing and talking and badinage, but the autumnal weather takes some of the pleasure out of the process – in the morning there will be dew on the grass. The olives come off easily and there is a good deal of satisfaction to be had, for an amateur at least, in filling up your small wicker hand-basket to the top and then listening to the noise produced by pouring its contents into a larger wicker container: it is a soft roar, rather like a far-off underground explosion. The dogs follow the pickers enthusiastically to the fields and then, for some inexplicable reason, fall into a deep sleep under the trees, and are loath to move when it's their tree's turn. Pickers work as a group (many of them made up from families) and are getting more and more difficult to find: they are usually paid with half of the oil produced. There is a German lady in our picking group, the lady I mentioned earlier on, who has been in Calatafimi for forty years and speaks perfect dialect – she says picking olives is not as hard as picking grapes and certainly much easier than picking tomatoes. But she enjoys doing them all.

Later on, in the evening, there can be infernal happenings at the press because, since Nature matures all the same kinds of fruit, not least olives, at precisely the same moment; everybody converges on the press together; and nobody wants to waste time waiting in line. It can be chaos at some of the mills: the arguments, sometimes resolved by social clout or even physical strength, sometimes by cunning, take the growers and the producers until the small hours to sort out, with endless promises that you will be next in line, and often with rapid sack movements if you have the courage or the stupidity to go out and sip a calming cup of coffee. Though not all the mills are like that. And I, the simple bystander, have the privilege of being a guest without the worry of having to stand my ground in the queue. I cannot describe the smell of the pressing; it is not to be found in the orchards, where the pleasure is purely tactile, one of stripping the trees of olives with the fingers and accumulating a palpable quantity. The smell of just-crushed olives is fresh, sweet, menacing and primitive. Words are too rubbery to pin it down precisely: it's a sort of memory-smell.

The pleasure of the harvest is a composite one: denuding hundreds of trees; carrying thousands and thousands of small round bulges of liquid goodness to the mill; anxiously waiting for them to be weighed; hearing the loud roar as they are poured into the enormous metal funnel-container; watching mesmerized while mountains of them disappear slowly down into a hole at one end of a long, gleaming aluminium digestive tract; smelling that smell; and listening to the green liquid softly filling the containers as it comes out at the other end: half for the pickers, and half for you. Only about 20% of the olive is oil, the rest being water and what is left after the pressing, and the percentage can be higher or lower, depending on when it last rained. It can be disappointing if it rains just before the picking, as the fruit needs time to turn the water into oil. But there it is at the end of the gleaming line of machinery – the result of a year's growth – safely waiting to be taken home, already divided into containers under the images of the Madonna on the walls and surrounded by gleaming happy faces. The mills work all night at harvest time.

My relationship with oil has become more intimate since I first accompanied it from tree to bottle: I now recall the dew, the leaves, the blackened hands, the chatter, the smell of the crushing and the smooth, slow filling of the containers. I suppose that if you are the farmer, it has a different taste. The oil, incidentally, is calculated in *cafisi* not litres: in Calatafimi a *cafiso* is 8.75 litres, although in other villages the measure is completely different. I would bring you a few *cafisi* of our oil on my next trip to London, if they did not discourage carrying oil and cheese on planes – Palermo airport is full of stern notices to this effect. Sicilians are acutely aware of how their family and friends appreciate the old home tastes, and airline officials are equally aware that these tastes spill easily and/or smell. They will only accept oil in hermetically sealed cans. These can be procured. But this year Brussels has come up with another exquisite complication: if you transport oil, it has to have a regulation label on it, so I presume I should not only have to put the oil in such a container but produce a form in triplicate to prove it was family oil and not bought from some evil peasant trying to outwit the European Union. It would be easier if you just came and enjoyed it here.

I believe the lives of most of our neighbours are directly or indirectly concerned with four basic actions, after their seeds have been safely sown: cutting, breaking, gathering, crushing. Whatever else it does, the whole town depends on the outcome of these actions. Pruning and grafting, ploughing and hoeing, picking and cutting, grinding and pressing. Have you ever thought about the importance of crushing? Corn, grapes and olives are all crushed for our benefit. Even stepping casually on a seedpod sets off a useful natural process. These basic actions have to be modified, of course, for farmers who are not involved in cultivation: shepherds and herders need to have squeezing added to the list. Cutting and breaking are not required with them, and gathering and crushing are dealt with by the animals themselves. But they do need to be squeezed. For the majority, however, the four basic actions are central and at the end of each process leftovers have to be burnt, which sets off silent white smoke-explosions that hover over the evenings.

Caterina's cousin and a friend decided some years ago to pick the olives from her trees by themselves. We were away that day, but in a moment of blissful innocence Blasco – you know how considerate our son is – decided that the girls needed some refreshment. So he filled a basket with biscuits, ice, lemon, a bottle of gin and some tonic water and proceeded to entertain them pastorally in the orchard. That was two years ago. Last year and this one, too, they again expected gin and tonic, and got it. Another tradition has been grafted on to Calatafimi's agrarian calendar, although it is too late to hope for its inclusion in a new folk song or a saint's festivities. Word will get around, however. Sales of gin will rise, a computer will note it and react, and the mystified local supermarket owner will in time understand that he can only get rid of the extra stock briefly during the olive-picking season.

18

Calatafimi at Table

Lurking in the wings of the 'Republic of Italy' are a whole series of small republics with their own unwritten constitution, bent on their own strategy, just as there are hordes of regional dialects chattering away behind the back of the 'Italian language'. And 'Italian cooking' is not even an elusive reality. The code-word 'pasta' doesn't bear scrutiny, since pasta is openly dished out to you in different forms and with different sauces in different parts of the country, to say nothing of what happens to it beyond the boundaries of Italy. Even 'Sicilian cooking' doesn't really bear scrutiny because the same dishes differ quite considerably from village to village, and the different versions are defended vigorously and volubly against all comers, particularly if they are from the next village. All this will no doubt evaporate in time, but for the moment brave local slave-traditions are still bearing up surprisingly well against the globalized gladiatorial forces that have moved into the aisles of supermarkets, even in such insignificant places as Calatafimi.

Take the sausage, for instance. Each part of Italy has its own version, and so does each area of Sicily. Calatafimi sausages have a particular blend of mountain fennel, chopped-up pork, pepper and salt that makes them unique. Other towns have similar ones, though the ingredients are balanced differently. Which is the best? That is not a permissible question: each village maintains that its own version is the best and cannot be brought to think differently. There is no point in trying. The real conundrum is who *in Calatafimi* makes the best mortal coil of *Calatafimi sausages*? There's the rub. Discussion is not only possible but enjoyed. Like the warm debate about who the best baker in town is, there are partisans of particular sausage-makers within the precincts, and parties are formed. Our family, for instance, is sharply divided over the skills in a certain butcher's shop and those of a butchery assistant in one of the supermarkets (yes, a supermarket, where they are made by hand and very well). But other houses champion other contenders. So I could go as far as arguing that there is no single 'Calatafimi sausage' as such, because sausages differ from ward to ward. While that might be going too far, it does illustrate how vital it is to get food right, whether it is home-cooked or bought, and how, if your guests agree with your choice of ingredients or suppliers, you will gain kudos for having chosen wisely – in the endless discussions that accompany every meal.

Regional diversity and local partisanship are at the heart of eating in this part of Sicily and are among the major ingredients in those critical conversations. Inevitably, eating in the country, while still being the pleasure it ought to be, is also something of a front-line activity since you will often have had a personal relationship with what you are putting into your mouth. You may have seen the bird flapping as you fed it, patted the animal in its frisky early years, seen the milk turning into cheese, the bud into fruit; or have known the chicken sitting on the egg that she might have thought possessed the right to become another chicken. Humans caught red in tooth and claw, but blissfully unaware of the fact, and licking their lips.

I'll start you, *dulcis in fundo*, with the sweet things at the end of the meal. Most places in Sicily have their own special cakes for particular times of the year. They are usually connected with religious festivals. There are some that involve the whole island like the *buccellato* at Christmas, marzipan sheep for Easter, or the *cannolo* and the *cassata* (you at least know by now that this is *not* an ice-cream but a *cake*); but even these have hotly defended local variations. There are many more that are entirely localized. The cakes that are either exclusively or particularly associated with Calatafimi are these. *Cuddureddi*, also at Christmas, a sort of *buccellato*, is made out of crown-shaped pieces of pastry filled with chopped-up dried figs and fruit with sugar. At San Giuseppe, on 19th March, *cucciddati* are made in various forms but mainly as crown-shaped pieces of bread: the altar of the little church in via Garibaldi ('la chiessetta'[1]) is covered with sculpted bread in all forms and shapes for the festa of San Giuseppe, although this custom is more typical of the nearby town of Salemi, where they have perfected the art. At Easter people here still make the marzipan Paschal lamb at home in moulds of fired clay, as they do in other parts of Sicily, but they also produce the unique local *cannattura*, which is bread with a coloured egg in the middle and sculpted bread-decorations on the sides. At the Procession of the SS Crocifisso, *cucciddati* were always thrown to the crowd, but over the ages they have been joined by all sorts of nuts –

sugared almonds, pistachios, peanuts, hazel nuts, in particular. On the second Saturday in November, for the festival of the builders in Calatafimi, *muffolette* (that is, small round loaves of soft bread) are distributed to the citizens filled with sugared cottage-cheese.

Bread forms the base of many of these special cakes, and bread is still the symbolic food for sustaining life, and is an essential part of any meal. It is much revered, but few people make it at home now. Caterina remembers its preparation when as a child she spent the summers in the country: the whole ritual from the preparation of the *levatina*, a piece of dough kept over from the previous bake, which, with added flour and water, was covered with cloths and left to rise overnight, in time for the kneading of the new dough in the very early morning and for baking it in the wood-fired oven a little later. She still becomes excited when she remembers tasting it hot and fragrant from the oven, dowsed in olive oil and seasoned with oregano and salt. Special small rolls were made for all the children and enough dough was left over to make pizza with your own tomatoes, cheese, oil and pungent oregano.[2] That was for everybody, but in the afternoon she and her brothers were given special bits of bread and sugar by her grandmother on the sly, although these had to be eaten away from the eyes of the other less fortunate children.

'Wild' – if that's the right word – vegetables, are still picked and eaten here regularly: borage and *cavuliceddi*, for instance, the former 'a blue-flowered hairy-leafed plant used in salads' (Arabic: *Abu arak*, father of sweat, 'from its use as a diaphoretic', *OED*), and the latter a wild, bitter member of the cabbage family. When they are in season, the countryside is dotted with people armed with knives and plastic bags intent on collecting them for the table. And there are three different types of wild asparagus that are found under trees, especially olive trees: the harvesters of these are less noticeable, but they are assiduous, and you may curse aloud at neatly snipped slender spears in the most unlikely places and be surprised that even the local shops sell some of the resultant bunches. In autumn, when the time comes round to pick oregano in the countryside, it is comic to see people nonchalantly trying to put other people off the scent as they make their careful way to their favourite spot. The plant is fastidious and does not grow everywhere, and when it does it is often not very copiously, so there is a lot of looking over one's shoulder. *Giri* or *erbette*[3] (one of the many forms of wild chard) are picked in the countryside and cooked as vegetables during most of the year. In the

spring the hunt is on for fennel. There are two types; the normal
dill, which is seldom used here, and the *finocchio di montagna*, the
'mountain' fennel with its curly leaves, which are picked for season-
ing almost everything, though fava-beans, salads and pastas in particular, and most famously, *pasta con le sarde* (one of the best known
'Sicilian dishes', but not a speciality of Calatafimi): the seeds are used
in nearly all varieties of Sicilian sausage. In the summer the stalks
and leaves of 'long' courgettes, called *tenerumi*, are used for a delicious summer soup-pasta, though these are cultivated. The various
herbs and fruit all ripen at the same time, so you can become in-
undated with one type. You eat them fresh or dry or conserve them;
otherwise they rot. They are put into salads, meat dishes, jams, pastas
– anything to make sure they do not go to waste. Pasta is combined
with peas, cauliflowers, beans, fennel, aubergines, almonds, olives,
the Sicilian 'long' marrows and their leaves, and just about anything
else whether vegetable or not: the same can be said of soups. Everything is used in its season, even to excess, because it is right and
seemly that everything that comes up in the earth should go down the
throat with nothing being left to waste. None other than Edward
Lear seems to have been a victim of this seasonal despotism when,
travelling with Proby in 1847:

> they soon found the island hot, dirty and poor, and, in Calatafimi,
> where they stopped, they could buy nothing but bread full of aniseed,
> and broad beans which they boiled and lived off for the next six days.[4]

The seasons dictate fruit consumption as well: the produce of the
trees has to be eaten as it ripens or a year's effort will have gone to
waste. One therefore gets quickly fed with a succession of cherries,
apricots, medlars, plums, pears, peaches, nectarines, figs, persimmons,
grapes and pomegranates. Many of these produce different varieties
at different times with different names, the first figs, for instance, are
called *bifare* and the last, which ripen in November and December,
nataline, with numerous varieties coming in between. Nicola, who
looks after the plants here, mentioned fifteen types of orange when
I asked about them, and there are probably more. Many of them
have geographical names, from the most common, *portogallo*, which
is a corruption of Portugal, to *moro*, *marocco* and *brasiliano*, and
the more surprising *washington*. Others are more heterogeneous:
belladonna, *ovaletto*, *sanguinello*, *navellino*, *manighia* (a corruption

of *vaniglia* i.e. vanilla), *tomas*, *tarocchio* and of course the *amaro*, the bitter 'Seville' orange that is quite difficult to find. Each of these oranges has their champions: my mother-in law, for instance will, with great glee, eat either *manighie*, because they are blandly sweet, or more bitter varieties if she sprinkles salt on them to bring out their sweetness. *Chacun à son goût*. One might be forgiven for consider-ing the eating of fruit to be a peaceful pastime, but we have a long-standing disagreement on the burning question of the best way to eat persimmons: it is akin to Swift's boiled egg controversy (big end or little end first?), and is between Caterina, who favours the coffee spoon, and her father, who is an energetic exponent of twisting the stalk off and using the resultant hole to suck out the interior. Not only that, in the peach season there are hot debates on whether the cut-up bits are better dowsed in red or white wine.

Mention has been made of *pasta con le sarde*, but there is another speciality, *couscous*, which, while again not strictly confined to Calatafimi, is much eaten in this area of Sicily, that is, the Trapani region. Although it is still often made by hand, you can buy packets of it at the corner shop or in the supermarket. It was clearly intro-duced by the Arabs, and it has been around in the area for centuries. The Trapanese version is almost always cooked with a fish broth, unlike the North African meat version, and it is a very popular alternative to pasta as a first course. Another typical dish of the area is pasta with *pesto trapanese*, different from the well-known green Genoese *pesto*, which consists of fresh uncooked vegetables – mainly tomatoes, basil leaves, chopped almonds, celery, garlic and a hint of chili pepper, but you can actually add most things – finely minced up and poured over the hot pasta. It is deliciously refreshing in the summer. The local, Trapanese, form of pasta is called *busiati*. It gets its name from the *busa*, the dialect name for the stalk of the *ampelodesmo*, a grassy plant with long whippy stalks round which the pasta used to be twined to dry. The absorbent quality of the thick-ish pasta, and the fact that it is a tight corkscrew shape means that it picks up sauce generously.

The banging of guns – surprisingly close sometimes – the baying of dogs and the abandonment of cars in unlikely spots in the country-side announce the hunting season. In some households, rabbits, hares and pigeons appear on the table, but not so often as even a few decades ago, and partridges are beyond being a rarity. If shooting is still enthusiastically engaged in, it is no more the long-awaited opportunity for the man of the house to put meat on the table. Those times, when meat was a seasonal luxury, have gone. Incidentally, you might be interested to know that if you carry a gun during the hunting season you have the right to traverse anybody's land – unless it is a hunting reserve, which is an expensive privilege – but if you try to do the same thing with a camera, or nothing at all, you may be ignominiously turfed off.

Even fish have their seasons and the townspeople of Calatafimi know them well enough. In addition to a couple of permanent fish-shops in the town, there are various three-wheeled vans that drive up from Castellamare del Golfo to sell the fish they bought at the market that morning. Even the agricultural worker, when he buys fish, knows what is in season. I mean, you wouldn't be seen eating tuna after mid June, would you? And other things have their season, too. The other morning I noticed a family in the main square of the town with an orange-box full of snails and a plastic scale, waiting to weigh out their gastropods for passing clients. They were, incidentally, the crawling variety not the *attuppateddi* – or the hermetically-sealed dormant version – which are the more appreciated variant. There was just one box of them, but the whole family was there, making sure they did not crawl out, and chatting away while they waited for customers. These were the larger snails, but there is a smaller version as well: they are both cooked in garlic and tomato sauce. Vying with the boxes of snails are the boxes of prickly pears, which can also be found in the shops for the short period of time when they are ripe. Soon afterwards the walnuts will arrive. Throughout the year, as the seasons come round, cauliflowers, artichokes, cardoons, medlars, figs (the various distinct varieties) and a whole range of other fruit and vegetables are sold from lorries, vans or boxes in large quantities and at prices that are lower than in the shops, where they will have made their appearance as well. Lorries tend to be parked in the main street; boxes are found in the piazzas; while the small vans usually tour the backstreets screaming their wares over a loudspeaker.

I am sorry to admit that when the pomegranate season comes round, we use the juice for the seemingly untypical cooking of Persian dishes, and overcome seasonal dictates by keeping it in the deep freeze. If the thought of our occasionally eating Persian food jars with your idea of a simple local life in Calatafimi, I might point out that there *is* an affinity, because dill, fava-beans, sultanas, aubergines and pine-nuts are ingredients that are common to both Persian and Sicilian cooking.

Cooking on a larger scale I have briefly dealt with when talking of the late-night ceremonial meals, the *tavulidde*, that have grown up around the local festivals, in particular on the night of the Immaco-latedda procession. The *tavulidda* is not peculiar to Calatafimi and is no longer confined to festas, but the Calatafimesi particularly enjoy these feasts: they used to be held at night and they now always in-volve roasts, usually of lamb. The meals that accompanied the corn-harvests, the *vendemmia* and the olive-picking, were also occasions for ritual eating, particularly on the last day of work: on other days, the meals were more a necessary means of sustaining the workers' energy. These final meals are nowadays much more modest affairs and tend to be taken care of by the workers themselves rather than the landowner. It is perhaps less colourful, but it is also less paternal. What still remains a family institution, and a strictly seasonable one, is the making of sauce for the year. When the tomatoes are ripe, the family gathers and makes its way to the country; the picking is done by all; large outside barbecues are made and lit; cauldrons (usually petrol drums) are boiled; and every possible glass bottle is unearthed for the year's supply of tomato sauce. The tomatoes are scalded, peel and all, and, after excess water has been eliminated by straining them through reed matting, they are put through a sieve and cooked with onions and basil leaves before being sealed up in the bottles, and boiled for the last time for twenty minutes. The taste is so much bet-ter than the shop version. There is no comparison. After all the effort, the whole happy family eats a plentiful meal together, cooked on what is left of the fire in the countryside where the tomatoes were growing, and grinning in the knowledge that the crop has been safely gathered, and that bottles of marvellous pasta sauce have been hoarded away for the rest of the year.

That pioneering Scottish traveller Brydone, who never got to Calatafimi, has a lovely description of a lunch organized by the Bishop of Mazzara (Calatafimi is still in that diocese) at the end of the eighteenth century, at which 'there were no less than thirty meat courses'. It ended up with a *credo* expounded by his hosts that God had given men things to eat, and that it would be an offence to God not to enjoy them with gusto. (This meal was picked up by Anne Radcliffe in *A Sicilian Romance*.)[5] Something of the same spirit sur-vives in Calatafimi, particularly on Sunday at lunch time. In our case, part of the ritual is played out by a stream of acolytes from Palermo who have escaped for the week-end, doctrinally confident that the country vouchsafes life-as-it-ought-to-be accompanied by natural food and healthy enjoyment, by contrast with the evil city that bleakly concedes nothing but demeaning work, artificial food and false emotions. This heresy has fuelled the international modern male's maniacal dedication to the office of 'cooking', be it in the kitchen or over the barbecue, although to his week-end mind the word 'creation' would be more appropriate. In the city, he kowtows to orders or market forces; in the country he alone sets the agenda, controls the alchemy and announces the exact moment for the un-veiling – to the applause of the other guests and the immense relief of his wife. The more complicated the meal, the less he remembers the previous week's grinding anxieties and the more his inner fulfilment wells up inside him. This happens in Calatafimi, just as it does in the Home Counties or Maine.

I'll take you through a recent Sunday. There were nineteen of us, a normal number. Three barbecues were jealously defended by men, huddled together conspiratorially. There was a whole kitchen inside, tended of course by the women, who were keeping out of the way of the re-born males and preparing the less glamorous dishes and things that were not do-able on barbecues – pasta, sauces, pastries and unimportant things like that. On the embers outside, there were sausages, the butcher's in this case not the supermarket's, *involtini* (roulades of meat with bread-crumbs, bay, sultanas, pine-nuts and locally picked oregano, and, though this was hardly mentioned, pre-viously prepared by the womenfolk), fish of all kinds and hunks of smoking meat. Wine abounded. Children were playing, dogs were patiently waiting and the world was being dissected with extra-ordinary forensic ability in about seven different simultaneous con-versations, in dialect and Italian, all of which real habitués can follow. I can, with difficulty, just about manage to follow three.

Finally the meal – that's the wrong word: the *event*. Devouring, declarations, diatribes, dialectics, dissension, dialogues, disasters, debates and above all decibels and sheer delight. Song breaks out. The children wander off to play by themselves, the dogs get their bones, the adults move from main food to desserts, dissertations and digestion. Every mouthful is diagnosed because recreational cooking is surprisingly cerebral. Was there enough salt; they do it better to the east of here; traditionally the peasants would have used lard (*sugna*) instead of sugar in the pastry; the aubergines should have been soaked longer – they were too bitter; was there perhaps a little too much oil; the tomatoes were not ripe enough; nobody can cook it like this in the city; the ricotta was magnificent – you simply cannot buy it like that; where my family comes from it's done without fennel and the taste is quite different; my mother did it another way; three minutes longer and it would have been perfect...my God, now all I want is a marvellous rest. If abandonment to country eating provides a sort of catharsis for city problems, sleeping creeps up very quickly afterwards. Around five o'clock in the evening drowsy, digested families climb into their cars, already dreading what they will have to encounter on Monday in Palermo, a dread which will vanish without trace on Monday morning.

Gluttony may be looked on as a capital sin, but I am sure that if there is a God, He would have loved to have had lunch with us, or to have had many of the other lunches that were being celebrated all around Calatafimi that Sunday, with fewer city people perhaps, but certainly with equal abandon.

A sobering thought or two.

Until recently only the rich ate meat around here, as I have said, except perhaps on a few festive occasions: recently means till about the mid 1950s. It is interesting to read in the Privileges, reluctantly granted to the town of Calatafimi by the baronial Prades family in 1393, which I told you about, that the three Giurati (the town's unpaid magistrates) were each awarded from public funds, as appropriate to their rank, half a pig at Christmas and at Carnival, as well as a gelded sheep at Easter. In this context, an interesting incident that took place in the grim years after the Second World War illustrates the protein/carbohydrate social divide well, although it needs some explaining today. A relatively well-off farmer down the road used to complain publicly to his wife as follows: 'Ovi, ovi, sempri ovi!', ('Eggs, eggs, always eggs!'), 'Uffa, dammi un pocu di cuccuzza!' ('Uff! Give me some vegetable marrows!'). On the face of it, you would think he had just got bored with eggs, but that was not the point: it was his way of proclaiming to all and sundry that he was somebody and could afford to eat things that were not just the bread and oil, vegetables and pasta that was all most other people could hope for. As late as the 1960s, Friday evenings would see many people riding back from the country with a live chicken in evidence. Other people were supposed to believe that they were so well off that they were going to eat chicken over the week-end, although the chicken was almost always silently spirited back to the country on Monday morning. The scantiness of most people's diet until quite recently has meant that country people now have more than a healthy respect for food, way over and above what is appropriate for the satisfaction of their appetite.

To close on the question of food, I want to quote you Caterina's great-grandfather. He was a man who loved his food and also obeyed other compulsive appetites which resulted in his leaving behind him many genetic copies of himself. The scene is the table, the conversation with his servant thus:

'That's enough...enough...No more please!'
'Eccellenza, if you do not desire any more, just don't eat it.'
'That, you fool, is precisely what I cannot do, dammit!'

Which brings me to the family.

19

The Mollica Family

Apart from the members of Caterina's family you know already, I have bored you stiff with frequent references to the various other Mollicas that keep cropping up in Calatafimi's past, and run the risk of being taken for a bemused, yawnmongering, provincial snob. I mention them because, together with members of other similar families, they have made up the warp and weft of the fabric of the place, until a few years ago, anyway. The Mollica family never covered itself in glory or seized the reins of local history: it simply maintained its defined but modest position in Calatafimi over the centuries, like that handful of other families, with which it continually intermarried. They made up the landowning and administrative class in this small community, where nobody budged. Their history is no source of pride to Caterina or to her family, though it may occasionally be of some interest to them or amusing, as is the case in many families when their names pop up in one place over any length of time. At a less visible level, other equally interrelated families provided the broadcloth of agricultural life, and they didn't budge either. People here were not socially or geographically mobile until not long ago, and existed in an environment in which who married whom, who was related to whom, and who owned what, were real issues. They would have been of complete irrelevance in more fluid societies. There are people in Calatafimi who can, and unfortunately will, recite their family trees generation after generation, with all the intertwinings and ramifications.

According to the doyen of Sicilian genealogists, Filadelfio Mugnos,[1] the Mollica family was connected to the Sicilian branch of the Frangipani family: the arms are quite similar except that the Frangipani have two crowned lions breaking a loaf of bread in two, while the Mollicas just have two truncated hands doing the same thing: *frangipane* means 'breaker of bread' and *mollica* the soft part of the loaf that is enclosed by the crust. While this is very romantic, if the putative connection is correct one cannot escape the fact that the dis-

coverer of *frangipane* essence and the man who introduced frangipani, pomelia or pagoda tree plants into the known world may have
been induced to undertake exotic travel on account of persistent
rumours of his having been involved in a murder. Anyway, all a far
cry from Calatafimi.

Whatever the truth may be, both Mugnos and Palizzolo Gravina
have identified the family founder as a certain Domenico Mollica.[2]
He was a Royal Knight at Messina in 1400, from whose loins sprang
a host of Domenicos, Pietros, Paolos, Giovannis and Vincenzos who
established themselves in various parts of Sicily, with one branch ending up here in the Trapani/Alcamo/Calatafimi area. There were also
a lot of Caterinas over the years, her grandmother being one of the
most recent, and a cousin of the same age another: this confuses
many people. The first Mollica I came up against in Calatafimi was
the Segreto Baroniale, Giovanni, who was recording *terraggiolo*
payments in 1554; he was the Count of Modica's local lieutenant in
the town. Pellegrino cites another Giovanni, presumably his grandson because of the Christian name, in a notarial record dated 25th
May 1594, indicating that the Carmelite Provincial, Father Master
Geronimo Amuruso, had elected as procurators for the reconstruction of the Carmine church – even at that early stage it was apparently about to fall down – the Magnificent Giovanni Mollica, the
Magnificent Geronimo Truglio, the Magnificent Giacomo Vanni and
the Magnificent Antonio Sichichi, all of whose families, including
that of Amuruso, have left traces today. It was the same church as that
in which Pellegrino stated that there was a chapel with the Mollica
arms in it. Their 'nobility' had been reconfirmed by Charles V in
1529, and Pellegrino has six pages on the family: who married
whom, or occasionally who was what, mostly coming from notarial
documents, for Pellegrino was a notary. Another Mollica, Cavaliere
Vincenzo, to whom Longo's book on the Trojan colonies in Sicily
was dedicated, and who was at the time the Prosegreto of Calatafimi,
introduced that most hated of taxes, on milled corn, by order of King
Ferdinand III on 8th December 1815.[3] Mollicas popped up all the
time in Calatafimi.

Marriages were important for families like the Mollicas. In conservative agricultural societies, marriage and a strict adherence to
primogeniture were the surest methods of defending or improving a
family's position, and they were meticulously planned and documented. I have Caterina's great-great-grandfather Paolo Mollica's

marriage settlement to hand, which is revealing in its way. He was twenty-five when it was decided that he should marry fifteen-year-old Gaetana Stabile, a granddaughter of Baron Pietro, who founded the Casa Stabile. On 25th May 1842, in the house/studio of the notary Antonio Mistretta, in a street called strada San Francesco in Calatafimi, a meeting was held to draw up the eleven manuscript pages of the agreement 'per il sostegno dei pesi del matrimonio' ('for supporting the weighty consequences of the marriage'). Present for the Mollicas were l'Illustre Don Paolo Mollica, his father Cavaliere Don Vincenzo (presumably the one who introduced the flour tax), and Paolo's three brothers, Cavaliere Don Gioacchino, the eldest, the priest Don Ignazio, later to become the archpriest, and another priest Don Salvadore (still spelt in the Spanish way) – all being described as landowners and living in strada San Francesco. The Illustre Signora Baronessella Gaetana was accompanied by her father and her mother, both of them landowners, who lived in the same street. The happy couple were to receive the sum of 4,000 ounces from her parents (3,700 from the father and 300 from the mother), but only after various inheritances had been legally 'divided', until which time they were to receive an annual cash payment of 200 ounces. To this day the 'division' of inheritances takes an interminable time. Articles 3 to 9 set out the contribution in 'land and rents' from the Mollica family. Father Vincenzo contributed an estate in the Angeli area outside Calatafimi plus twenty-six other pieces of land near at hand. The three brothers together made over to the couple other farms and rents in the same area, often carrying out land permutations with their father in order to rationalize their remaining holdings. All the donations were to become effective from the day of the marriage, but the whole of that year's harvest and rents were to go to the newly-weds. In article 10, Paolo promises a one-off payment of 200 ounces in the event of his predeceasing his bride; and the annual sum of 18 ounces, payable in advance during his lifetime, the first payment falling due on the day after their wedding. The different title deeds were handed over and the document was signed, sealed and registered. A cosy affair among friendly local families all living in the same street, and a well constructed arrangement which was designed to last, although 150 years later precious little of it is has survived, in favour of a young man who was not even the first-born in his family.

Although I have no intention of inflicting a full family history on you, I should like to sketch out the lives of some recent members of the family, in sepia tones with the occasional tint of watercolour if I am lucky, as background detail for this picture of Calatafimi. Just a few from the older generation, some of whom I'll follow till after the Second World War, when social stirrings were starting to rub off more than merely the edges of the established way of life.

For the distaff side of the family we need to go back to Domenico Saccaro. I've already told you about his public, financial and charitable side. What little I know of the Saccaros' origins and private life comes from a small notebook in which Vincenzo Vivona (son of Domenico's adoptive heir and Caterina's maternal great-uncle) jotted down notes towards the end of his life, at the suggestion of one of his nephews, who gave me a photocopy of it.

The story begins with the three original Saccaro brothers and a sister who rented the manors of Morfino, Amburgio, Giumarella, and Bernardo in the Calatafimi area and used this large swathe of land to raise cattle. The notebook says they had so many head of cattle that when the herders took them to pasture the clouds of dust they put up dimmed the sun. Such was their supply of beef that they managed – I have no idea how and the notebook does not say, either – to land the contract to supply Napoleon's troops on his Egyptian campaign in 1798, embarking the cattle in French ships from the nearby port of Castellamare del Golfo.[4] They were paid in cash, in gold *marengos*, and so great was their profit that they were able not only to buy those four rented manors and add them to the land they already owned, but also to accumulate liquidity in gold worth even more than the land itself. Of the three brothers little is known of Silvestro, the eldest, except that he had three daughters, one an abbess and two who were married to local landowners, and one son who left no trace at least as far as the notes go. I expect he died. There was a daughter, Sebastiana, who never married and two other sons – Giuseppe and Francesco. Giuseppe was the natural leader and looked after all the business side, despite the fact that he was an abbot: his resultant wealth earned him the nickname of L'Abbate Zecchino, or the 'Mint Abbot'. The other son, Francesco, was the father of the Domenico with whom I am concerned here, and whom the Mint Abbot made his sole heir.

Domenico inherited a great deal of his own money on his father's death and was brought up by his aunt Sebastiana and his uncle Giuseppe, the Abbate Zecchino (Caterina's brother has inherited a massively authoritative portrait of him looking rather like a Borgia

Pope, which he hangs in his office in Palermo and impresses his clients). Such was the wealth involved that, according to Vincenzo Vivona's notebook, certain relatives who had hoped to enjoy some of it were so fraught with jealousy that they ambushed both uncle and nephew in 1848 when Domenico was aged thirty-two: they shot the abbot dead and slightly wounded his nephew. While local tradition does allow for the element of jealousy, there may also have been a political dimension. In Francesco Morsellino's memoirs of Francesco Avila[5] it was said that unknown marksmen had in the dead of night fired on a group of Bourbon reactionaries, including the two Saccaros, during the course of the 1848 uprisings and the election of Calatafimi's representative to the Sicilian Parliament. The local hero Francesco Avila was returned. According to the notebook, the wounded Domenico was quick to react and managed to catch one of the attackers, a certain Simone nicknamed 'Patucchio'. He gave the man a hiding with the butt of his pistol, which left him paralysed for a considerable time before he died.

Caterina's aunt has two portraits of Domenico: as a sharp-faced, dark, balding thirty-five-ish-year-old and as a rounded, contented patriarch. He married Caterina Gandolfo, but as the union was not blessed with children, they adopted a child from outside their family, which did give rise to no little jealousy: his name was Domenico Vivona and his arrival on the scene was described in the notebook as follows.

> One day Saccaro, being in need of taking on a workman for his own personal affairs and having involved a friend of his in Palermo, engaged a certain Giuseppe Vivona who lived in Palermo but had been born in nearby Alcamo. He turned out to be an honest person and of proven rectitude and Saccaro became so fond of him that he was treated almost as an adoptive son.

One day the man's small son Gabriele, a fine intelligent blond-haired boy, went playing with some friends near the castle and failed to come back at nightfall. His family, Saccaro's and other people turned out with torches and lanterns to look for him and

> they found him at death's door in a deep ditch into which he had fallen or had been pushed by some other child related to Saccaro from motives of jealousy.

The child died, but on 25th September 1855 another child was born to the Vivona family, whom Saccaro had baptized with his own name Domenico. The notebook continues:

> As the boy grew up, Saccaro kept him close to his person, treating him as his own son. He educated him and, since the boy was intelligent, of good disposition and hardworking, he subsequently made him the curator and administrator of all his worldly goods.

And his sole heir.

When old Saccaro died, he was buried in the family tomb in the town's cemetery, an event which dissatisfied his widow and Domenico, his heir and father of the Vincenzo of the notebook. It is eerie to read Vincenzo as an old man describing what happened afterwards. He writes that one day during the winter of 1881, Domenico's embalmed body was surreptitiously dug up by his father with the connivance of the widow, carried off in the dead of night and quietly re-buried in the chapel of the Albergo della Mendicità, the poor people's home that he had founded. This body-snatching involved the use of step-ladders for getting over the cemetery walls, blackened lanterns, silent trusted labourers and the tacit agreement of the custodian of the cemetery. When they discovered what had happened the next morning, the authorities made a move to arrest Vincenzo's father, but as the notebook disarmingly states:

> Le autorità civili e militari erano stati blandite dalla munificenza della vedova di Saccaro stessa e anche perchè tutta la popolazione del paese era d'accordo con quanto era avvenuto. (The civil and military authorities were won round by the munificence of Saccaro's widow and also because all the people of the town were in agreement with what had happened.)

You can see his sarcophagus with the bas relief of his head in the diminutive chapel of the old people's home today, adorned with fresh-cut flowers. As Vincenzo simply put it: this was the 'only worthy site for the eternal resting place of the Benefactor Domenico Saccaro'.

In 1879, Domenico Vivona married Giuseppina Adamo. This union *was* blessed with children – thirteen all told, of whom ten survived (probably a high percentage for that time) – but, apart from his innate good qualities that were so appreciated by his adoptive father, Domenico Vivona was also blessed with the knack for spending money with ease, and it is said he did so liberally in Palermo with his growing family until he was recalled by Domenico Saccaro to the less giddy task of paying better attention to the family interests in Calatafimi,[6] the interests which were to become his on Saccaro's death. He also inherited cash and chattels from Saccaro's wife when she died in 1894 (though not her real estate which went to the Casa della Mendacità, the Poor House her husband had founded), including 'my pair of earrings with the large diamonds', which were to be his and his heirs' in perpetuity, with the proviso that they were to be worn by the Madonna di Giubino, the patron saint of Calatafimi, whenever she was in procession or the object of a special ceremony. His first move after the death of his adoptive mother was ill-conceived. He and his family were living in a ten-roomed apartment in the palazzo that had been left 'in usufruct' for life to Domenico and Caterina Saccaro by Domenico's aunt Sebastiana; but under Sebastiana's 1859 will the whole building had been bequeathed to the municipality for the local school. After Saccaro's wife died, Domenico Vivona attempted to get the will overturned, a move that was quickly scotched. Most of Domenico Saccaro's considerable wealth had of course already been given away to charity, but the substantial amount that remained got frittered away over the years by his adoptive family, even though they did insist that a great deal continued to be given away in donations.

I shan't take you through the long lives of all ten of the children of Domenico and Giuseppina, although I shall linger a bit on two of them. Their names were Domenica (Mimma for short), Annita, Lina, Mimì (Domenico), Vincenzino (the author of the notebook), Peppino, Giulio, Tanino, Ninnì and Caterina (Caterina's grandmother). With one exception, Ninnì, who was the exception in everything, they lived to a great age. As a family they seem to have had a talent for dissipating what was left of the Saccaro inheritance, some with more of it than others. Such work as was done by them was mainly in the fields of law and education. The eldest son, Mimì, was a lawyer, and Mimma married a lawyer, but she combined this with being a headmistress. Vincenzino, Giulio and Tanino were all elementary teachers, though Giulio drifted off to the Saccaro Bank and a life of embroidery and poetry;[7] and I'll tell you about Tanino in a moment. Peppino became an accountant and, since there was no future for that profession in Calatafimi, went north, made a fortune – the only brother that did so – and slipped out of family history. Lina looked after her mother. Ninnì couldn't keep down a job and argued with everybody, including the Fascists, which landed him in political exile on the island of Ponza together with eminent Communist political prisoners. After the war, he argued with the Communists because the ex-political prisoners would not find him a job.

Annita was the colourful one. I met her once very late in her life. She and her close friend Margherita, the daughter, believe it or not, of a Piedmontese lady-in-waiting to Queen Elena, spent a large part of their lives in Palermo. They were both pianoforte teachers and composers. The two ladies were famous for the time they took to make decisions, a typical example being their preparations for the yearly holiday they spent in Calatafimi in September (that was the month for *villeggiatura* then, not August). Apparently, they began packing in May and by the end of August they had accumulated huge amounts of clothes and accoutrements that were completely unsuitable for a visit to the country in the autumn. They were also much concerned about making preparations for their future, which for them meant composing and publishing music. They were doing this well into their eighties. I have in front of me the score of an *Ave Maria* by Annita Vivona ('rights reserved in all countries'), that was published in 1952 by G.&P. Mignani in Florence. On the back cover, the publisher states that from the same composer there were 'publications for solo pianoforte, lyrical works for voice and piano, didactic works (scholastic songs and musical theory), musical comedies and fables'. Margherita died when she was eighty, Annita much later at ninety-three. Caterina's father, who was Annita's nephew was born in her house in Palermo, although he had been conceived in Turin.

Tanino, who ended up as an elementary teacher in Calatafimi led a more flamboyant life in his early days, based on the Vivona house in Palermo. He was a well-dressed *bon viveur*, whose attention was concentrated on perfectly shined shoes and on Donna Franca Florio, around whom the social life of Palermo and to a large extent that of Italy danced giddily.

It would take too long to describe the Florios and their place in Italian social life at that time.[8] Heirs to the original down-to-earth Yorkshire wine-merchants in Marsala, they had become immensely rich and, *mutatis mutandis*, Donna Franca Florio was a sort of female Princess of Wales in Italian society: indeed Bertie the real Prince of

Wales was her guest while yachting in the south of the Mediterranean. It may sound grotesque, though it was much appreciated at the time, but one of the near-traditions that Donna Franca created for the festival of Santa Rosalia, the patron saint of Palermo, was to have strips of gold loosely attached to the hooves of her carriage horses which she contrived to shake loose every year in front of the cathedral during the saint's procession through the city. In response to the interest shown by the poor bystanders, she leaned out of the carriage and theatrically tore long, three-stringed pearl necklaces from her internationally admired neck. If it sounds disgusting as described, she was genuinely loved by Palermo, Italy and Tanino Vivona. How on earth he ever came anywhere remotely near her wavelength I cannot conceive, though it has been suggested that they shared an interest in the new rage for cycling, and that they practised together. Be that as it may, the fact is that he became infatuated with her, and it is repeatedly said in the family that one – possibly the main – reason for the decline of their by then modest fortunes was Tanino's diversion of jewels to Donna Franca. What actually happened is, to say the least, unclear. He eventually ended up marrying the daughter of another 'prominent' Calatafimi family, the Zuaro, and after the First World War they happened to be living in the Venice area when Benito Mussolini began his March on Rome. Tanino threw in his lot and marched with him. He remained an enthusiastic supporter for many years, until 10th June 1940, when Mussolini declared war. On that day, Tanino wrote him a rather pathetic letter, beginning 'Dear Benito', withdrawing his support from the Duce and dissociating himself from the decision to declare war on the basis that it was not necessary and would lead to ruin. Clearly Benito never saw the letter but, what is more important, a cover up was managed and there were no consequences for Tanino: he finished his days as an elementary schoolmaster in Calatafimi.

That is something about the maternal side of the family, the Vivonas. The paternal side, the Mollicas, was less numerous.

Vincenzo Mollica, who was Caterina's paternal great-grandfather, was another somewhat flamboyant character. He was known either as the Cavaliere Testone ('Sir Stubborn') or else the Toro di Calatafimi (the 'Bull of Calatafimi') and he was much attracted to the female sex. Before marrying a saintly lady who gave him Pietro, Paolo (Caterina's grandfather who married Caterina Vivona) and Rosina, he had at least three illegitimate children, whom, however, he dutifully set up and looked after for the rest of his life. He was widowed early and consoled himself thereafter with a stream of the daughters of his employees. They had to be rigorously over eighteen, but when they reached that age they were rigorously summoned upstairs, although it must be said that they and theirs were also always carefully looked after. He was a Justice of the Peace, and held various public offices such as that of the governor of the Stabile Orphanage. But his main occupation, apart from hunting and eating, seems to have been looking after his lands, of which he had many. Caterina's father remembers him as a man who was dedicated to hygiene, with a tendency to vegetarianism. He was an early riser. In the bathroom he smoked a *spuntatura*, an evil-smelling cigar, through a clay pipe, while using a terracotta spittoon and contemplating the world. By the time he had dressed, his horse would have been got ready, and he stepped out to visit one of his many properties. He sounds as if he was a hard man, but he was also a poet, a very upright person and a lover of flowers: indeed, he died as the result of a prick from a rose. His poetry, which was found in the ruins of the house after the 1968 earthquake, and was written for his eyes only, reveals him as being a lonely man towards the end of his life. He must have had a traditional frame of mind as he considered my father-in-law, his grandson, a 'Vivona' not a 'Mollica' because his name was Domenico (the maternal grandfather's) rather than Vincenzo, his own name. The reason for this was that my father-in-law had had an elder brother, called Vincenzo obviously, who had died at the age of six, and he himself was therefore given the name of his maternal grandfather. His younger brother, who was born after the death of his eldest brother, was also named Vincenzo, and was for this reason preferred by the Bull of Calatafimi. Apart from the land he controlled directly he had also other land let out 'on emphyteusis' (i.e. rented), which no doubt allowed him to lead a tranquil life. But it created problems later.

Of his three children, Rosina died in childbirth delivering Nina. As a child, Nina used to play with her cousin, the Domenico who was to become Caterina's father, and who remembers that when it was time to go back to school, grandfather Vincenzo would give her a Bank of Naples note for five lire, an enormous sum for a child those days. He himself never received anything like that, although his younger brother Vincenzo was better treated than he was, as I have said.[9] Nina went on to marry another cousin, the Li Bassi brother who died in the war earning the posthumous *medaglia d'oro*, as I have described elsewhere. She later married his younger brother and lived in Palermo in the house where Caterina saw the light of day. On the evening before Caterina was born, the new husband, Andrea Li Bassi, managed to borrow some money from my mother-in-law and won a lot of money at cards, a rare event for him. He maintained it was Caterina's birth, while he had been playing that evening, that had brought him luck, as I have said, and so gave back all the money he had borrowed, an even rarer event. He lost everything to cards in the end. The Li Bassi brothers were the two billiard-playing antagonists of Cocò Adamo, the elegant Avvocato I told you about. Nina herself played cards with a similar dedication and lack of luck: she often took wagers and lost the house and land just below where we live, which was regularly redeemed by her father, until the situation became untenable and it ended up in the hands of her stepmother's family. It recently came on the market, after being abandoned for at least forty years, and we brought it back into the family. We are going to live there when we have finished restoring it stone by stone.

Pietro, the other son, left Calatafimi at an early date. He took his degree in medicine at Palermo University and established himself at Grisolera, in Val Gardena near Venice, as a general practitioner. He married the rich daughter of the local pharmacist and had little to do with events at Calatafimi. Venice had some sort of fascination for the Mollica family as so many of them ended up there from time to time. Pietro had two children, another Vincenzo and Concetta. Concetta married her cousin Silvio who, after his father-in-law's death, decided that the part of the land he and his wife owned here at San Giovanni was of little use and ought to be sold. This he dealt with through the family lawyer who, without offering it to Caterina's father or even informing him, sold it off to an outsider whose family still owns it.

Caterina's grandfather Paolo took a degree in law and enrolled in the judicial service. He moved about quite a lot, spending time in Turin during the First World War as a military judge, in Trapani after it as a civil one, followed by Palermo and then Venice, where he died in 1942. He loved San Giovanni and indulged his passion for shooting there during his holidays. It is easy to dismiss the virtues of country shooting in Sicily and to agree with D.H. Lawrence's assessment, expressed with some energy in his essay *Man is a Hunter!* (*L'Uomo è Cacciatore*), but there were other sides to it, not least that it was until recently a way of putting meat on tables which did not often have it. Other more complex matters are revealed in an incident experienced by Paolo Mollica in the 1930s. A certain Diego used to accompany him on his expeditions, and one morning, at about 8 o'clock, Diego mentioned that there was a certain 'thing' he had to do in the village ('Signor Giudice avissi un chiffareddu a lu paisi') to which a noncommittal 'yes, yes' answer was given. The remark was repeated a couple of times with the same reaction, as the morning was proving particularly exhilarating, until around 10 o'clock when a stop was made for breakfast, and Grandfather Paolo thought he had better find out what Diego needed to do in the village. This was his simple reply: 'a li dieci m'avìa a maritari' ('at ten o'clock I have to get married').

Caterina's father has cherished memories of shooting with his father, from making the cartridges by hand by candlelight the night before, to eating figs the next morning under a favourite tree before starting off. After the shoot there was swimming in the *gebbia* and the eating of game for lunch – obviously a previous day's bag, as it had had to hang. The prey was mostly rabbits and partridge, though woodcock was still quite plentiful, and it was cooked over charcoal and sprinkled with a bunch of oregano dipped in oil and garlic.

After the war, Caterina's father returned to Palermo as a judge, with his wife, one child, Paolo, and another on the way (Caterina), to discover that, his interests having been left in the hands of the family lawyer, his resources in Calatafimi were for some reason somewhat depleted. *Pazienza*: a lot of strange things happened during that war and times were difficult. Another child (Francesco) was born. Based in Palermo, he was prosecuting judge for a long time in the famous Salvatore Giuliano bandit affair, which deserves a book to itself. He enjoyed a long career as judge, and he was so effective that he prompted mafia prisoners he had successfully convicted to malign him in their attempts at plea bargaining, envisaged under a new 'state witness' law, a much debated and very sensitive piece of legislation. The main would-be 'grasser' had actually had his original sentence increased on appeal, at his hands, and he had also sentenced him in the first instance; but as it was a sensitive issue, the formalities had to be respected. The matter had been fairly dealt with in the end and the accusations had been brushed aside, when he decided – he had already retired by that time – to spend much more time in San Giovanni, where he had spent so many youthful summers, in a new house that grew from the ruins of the old one which had been destroyed in the 1968 earthquake. His two boys also went into the law and are still practising as solicitors; they come down from Palermo at week-ends. His daughter married me. She wanted to live in London. I wanted to live in 'the Mediterranean'. We compromised on Rome (there is no work in 'the Mediterranean'), until the time came when we too decided that San Giovanni was a unique place. So, when not in Rome, we now spend almost all our time here not doing as the Romans do.

It must be apparent to you that that is that. The story has drawn to a close. I have told you just about all I can about what the hell I am doing here.

But let me end on a positive note.

The Bull of Calatafimi kept in the *dispensa*, or store-room, at San Giovanni a smallish (forty-litre) barrel of special wine: when Caterina's grandfather was born the whole contents were replaced by what was considered a really exceptional wine. It was drunk only on special occasions and it was topped up, usually at the end of the year, with other exceptional wine. It was a 'Vino Perpetuo'. In the 1968 earthquake a wooden ceiling beam cracked and brought the ceiling down on the barrel, bursting it open. The Vino Perpetuo is no more. Yet after the earthquake, after the old house fell down, and after a very long interval with no contact at all, the three surviving Mollicas all began taking an interest in Calatafimi again, and this small hamlet came into being. Surprisingly, their children have showed an interest as well, and their children, too.

So a break in a tiny strand of history has been avoided.

20

Afterthought

That, then, is what I have been doing here in Calatafimi. Either pay-ing urbane attention to the district in which I reside, or, if you think a bucolic metaphor more appropriate, scratching and pecking for small scraps of information in my adoptive back-yard. Whichever version you favour, I had the aim of showing that Calatafimi is a long way from being an insignificant little town.

It was a lengthy process for me because, if you will forgive an abrupt change of metaphor, there is something of the stick-insect or flatfish about Calatafimi. Despite their exotic biology and evolu-tionary strategy, these creatures are frustratingly difficult to see unless they make a move, which rash action they only venture upon when there is something to eat, and there are no enemies in the offing. Like-wise Calatafimi has evolved, safely, silently and with little perceptible movement. It has cautiously changed its camouflage with the times, surreptitiously eaten just well enough and tactfully managed to avoid predators. No mean achievement. Glamorous Segesta was not able to manage that.

It would be silly of me to claim Calatafimi as a treasure-trove society. I simply want to demonstrate that, although its apparently inert evolution has made it difficult to see, it has in fact been a suc-cess story. Calatafimi is a historical organism that is in no way to be brushed aside as another patch of earth on which a few drab humans have eked out an unwelcome existence, and left nothing behind.

Outsiders have every right not to like the place. They do not have the right to dismiss it because they cannot follow what is going on behind the walls.

Notes

Introduction (pages 1 to 2)

(1) 'There is nothing interesting about Calatafimi, except its etymology.' Saccaro was known locally as the 'Abbate Zecchino' or 'Mint Abbot', so-called because he was, by local standards, immensely rich. His nephew and adopted heir turned out to be one of the most interesting of Calatafimi's philanthropists and a local banker of note. Both these gentlemen turn up on other occasions later on.

(2) Vicomte de Marcellus, *Vingt Jours en Sicile*, Paris, 1841, chapter 7. The Dante could be translated as: 'Let us not discuss them, but just steal a look and pass by.' I am clearly unreasonable in my instinctive disliking for the man. He rather despised his accommodation at the time, but he revised his opinion as his journey proceeded. 'Nous userpons tous les appartments de l'Abbé Sacara [sic]. Nous expierons plus tard nos épigrammes sur l'exiguité de son elogement, et la gêne qui en risulte: la comparaison nous le fera nommer bientôt un vrai paradis.' ('We took over all the rooms of the Abbé Sacara's [sic] apartment. We made amends for our epigrams on the cramped conditions of the lodgings, and the torture that resulted from them: comparisons later on made us call them a real paradise'.) A local notable came to visit them and, instead of offering him a glass of the 'insipid local white', the Vicomte gave him their good old Bordeaux, which visibly failed to be appreciated. But he was no doubt a worthy man. Before early retirement in 1830, he had been Under-Secretary of State for foreign affairs under Polignac. Earlier in his career as a diplomat he had been a secretary to the French Ambassador in Constantinople when in 1820 he persuaded his superior to send him to the island of Melos to negotiate the claim the French government had to the statue of the Venus de Milo, which, after being ploughed up by a local farmer, had been stumbled on by Dumont D'Urville, who was then a French naval captain. Marcellus travelled to the island with immense zeal, not for the famous statue but more for the love of a local girl with whose portrait he had become enamoured. He arrived to find that the statue had been sold and was already on board a Greek ship which was about to leave the island. However, he did manage to negotiate its sale to France and he therefore had some claim to be the French Lord Elgin.

(3) Raleigh Trevelyan, *The Companion Guide to Sicily*, Companion Guides, Woodbridge, 1998. His family has a long connection with Sicilian history, of which an example is G.M. Trevelyan's standard book on Garibaldi and the Thousand. He also wrote *Princes Under the Volcano*, London, 1972, a study of the Yorkshire dynasties of Woodhouse, Ingham and Whitaker, who founded the Marsala wine industry and played an important part in Sicilian history for 200 years.

1. From Contrada San Giovanni into Calatafimi (pages 3 to 15)

(1) Ernesto Basile, 1857-1932.

(2) Porcupines can be eaten without difficulty. It is said that the hunters beat the ground at night and shoot them when they come out of their burrows, although this does not seem to tally with their timidity. Also, hunters run wild if they hear of a rare wild boar, which is a much more common sight in other parts of Italy, where they are often looked on as pests.

(3) In *Henry IV*, part 1, act 1, scene 2, Falstaff praises the tavern hostess as a sweet wench and the Prince agrees that she is 'as the honey of Hybla'.

(4) According to Giuseppe Pitrè (1841-1916), the author of twenty-five volumes on Sicilian customs, traditions, usages and songs, the owner has the right to follow a swarm as far as he likes to take possession of it. If he does not exercise this right, the swarm becomes the property of the owner of the land where it decides to stop. Pitrè also refers to a belief that bees can fall in love with a single person and, if that person dies, they will leave their home.

(5) It is also called by other names depending on the development of the crystals (alabaster is one such development): it originates from sea-brine. It shines in the countryside around here, and is used locally in house-building.

(6) Shakespeare in *Antony and Cleopatra* has it as a soporific:

> Give me to drink mandragora...
> That I might sleep out this great gap of time
> My Antony is away...

It is a small perennial of the potato family, shrouded in superstition. The root is said to shriek if pulled up, and the ancient Greeks used it as a painkiller and aphrodisiac. There are now four plants flourishing in our garden.

(7) This was due to the 1861 Inheritance Law. Before that, the system in the more visible families was much like that which obtained in other European countries: really only the first-born male ought to marry and have children – he inherited almost everything. The others became soldiers or went into the Church.

(8) Especially when buying land from émigrés. You have to get in touch with lawyers in Australia, Germany, Brooklyn. It can be done, but much patience is needed.

(9) In a pamphlet published by Fabio Orlando Editore for the municipality of Calatafimi the following is a list of some of the wild flowers to be found in the district:

Myrtle (*Myrtus communis*)
Alaterno (*Rhamnus alaternus*)
Sumach (*Rhus coriaria*)
Hawthorn (*Crataegus monogyna*)
Sparzio Villoso (*Calicotome villosa*)
Arborescent Spurge
   (*Euphorbia dendroides*)
Cistus (*Cistus salviifolius*
   and *incanus*)
Ferule (*Ferula communis*)
Erba-vajola (*Cerinthe major*)
Silene (*Silene sericea*)
Butcher's Broom (*Ruscus aculeatus*)
Camedrio (*Teucrium fruticans*)
Thyme (*Thymus vulgaris*)
Mandrake (*Mandragora autumnalis*)
Arisaro (*Arisarum vulgare*)
Asphodel (*Asphodelus aestivum*)
Brassica (*Brassica villosa*) (rare)
Mare's Tail (*Equisetum arvense*)

Heather (*Erica arborea*)
Lentil (*Pistacia lentiscus*)
Bramble (*Rubus fruticosus*)
Honeysuckle (*Lonicera implexa*)
Broom (*Spartium junceum*)
Dwarf Palm (*Chamaerops humilis*)
Tamerisk (*Tamarix africana*)
Clover (*Psoralea bituminosa*)
Cyclamen (*Cyclamen hederofolium*)
Anemone (*Anemone hortensis*)
Latte di Gallina
   (*Ornithogalum montanum*)
Daisy (*Bellis perennis*)
Bindweed (*Convolvulus althaeoides*)
Cuckoopint (*Arum italicum*)
Carnation (*Dianthus rupicola*)
Muscari (*Muscari neglectum*)
Bee Balm (*Melissa officinalis*) (rare)
Mauritanian Reed Vine
   (*Ampelodesmus mauritanicus*)

There are also a large number of wild orchids, including two splendid Ophrides (*Ophrys lutes* and *Ophrys sphegodes*). As well as a lot of other plants such as garlic, snapdragons, irises, lilies, asparagus and a host of edible herbs.

In the spring, the yellow of the wood sorrel and the local daisies, the blue of the borage, and the orange and the mauve and blue wild peas border on the unbelievable.

2. The Town and its Monuments (pages 16 to 40)

(1) The Italians have a beautiful saying: 'pieno come un' uovo' (as full as an egg). I think some of those Belice grapes could substitute for the egg without changing the meaning.

(2) Pitrè mentions this on various occasions. The fullest account is in *Usi e Costumi*, vol. IV, pp.116-17 (reprinted 1993, Clio, Catania; first printed 1889). It translates thus: 'One characteristic of witches is to fly in the air at night-time, whizzing around like a spindle (*arcaiolo* in Italian; *animulu* in

dialect) in yarn-making. Hence the definition of *animalaru* given to women, who, because of their evil arts, are believed to be sorcerers and witches; and the offensive catchphrase *Calatafimara animalara* used about the women of Calatafimi is extremely common in the province of Trapani, because they are all considered sorcerers.'

(3) Vito Pellegrino (1697-1773), *Calatafimi Scoverto a' Moderni*. Published in 1993 by the Banca Popolare Cooperativa di Calatafimi, transcription, introduction and notes by Diego Tarantino and Leonardo Vanella, pp.75 and 163. The 377-page MS was presented to the local library in 1950 by Nicolò Mazzara, the local historian and pharmacist. Pietro Longo had read it in manuscript, however.

(4) Pietro Longo. A much loved Calatafimi parish priest (1756-1825). He wrote a local history, *Ragionamenti Istorici sulle Colonie de' Trojani in Sicilia* (Palermo, 1810), and the life of the local Beato Arcangelo Placenza (Palermo, 1804), and was tireless in digging up historical evidence in the famous case of Calatafimi versus the Counts of Modica over the illegal feudal tithe called the *terraggiolo*. All these subjects are dealt with later. *Ragionamenti*, pp.310-11.

(5) However, as all the foreign visitors to Segesta recorded, the inhabitants were terrified of catching fever (malaria), from the evening onwards, in the countryside. In 1910, Nicotra was writing in his *Dizionario dei Comuni Siciliani*: 'Predominant diseases: malarial fevers, infective fevers, pneumonia, bronchitis. The causes of these diseases are the somewhat unhygienic conditions in the town, the scarcity of water, and large tracts of territory being subject to malaria. The free distribution of state quinine to those who worked the land, carried out by the Town Council on behalf of the landowners, was of great help. Everybody took quinine with a notable advantage to the health of the poor.' The economy of Sicily was not good in the early 1900s.

(6) *Belzuarie*. In Antonio Traina's 1868 *Sicilian Dialect Dictionary* their existence is recorded as a balsamic substance: a latex extracted by cutting a tree called *Belzuino* or *Belguino*. So it was known in Sicily. But where did it come from? Certainly not from a stream. The Latin name of the tree (correctly quoted by Traina) is *Styrax benzoin* or 'Gum Benjamin' in English (*Tropical Planting and Gardening*, H.F. Macmillan, Macmillan, London, 5th edition, 1956) and is a native of Malaysia. It was balsamic and aromatic, and was used as incense and in medicine. It seems to have fallen out of memory in today's Sicily, though Longo warns against false *belzuarie* being sold by counterfeiters because they were in such demand.

(7) I owe this information to an article by the eminent Oxford philosopher Sir Michael Dummett, which appeared on Sunday 10th August 2003 on the cultural page of *Il Sole 24 Ore*, the Italian equivalent of the *Financial Times*. Dummett, who, apart from being an eminent philosopher, is also a devotee of and expert on tarot cards, wrote this article to record his trip to Sicily in

order to check up that Sicilian tarot card playing was still alive twenty years after he had first come across it in 1973. He visited five towns, including Calatafimi, leaving his recently translated book *I Tarocchi Siciliani* with the players and asking them to correct any technical errors that might have been made: at the time of the article Calatafimi had not yet made any comments. The article is a sort of thank-you letter for the hospitality he received during his visit. He notes that the game is still alive on the island, although it is dying out, and that it is a 'manifestation of Sicilian creativity and originality', and reminds us that the idea that tarot cards had anything to do with divination was an eighteenth-century invention.

(8) Many country railway stations, specially in the south, used to have a monkey on show.

(9) Noises off suggest that the plan has not been entirely abandoned. In the same vein as this Mystical Park idea there was a Parliamentary Bill (n.654), presented by the same Mayor (who is also a National Deputy) in Rome on 7th June 2001 which affords another fascinating example of an 'important initiative for the enhancement of the immense historical, cultural, scenic and environmental patrimony that characterizes the zone…an initiative that would favour the development of tourism by fighting the phenomenon of unemployment and re-launching the economy of the area'. This therapeutic bill was for the setting up of a betting shop in Calatafimi-Segesta. It was to be owned by the municipality of Calatafimi, but it must be noted that it was specifically stated that the running of it could be farmed out to third parties (article 3). Thankfully, nothing more has so far been heard of this panacea.

(10) Quoted in *Il Giornale di Sicilia*.

(11) Mango is still not visitable for the general public.

(12) Edrisi, the Arab geographer of Roger 11, writing in *The Book of Roger*. Although the book had taken fifteen years to produce, it was 'published' on precisely 14-15 January 1154, just a few days before Roger's death (*The Norman Kingdom of Sicily* by Donald Mathew, Cambridge,1992).

(13) See *La Rivoluzione del 1848 nella Sicilia Occidentale* by Giuseppe Mistretta di Paola and Carlo Cataldo (Edizioni Campo, Alcamo, 1988).

(14) A brief description of this palazzo is given in Calcara and Gambino's 1981 university thesis, a copy of which is in the local library. It was used quite often by the earlier Counts of Modica to control their agricultural income. The plan of the first floor was for a reconstruction to accommodate Ferdinand on the occasion of his visit in November 1806. The hunting must have been good because Ferdinand came back again in 1808 and 1811.

(15) Nicolò Mazzara, one of the local historians (he was a pharmacist professionally), in *Calatafimi: Opere, Arte, Toponomastica e Canti Popolari* (Edizioni Sarograf, Alcamo, 1991).

(16) In 1971 the Banco di Sicilia took over the running of the affairs of this bank and absolutely nothing has been done since.

(17) Since he was a cousin, Caterina's grandfather thought his son might benefit from some private coaching in Latin, so he sent him to Vivona. Vivona asked him to prepare a piece so that he could gauge the situation, and, on reading it, according to Caterina's father, declared that he had no need for private coaching. Could it be that the eminent professor wanted to enjoy his holidays in peace?

3. A Potted History of Sicily and Calatafimi (pages 41 to 57)

(1) *Breve Elogio del Dottor Natale Macaddino*, an oration delivered by Niccolò Cervello at the Academia Reale delle Scienze Mediche at Palermo, 10th June 1846, Palermo, 1846.

(2) The oldest Italian banks started off as municipal or state pawn-shops or *banchi di pegno* with a charitable objective and were therefore not allowed to make a profit: this limitation has remained on many of their statutes. Many later banks followed suit. This book was published by the Banca Popolare Cooperativa di Calatafimi, that developed out of the Monte Frumentario, a wheat-seed mortgage bank set up by a local magnate, Domenico Saccaro, which will be dealt with in a later chapter. The objective of the wheat-seed bank was clearly philanthropic. The books are not on sale to the public, but are beautifully produced.

(3) Philippus Cluverius (1580-1623), *Sicilia Antiqua; cum minoribus insulis, ed adjacentibus, item Sardina et Corsica. Opus...elaboratissimum; tabulis geographicis; aere expressis, illustratum*, printed by Louis Elsevier at Leiden in 1619. Apart from Longo's own particularly virulent attacks on Cluverius' accuracy, he also quotes Giacomo Bonanni, Duke of Montalbano (*Dell'-Antica Siracusa Illustrata*, Messina, 1624), who agreed with his judgement:

> ...si sconce e precipitose decisioni, che allo spesso si allontanò dal retto senso, quanto la mesogna dal vero.

> ...such indecent and hasty decisions, that often they wander from the correct meaning, as far as lies from truth.

(4) The classic account of ancient Sicilian history is *Sicily: Phoenician, Greek and Roman* by Edward Freeman, London, T. Fisher Unwin, first edition 1892. Denis Mack-Smith has published much. Michele Amari's *Storia dei Musulmani di Sicilia* is the classic on the Arabs in Sicily (publication began in 1854 but, what with additions, emendations and war, the final three-volume edition was not published until 1939). John Julius Norwich (*The Normans in Sicily*, Penguin, London, 1992: it incorporates his two books on the subject) and Donald Mathew (*The Norman Kingdom of Sicily*, Cambridge Medieval Textbooks, 1992) deal with the Normans. An excellent

NOTES

overall view is *A History of Sicily* (Finley, Mack-Smith, Duggan: Chatto & Windus, London, 1986).

(5) Euphemius' revolt is decribed on pp.6-8 of *A History of Islamic Sicily* by Aziz Ahmad, Edinburgh University Press, *Islamic Surveys*, 10, 1975. In *La Contea di Modica, Ricerche Storiche*, by Raffaele Solarino (circa 1886), vol.1, pp.221-2 (a new edition is now available from Libr. Paolino Edit., Ragusa, 1982), a popular tradition is set down as to how, at about this time, the city of Ragusa managed to save itself temporarily from an Arab siege by throwing *ricotta* cheese (made, in fact, from human milk) over the town walls, which convinced the Arabs they would never take it through starvation.

(6) Although he might have been over-anxious to underline the Arab influence in Sicily at the time, Ibn Jubayr, in his *Travels* (translated by Roland Broadhurst, London, 1955) has the following to say about Christmas 1184 in Palermo: 'The Christian women of this city follow the fashion of Muslim women, are fluent of speech, wrap their cloaks around them and are veiled: they go forth on this Feast Day dressed in robes of gold-embroidered silk, wrapped in elegant cloaks, concealed by coloured veils, and shod with gilt slippers. Thus they parade to their churches, or (rather) to their dens [a play on the words *kana'is*, 'churches', and *kunus*, 'dens'], bearing all the adornments of Muslim women, including jewellery, henna on the fingers, and perfumes. We called to mind – in the way of a literary witticism – the words of the poet: "Going into the church one day, he came upon antelope and gazelle."'

(7) In the opinion of John Julius Norwich, *Byzantium, The Apogee*, Viking, London, 1991, p.307.

(8) G. Tomasi di Lampedusa, *The Leopard* (first published by Fetrinelli in Milan in 1958, and by Collins in London in 1960), and F. De Roberto, *I Vicerè* (published in Milan in 1894).

(9) Edward A. Freeman, *Sicily: Phoenician, Greek, and Roman*, London, 1892, fourth edition, 1926, p.113.

(10) Diodorus Siculus, 20,71,1-5. In search of ready money after his unsuccessful invasion of North Africa, he wreaked horrible torture on the inhabitants of Segesta that was exceptional even for those cruel times, and changed the name of the city to Dikaiopolis, or 'City of Righteousness'.

(11) *A History of Islamic Sicily* by Aziz Ahmad, Edinburgh, 1975, pp.6-9.

(12) Bartolomeo de Neocastro, chapter 15, quoted in Michele Amari, *La Guerra del Vespro Siciliano* (Messaggerie Pontremolesi, Milan, 1989), p.128.

(13) See Mistretti di Paola and Cataldo, op.cit. For Avila, see *Ricordi su la Rivoluzione siciliana* by Vincenzo Fardella di Torrearsa, reprinted by Sellerio, Palermo, 1988, p.126.

4. A Day (pages 58 to 65)

(1) Their practicality is amusingly illustrated in this context by a series of seventeenth-century books, mostly written by priests, which are guides on how to walk around towns in the summer and always stay in the shade: there was at least one that gave a Roman itinerary, as well as one for a Sicilian town, Palermo I believe.

5. Samuel Butler and Calatafimi (pages 66 to 76)

(1) Most of what follows is based on Festing Jones' two-volume *Samuel Butler: A Memoir* (Macmillan, London, 1920). Recent criticism, however (*The Correspondence of Samuel Butler with his sister May*, ed. D.F. Howard, University of California, 1962), suggests that Festing Jones paints a portrait that Butler would have liked to survive: that of a deeply committed rebel against Victorianism – whereas he was rather more conservative than that. But the biography is very complete. Butler's own works were also consulted, of course.

(2) Just two examples. Robert Graves in *Goodbye to All That* said that he was introduced for the first time to modern authors by a form-master of his, and Butler was second on the list after Shaw. Furthermore, he mentions of his uncle, of the *Spectator* and *Punch*: 'When he tipped me a sovereign two terms previously, I had written to thank him, saying that I was at last able to buy Samuel Butler's *Note Books*, *The Way of All Flesh* and the two "Erewhons". This infuriated him, as a good Victorian'. Furthermore, Graves' *Homer's Daughter* (1955) was a fictionalized rewrite of the idea behind *The Authoress of the Odyssey*. The second example concerns George Bernard Shaw. His will, which bequeathed a large part of his fortune for the creation of a new English alphabet, also provided for his house and its contents to be left to the National Trust. In December 1950, Harold Nicolson, as an officer of the Trust, inspected the property and had this, among other things, to say about it: 'The pictures, apart from one of Samuel Butler, and two of Stalin and one of Gandhi, are exclusively of himself' (*Diaries*, vol.III, p.197).

(3) Not much is mentioned about the New Zealand section of Butler's life. I have a certain amount of information that arrived from there in Rome, by email via the Yemen (quite irrelevant, but in keeping with E.M. Forster's judgement of Butler as 'a master of the oblique'). There is an extract from what should be something akin to the New Zealand Dictionary of National Biography (I do not have the title) describing him as an 'Explorer, pastoralist, writer, artist, musician'. It mentioned, incidentally, that he was rumoured to have proposed to a certain Mary Brittan in 1864. Much of *Erewhon* is based on his New Zealand explorations. He ended up with about 55,000

acres of land, and in the space of four years had doubled to £8,000 the capital he had from his father when he came.

(4) Festing Jones writes that, after the 'O Roma O Morte' incident, Ingroia 'had left the church, married and settled down to his profession of school-master. They were the same age, within a year, and became fast friends. Ingroia was indefatigable in helping Butler with his Odyssean studies, and his suggestions, unlike Sugameli's, never led to any embarrassment. He looked forward to Butler's annual visits as to the visits of a brother...' He visited Butler on his death-bed in Palermo in 1902. In his *Diary of a Journey through North Italy to Sicily* (published privately, Cambridge, 1904), a journey which was to distribute mementoes of Butler in Varallo-Sesia (together with the MS of *Ex-Voto*), Arcireale, Calatafimi and Trapani (he left the MS of *The Authoress* here), he describes a lunch with Ingroia and family. During lunch 'I gave (him) a card-case of Butler's and a sketch made by him the last time we were in Calatafimi, also the negatives of several snap-shots Butler took at different times in the neighbourhood.'

(5) *La Teoria dell'Origine Siciliana dell'Odissea*, by Renato Lo Schiavo, ISSPE (Istituto Siciliano di Studi Politici ed Economici), Palermo, 2003.

(6) Daniel Howard's *The Correspondence of Samuel Butler with his Sister May*, op.cit., p.211: in a letter dated 18th January 1892, Butler explains that he is looking for a part of Sicily not far from Marsala with a town and a harbour, with a river some four or five miles away; there should be a big mountain near it and a sunken rock 'awash' and level with the sea and there should be no hills between river and town. Hardly simple one should imagine, but 'armed with these requirements I went down to the map-room of the British Museum and demanded to see the admiralty charts of the coast near Marsala: I explained what I wanted and the keeper of the maps had no sooner unrolled the chart than he said "Why here it is, the very first thing" – just nine or ten miles north of Marsala – every condition absolutely ful-filled, and nothing like it anywhere else. So I have no longer any shadow of doubt about my view being correct.'

(7) Butler met 'Madame', Lucy Dumas, in 1872 in Islington: she was twenty-one and he thirty-seven. They were in touch until her death from consump-tion in 1892, when Butler arranged the funeral and attended it with her brother and Festing Jones. An interesting reference to her occurs in the privately printed *S.B. Butleriana*, ed. A.T. Bartholemew, Nonesuch Press, 1932. On p.163 of this book based on Butler's *Notebooks*, in the section called 'Bossiana' dedicated to the colourful sayings of Butler's cousin, R.E. Worsley's laundress, there is the phrase: 'she [the laundress] calls a whore's fee her "compliment": Madame calls it her *douceur*.'

(8) This appeared in the Trapanese periodical *La Falce* (anno I, n.20, 15th May 1898) and is quoted in *La Teoria dell'Origine Siciliana dell'Odissea*, by Renato Lo Schiavo, ISSPE, Palermo, 2003.

(9) *Further Extracts from the Note Books of Samuel Butler,* ed. A.T. Bartholemew, London, 1912.

(10) On p.311 of vol.II of Festing Jones' biography, Butler drew up a table of his gains and losses from writing in 1899, when he was sixty-four. He had lost nearly £800 overall: the only book to make a profit was *Erewhon,* which netted the princely sum of £62; the *Authoress* made a loss of £60 and only sold 165 copies. He did posthumously make money out of *The Way of All Flesh.*

(11) *Sicilian Noon* by Louis Golding (1895-1958), novelist of Jewish life, best known for *Magnolia Street* (1932).

(12) In the *Dizionario dei Comuni Siciliani* by G. Nicotra (1910), the author lists three hotels in Calatafimi at that time: the 'Samuel Butler' in via Garibaldi, the Albergo 'Garibaldi' in the main square, and the Albergo 'Segesta' in via dei Fondaci (which itself could be translated as the street of post houses: Hoel's night at Calatafimi was in a fondaco).

(13) Israel Zangwill (1864-1926) wrote this in *Italian Fantasies* (Heinemann, London, 1910), in the chapter 'Sicily and the Albergo Samuele Butler: or the Fiction of Chronology', pp.195-204. He was a journalist, a leading Zionist and well known for his novels of Jewish life. When looking for his book *Italian Fantasies,* I discovered in the catalogue of the Biblioteca Fardelliana at Trapani a large number of his tales of ghetto life, in English. Since he met Festing Jones, perhaps he gave them to the latter who subsequently donated them to the Fardelliana library. I cannot think of any other reason for them to be there.

6. Foreign Travellers on Calatafimi (pages 77 to 92)

(1) Donne junior travelled in Sicily and Malta from Rome in October to November 1700. He did not get to Segesta because he was basically sailing around the coast. The book was only published in 1776, encouraged by the success of Brydone's book.

(2) Patrick Brydone, FRS, *A Tour Through Sicily and Malta,* 2 vols, 1773. He went on the journey as 'travelling preceptor' to young Lord Fullerton. Published in the form of letters to Mr Beckford of Somerly, an eighteenth-century bestseller, which influenced the Grand Tour to some extent and also literature (Ann Radcliffe, for instance).

(3) Ann Radcliffe, A *Sicilian Romance,* for example, in which she leaned on Brydone for banditti, monastic eating habits and the enormous power of the Sicilian barons.

(4) Newman's *Letters and Correspondence,* 1833. Partially quoted also in Mrs Nevill Jackson's *A Student in Sicily* (London, 1926).

(5) Louis Simond, *Voyage en Italie et en Sicile,* Paris, 1828, vol.2, p.196.

Comments on accommodation in Sicily over the centuries are legion, but they would have applied all over Europe, as only a few wealthy people travelled for pleasure and clearly the reality of conditions on the road would never bear comparison with their standards at home. Most people carried letters of introduction to prominent people or clerics, but those who did not, come up occasionally with some nice experiences (for us). John Francis, for instance, in Calatafimi prior to his 1847 publication of *Notes from a Journal*...describes his stay thus: 'The inn, so called, is a disorderly cowhouse, into which both pigs and mules intrude: an abominable loft overhead receives you hungry and tired, and here you must keep the windows open or choke. We had taken the precaution of bringing our own sheets, one of Shamoy leather included, and a few ounces of tea: these with patience and hope of the morning kept up our courage during a night of fierce contention with a marching host.' Jeremy Bentham's nephew, George (1800-84), mentions twice in his autobiography (ed. Marion Filipiuk, University of Toronto Press, Toronto, 1997, pp.68-9 and 421) that he had never come across such foul accommodation as that encountered at Calatafimi (spelled Calatafime and Calatafima) except perhaps in the Pyrenees (though he does not say in what year he visited), and George Russell (*A Tour Through Sicily and Malta in the Year 1815*) also complained of a room in an 'osteria' which 'was extremely dirty, and, literally speaking, swarmed with domestic vermin of almost every species'; but that was in nearby Salemi, so Calatafimi was not the only black spot. There probably were no white spots. Some places, in this case nearby Alcamo, offered alternatives to William Young (*Journal of a Summer's Excursion by the Road of Montecassino to Naples and from thence all over the Southern Parts of Italy, Sicily and Malta in the Year 1772*): 'There being no inn in the town, we once more took up our residence with the bearded tribe of St Francis.' One could go on, but really they were intelligent people and should have known what they were in for.

(6) Jean-Pierre Houel (1735-1813): *Voyage Pittoresque des Isles de Sicile, de Malte e de Lipari. Par Jean Houel, Peintre du Roi. A Paris, de L'Imprimerie de Monsieur, 1782*. On his return to Paris he sold his preparatory drawings to finance the publishing project: among the buyers were Louis XVI and Catherine II of Russia.

(7) Henry Swinburne (1743-1803), *Travels in the Two Sicilies 1777-80*, vol.1, published 1783, vol.2, 1785, with his drawings. Fourth son of a Roman Catholic baronet, he was educated and spent most of his life out of England, though he had an estate in Durham. Diplomat and traveller (with all his family). The Emperor Joseph was godfather to his son Joseph. His wife's holdings in the West Indies were devastated, after which Marie Antoinette granted him lands on St Vincent valued at £30,000, but uncultivated. He died of sunstroke in Trinidad leaving four sons and six daughters.

(8) Captain Frederick Chamier RN, *My Travels, or an Unsentimental*

Journey through France, Switzerland and Italy (London, 1855); Vernon William Warren (who travelled with Chamier in Sicily and copied much of the former's book, it would appear), *Recollections of Seventy Two Years* (London, 1917). The *Dictionary of National Biography* judges Chamier to be a bad novelist and entertains doubts about the truth in parts of *Unsentimental Journey*, but there was a Pampalone at that time and also it was a time of poverty in Calatafimi.

(9) Douglas Sladen, *In Sicily* (two vols, London, 1901-3). He wrote a series of books, mainly on Japan and Sicily, at the beginning of the twentieth century.

(10) W.A. Paton, *Picturesque Sicily*, New York and London, 1897.

(11) Begging was not a permanent problem; it depended on the cyclical conditions of the island's economy. In Paton's time, conditions were terrible and emigration was rife, but compare this with the picture painted in *The Rare Adventures and Painful Peregrinations of William Lithgow* (printed by Nickolas Okes in London in 1632). This extraordinarily perspicacious description of Sicily (chapter 14 of the Second Peregrination) says at one point: 'I compassed the whole island and thrice traversed the middle parts thereof from sea to sea, (and) I never saw any of that self-negation to beg bread or seek alms, so great is the beatitude of their plenty. And I dare avow it (experience taught me) that the poorest creature in Sicily eateth as good bread as the best prince in Christendom doth. The people are very humane, ingenious, eloquent and pleasant. Their language in many words is nearer the Latin than the Italian, which they promiscuously pronounce. Somewhat talkative they are, and effeminate, but generally wonderful kind to strangers.'

(12) René Bazin (1853-1932), *La Sicile*, was published in Paris by Calmann-Lévy without a date (though it must have been around 1890, as he quotes figures for sulphur production in 1889). He was a novelist with a particular interest in Catholic agricultural life: people clinging to or leaving the land.

(13) I cannot trace who this mysterious woman was.

7. Some People (pages 93 to 110)

(1) Many of them kept very much to their own countrymen and showed their contempt for the locals, which in towns like Florence, Rome or Naples led them to be unpopular. This was pointed out perceptively by Henry Mathews Esq, *The Diary of an Invalid*, London, John Murray, second edition 1820, although on p.171 on his very first morning in Naples we find him 'transported ten years backwards, into the middle of old school-fellows: There was a regular double-wicket cricket match going on; Eton against the World; – and the world was beaten in one innings!'

(2) *Prime Lezioni di Grammatica, di Lealtà e di Galateo offerte alla Scuola*

Nazionale di Torino da un Italiano di Calatafimi, Premiata Tipografia Cavassego, Belluno, 1890 (the title can be translated as *First Lessons in Grammar, Loyalty and Good Manners offered to the Scuola Nazionale of Turin by an Italian from Calatafimi*).

(3) *Agli Operai Italiani sul Monte Sacro. Versi del Prof. Biagio Ingroia (fuori commercio)*, Adria-Rovigo, 1891 (*To The Italian Workers on Monte Sacro. Verses by Prof. Biagio Ingroia (not for sale)*).

(4) Many years ago I was asked to attempt a sale to the British Museum of two Nuraghi bronzes from Sardinia, at a time when I was living there. They had been ploughed up by a collector, who had many, and thought he might try the British Museum, as I was going back to England for a holiday. The museum was very polite and took me to a back room to examine the objects. They did not buy them in the end (no price was even mentioned) because they said they had so many similar pieces that were not even on show; at which point a few drawers were opened to make their point. There is an excellent picture of the local connoisseur, though with a romantic twist, in Norman Douglas' *South Wind* (London, 1917): Count Caloveglia who, apparently unwillingly, has to sell secretly the priceless ancient Locri Faun.

(5) This MS was recently printed in facsimile as *Ricerche sulle Antichità di Segesta*, ISSPE, Palermo, 1991.

(6) Mommsen, *Viaggio in Italia 1844-45*, Turin, 1980.

(7) Pellegrino (op.cit) writes on p.166: 'The Blessed Archangelo Placenza was said to be related to the families of Gullo, Mollica, Rizzo and Placenza.' The only biography was by Longo: *Memorie e Virtù del Beato Arcangelo Placenza della Città di Calatafimi* (Palermo, 1804).

(8) On the question of the ownership of slaves, some interesting documents have been published by Carlo Cataldo, *La Casa del Sole*, Edizione Campo, Alcamo, 1999, pp.61-8. Quoting Carmelo Traselli, he shows that slaves were bought and sold in the area fairly commonly: there is a notarial act dated 20th August 1379 in which Allegranza di Otranto, resident in Calatafimi, sold Maddalena, a tartar slave, for thirty-six florins to Tommasa di Alcamo; and another of 1382 when another Calatafimi resident, Machonus de Sancto Stefano, sold a male tartar named Antonio for fifty-three florins. There are other documents dealing with absconding slaves, sexual relations with slaves, their fleeing, baptism and emancipation, up till the eighteenth century. There was also the question of Sicilians being enslaved by the North Africans and attempts to free them. And see Iris Origo, *The Merchant of Prato* (The Folio Society, London, 1984, pp.178 et seq.) in the chapter entitled 'La Famiglia', which discusses the phenomenon in fourteenth-century Tuscany. Since many of the slaves came from North Africa and Spain as well as the Balkans, this will be pertinent to Sicily to some extent.

(9) Mancuso, *Descrizione delle Feste per l'Incoronazione di Maria SS Di Giubino*, Antonio Valenza, Palermo, 1780, p.15.

(10) A commentary on the various diggings up, authentications and donations is given in Nicolò Bonaiuto, one-time archpriest of Calatafimi in *Opere*, pp.59 et seq. (Sarograf, Alcamo, 1988).

(11) Longo in his biography devoted pp.5-18 to brutally battering people who dared to suggest that Arcangelo Placenza was from Alcamo, quoting author after author: he was particularly aggressive against the Alcamese poet Sebastiano Bagolino (d. 1604).

(12) Sebastiano Tusa, *Labirinti*, published by *Orestiadi* at Gibellina, a quarterly, n.2, November, 1991.

(13) Cocò's surname was Adamo and the Li Bassi brothers were called Giuseppe and Andrea: they were all cousins.

(14) Mongitore, *Della Sicilia Ricercata nelle Cose Più Memorabili*, Palermo, 1747; reprinted by Sicilcassa, Palermo, 1981.

8. Earth, Fire, Wind, Water (pages 111 to 122)

(1) Swinburne, op.cit., pp.405 et seq. In his section on exports from Messina, he says of sumach: 'The most esteemed comes from Alcamo, Castelamare [sic] and Monreale.' The first two towns are just a few kilometres from Calatafimi.

(2) Manna was a sweet substance, used in confectionery, in cosmetics and as a mild purgative. It was made from the sap of the ash tree, by tapping the trunks in much the same way as rubber is obtained. Johan Herman von Riedesel in his *Viaggio in Italia* (English translation, J.R. Foster FRS, London, 1773) states: 'Here they likewise have abundance of *Manna*, which is a juice of a kind of *Accacia*, whose bark they wound in the months of *July*, *August* and *September*, and the issuing sap is this inspissated by the heat of the sun, and becomes *Manna*.' It used to be a major export.

(3) Signor Gaetano Pampalone has the original.

(4) Sicilian weights and measures are somewhat difficult to deal with, and not only because the same terms have different values in different parts of the island. Many attempts were made to reform them. In the *Tavole di Riduzione dei Pesi e delle Misure delle Due Sicilie* by Carlo Afan de Riviera (Naples, 1840) there is on pp.23-4 of the introduction a brief description of the term *rotolo*, a measure of weight, for those interested. Afan de Riviera acknowledges the power of tradition when he states that this measure of Norman origin has been allowed to stand in the new Law of 6th April 1840 ('Noi dunque conserviamo senza la menoma alterazione quell medesimo peso che si trova statuito fin dai tempi de' nostri principi normanni.' ('We have therefore retained without any alterations those same weights that had been on the statute books since the times of our Norman princes.')

(5) It might be worth pointing out that three of the winds bear the names of

the countries they hail from: *grecale* from Greece, *levante* from the Levant and *libeccio* from Libya. *Tramontana* is the cold north wind from beyond the mountains; *sirocco*, the insufferably hot humid wind from the south, derives from the North African Arabic word *shuluq*; *ostro* comes from the Latin *austrum*; *ponente* from the Latin *ponere*, the verb used for the setting of the sun; *maestrale*, also from the Latin *magister* or master, is a typical wind in the Tyrrhrenian sea.

(6) Swinburne, op.cit., p.232.

(7) The Duke of Buckingham and Chandos, *The Private Diary...(The Greville Diary)*, London, 3 vols., 1862.

(8) Mongitore. op.cit., p.193.

(9) The original is in the hands of Signor Gaetano Pampalone.

9. Festas and Processions (pages 123 to 138)

(1) Nicolò Bonaiuto, *Opere* (Sarograf, Alcamo, 1988), pp.39-194.

(2) There were four Giurati. They were not elected by the people but nominated by the Segreto Governador, or the Count's deputy. The four of them were each in office for a week, by rotation: when exerting his office, the Giurato carried a wooden cane. Their letter to the Bishop of Mazzara announcing the choice of the Madonna di Giubino was recently found by archpriest Bonaiuto.

(3) This in the letter of the Giurati, the original of which was found by Bonaiuto in the Episcopal archives at Mazzara del Vallo just after the Second World War.

(4) *Descrizione Delle Festa Fatte Nella Città di Calatafimi...*by Francesco Sanseverino, Palermo, 1780. Sanseverino was the Archbishop of Palermo and visited Calatafimi in 1779 (see later).

(5) Idem.

(6) The Angimbè church was allowed to fall into disrepair and, in 1464, the statue was transferred to the church of Giubino. After the dissolution of ecclesiastical property in 1866 and the selling off by auction of the various landholdings, no buyer could be found for the church of S Maria del Giubino. A committee of private citizens was formed in 1876 and bought it by private act. At the beginning of the twentieth century it was restored and elongated, and there is a plaque stating that some of the work was carried out with funds sent by Calatafimi émigrés in 'Brooklyn and New York'. The church was regularized in 1933; work was carried out in 1956 for the Madonna's marble chapel; in 1958-9 a new front was built onto it – the architect was Biagio Vivona, an uncle of Caterina's.

(7) Most of the key documents for the story of the Madonna di Giubino, or at least authenticated copies of them, were found during the twentieth

century. I have already mentioned that Bonaiuto found the original letter of the Giurati in the episcopal archives at Mazzara just after the First World War (the volume containing it actually opened at exactly the right place the first time he looked at it!) and the others (the notarial act of the election, 1656; the Royal Act of approval, 1657; the confirmation by fifty-six leading citizens, 1657; the explanatory letter to the bishop by the Giurati – they talked of one, not three extractions – 1658) were found by Sac. Diego Taranto at Calatafimi in 1957. At the same time there was also found the Decree of the Congregation of Rites, dated 1802, subsequent to the granting of the Papal Crowns in 1779, the granting of ratification of Maria di Giubino as a Patron Saint of Calatafimi and the granting of the rare privilege of a special mass. See also Sac. Diego Tarranto, *Il SS Crocifisso di Calatafimi*, (Pro-Loco di Calatafimi, 1982).

(8) Laurana was at work in the vicinity. He was born in about 1420 in what is now modern Croatia and died in Italy before March 1502. His life is something of a mystery, but he began as an itinerant sculptor in Naples in 1453 and went on to work in Sicily and Provence. He did many Madonna and Childs and female busts with oval-shaped faces. In 1469, he did a copy of the Madonna di Trapani for the town of Erice, and in the previous year he made a bust of Pietro Speciale, who was then lord of Alcamo and Calatafimi. Our Madonna was probably mid-fifteenth century.

(9) The nearly full title of Sansverino's book, already referred to, was *Descrizione Delle Feste Fatte Nella Città di Calatafimi, in occasione d'essersi coronata...la venerabile marmoreal imagine della Vergine Sacratissima detta del Giubino...Da Monsignor D. Francesco Sanseverino...Arcivescovo di Palermo...*, published 'In Palermo MDCCCLXXX. Nella Stamperia di D. Antonio Valenza, Impressore Camerale. Con Licenza de' Superiori'. This was the official report on the Crowning of the Madonna di Giubino with the Papal crown, which took five days.

(10) Calcara, *Breve e Fedele Ragguaglio del Triduo Festivo che annualmente ad onore del suo Miracoloso SS Crocifisso celebra la città di Calatafimi*, 1728.

(11) In 1776 the Mugnai presented the silver cross to the SS Crocifisso. It was paid for by a collection among all the members of the guild with the exception of the Colombo family, which for some reason declined to contribute. The result is that the cross is thus inscribed:

D:DOM.^{ci}NOLEDO AC MOLINDARUM

ELIMOSINA 1776

EXCEPTIS LI COLOMBO

For a description of the numerous water-mills in the Kaggera valley, see *I Mulini di Calatafimi*, Accardo, Boni, Palmieri, op.cit. The area was an important milling centre for a large radius of pasturage beyond the town limits.

10. Calatafimi and Garibaldi (pages 139 to 149)

(1) See *Garibaldi and His Enemies* by Christopher Hibbert, Little, Brown and Company, Boston, 1965, p.193.

(2) For the issue of the Election see *The Times*, 19th May 1860, with a report from Turin dated 16th May (the day after the battle of Calatafimi): Cavour managed to get all his men through and to exclude Garibaldi, despite his great popularity.

(3) This denouncement was printed in *The Times* on 21st May: it had been published in the *Piedmontese Gazette* on 18th May. In *Letters from Sicily* (a conglomeration of texts in the British Library at X.42973489) there is also printed a note by Cavour to the Chevalier Conofari, which reads as follows: 'The undersigned has received the note of the 24th instant by which the Chevalier Canofari, Envoy Extraordinary and Minister Plenipotentiary of his Sicilian Majesty, has informed him that in the Proclamation circulated by General Garibaldi in Sicily, he assumes the title of Dictator of the King of Sardinia, and calls on this fact the disapprobation and repudiation of the Government of his Majesty the King [i.e. a formal declaration should be made to that effect]. Although there could not be any doubt on this subject, the undersigned, by order of his Majesty, does not hesitate to declare that the Government of the King is totally unconnected with any act of Garibaldi, that the title assumed by him is entirely usurped, and that the Government of his Majesty cannot but formally disapprove it. Etc, etc. Cavour. Turin, 26th May 1860.'

(4) Pietro Adamo's eye-witness account, which was dictated much later in 1891 to Biagio Ingroia, was published under the title 'Memoria' in *Calatafimi in Camicia Rossa* (Palermo, 1982). The municipal library in Calatafimi has the MS of Ingroia's original fair copy of Adamo's statement for the period 13th-17th May. An interesting account, from the aristocratic point of view, of the sincere, but ineffective revolutionary movements in Palermo at the time is to be found in *Tre Mesi nella Vicaria di Palermo nel 1860* by F. Brancaccio di Carpino (translated as *The Fight for Freedom: Palermo, 1860*, the Folio Society, London, 1968). Brancaccio heard of the battle of Calatafimi in the Vicaria prison only on 21st May from a message written in lemon juice smuggled into his cell. The invisible news was rendered legible by singeing the paper over a candle.

(5) The local historian Carlo Cataldo, *Calatafimi e Garibaldi* (Sarograf, Alcamo, 1990), pp.10 et seq., gives a simple narrative summary.

(6) Biagio Ingroia: 'Nè Pianto Romano, Nè Pianto dei Romani' ('Neither Roman Tears, Nor Tears of the Romans'), in *Il Lambruschini*, anno IV, n.3, Trapani, September, 1894. This was picked up and used by Salvatore Romano (1838-1923) for a paper given to the *Società Italiana per la Storia Patria* on 11th November that same year. Educationalist and local historian,

he was also involved in the early days of Butler's theory about the *Odyssey*, publishing papers in *Il Lambruschini*, the Trapanese magazine.

(7) Salvatore Romano's paper, which had been printed in the *Archivio Storico Siciliano*, anno XX, fasc.III, was published as a pamphlet under the title *Il Vero Nome del Colle Impropriamente Detto Pianto dei Romani*, in 1910 at Palermo.

(8) The parliamentary debate in the House of Commons on the subscription issue was reported in *The Times* on 18th May. The advertisement for this particular subscription appeared in that paper on 9th May, but there were other funds being arranged.

(9) In *The Times* of 18th May the Neapolitans are said to have bombarded 'the wine factories of Messrs Woodhouse, Ingham and other British subjects'. On the 21st, the paper printed a report dated the 18th claiming that Garibaldi's ships were showing the Union Jack and wearing English red ('redshirts', of course was a synonym for 'Garibaldini'). For an excellent history of the Inghams, Woodhouses, Whitakers and Florios, see Raleigh Trevelyan, *Princes Under the Volcano*, op.cit. He quotes the phenomenally rich Benjamin Ingham's August 1860 letter to the British Consul complaining of the general unrest left in the wake of Garibaldi's advance (a letter which was forwarded to Lord John Russell), which reveals that Ingham also owned land in nearby Vita, which is a part of the Comune of Calatafimi.

(10) Carlo Agrati, *I Mille* (Mondadori, Milano, 1933) prints the list of billets, signed by a certain Cenni who was 'il commandante di piazza'. Dunne (1827-1906), known as 'Milordo', fought with Garibaldi throughout the campaign, commanding the 'English regiment' of local volunteers under English officers which he had trained after the capture of Palermo (see Trevelyan, *Princes Under the Volcano*, op.cit). It is possible that Dunne did not arrive in Sicily till June 1860 with the second wave of volunteers under the command of Giacomo Medici (see Adam Zamoyski's *Holy Madness*, Viking, New York, 2000, p.400).

(11) Denis Mack Smith in *Garibaldi, A Portrait in Documents* (Florence, 1982), p.7. He also says that the English government had financed Garibaldi with a case of Turkish piastres. See in addition his *Victor Emanuel, Cavour and the Risorgimento*, Oxford University Press, 1971, p.165. It is, however, a well-documented fact that the towns of northern Italy contributed enthusiastically to Garibaldi's activities. Enthusiasm for Garibaldi in England was long-lasting, despite the outrage it produced in Queen Victoria, and it was manifest among all classes. On 12th April 1864 the Prince of Wales visited Garibaldi, then in London; he reported to his mother that he had gone 'quite privately', found him 'uncharlatanlike' and, as an Italian patriot, he had been hailed by her subjects for being a protagonist in her Government's policy with regard to the unity of Italy (Stanley Weintraub, *Edward the Caresser*, New York, 2001). On that same day, 12th April, all the workmen

involved in putting the finishing touches to Lionel Rothschild's new Piccadilly House had downed tools to acclaim him as a hero (Stanley Weintraub, *Charlotte and Lionel*, New York, 2003).

(12) The local historian Carlo Cataldo, op.cit. pp.28 and 37 has made a meticulous list of both the dead and the wounded.

(13) In their respective novels *I Viceré* (*The Viceroys*) and *Il Gattopardo* (*The Leopard*). The first, although it was also translated into English by Archibald Colquhoun in 1961, has remained almost unknown to English readers, which is a real loss: it was originally published in 1894.

(14) Nello Morsellino, *Giuseppe Garibaldi e I Mille...Guai*, Edizioni Campo, Alcamo, 2000.

(15) His three donkeys, on the other hand, were burdened with the names of Pio IX, Franz Joseph and Louis Napoleon. Hibbert, however (in *Garibaldi and His Enemies*, op.cit.), says that the horses were called Calatafimi and Milazzo. The tradition of remembering Calatafimi was respected much later by his descendant Anita Garibaldi, who visited Calatafimi on the 2004 anniversary of the battle and presented her book *Nate dal Mare*.

11. Charities (pages 150 to 166)

(1) My wife's great-great-grandfather on the maternal side. See below in chapter 19.

(2) Mazzara Niccolò, *Calatafimi*, Sarograf, Alcamo, 1991. Among the many who are not to be forgotten, one should particularly remember Blundo who founded 'La Casa delle Fanciulle Orfane' (an orphanage for girls) in 1631, still functioning in its beautiful, though rather damaged, building next to the Chiesa Matrice and the castle (Butler shot some photographs of a Mother Superior inside this building much later on). Then there was Truglio who left a large amount of money for the Chiesa Matrice, the hospital (which gained the name of 'Ospedale Truglio') and for the Monte di Pietà (which made interest free loans for collateral: the origin of Italian banks in the Middle Ages). He also gave dowries and lots of offerings for the poor. His Elizabethan-ruffed sarcophagus is in the Chiesa Matrice.

(3) *Ounces* and, later on, *tari*, as well as *salme, rotoli*, etc, etc: they do not bear translation, because it is extremely difficult to be precise: they change from area to area and, even if one does manage to pinpoint an exact measurement, it will be of little significance anyway in a modern context.

(4) Unusual, but it did happen. In 1758 the Calatafimi priest, a certain Antonio Balduccio, was captured by the Turks while sailing on the galley *San Gennaro*. A collection was organized by the clergy in the diocese in 1762, which raised 200 golden Venetian sequins, but even this was not enough to ransom him. He was eventually ransomed, however, and returned to

Calatafimi in a pitiful state where he died on the 19th August 1766. This is reported in the preface to Pellegrino (by Diego Tarranto and Leonardo Vanella).

(5) I am told that the building survived the 1968 earthquake, but that it was bulldozed by an engineer with a chip on his shoulder who was having an argument with, among other people, the Monte's director.

(6) I found among some family papers the other day a draft of another supplication to the Pope in the hand of Domenico Saccaro. He thought he was having unfair payments asked of him by the ex-Capuchin friars and the municipality for land that the Vatican had granted him in perpetuity in the grounds of the old Capuchin monastery gardens. It comes with a letter of recommendation to a certain di Giovanni at the Vatican, and is rather interesting (one must remember that the monasteries had been disestablished by then). It asks for the supplication to be presented at the feet of His Holiness and says 'He (Saccaro) had always been a benefactor to the Capuchin monks, and has given them considerable charity at all times. He cannot suffer to see himself opposed by the present monks in this matter of payment, and if the institution (the poor people's home) had not already been well built, he would have abandoned it completely, to the great sadness of the entire population. A faithful Catholic merits all respect, including precise rights of compensation. I therefore recommend this supplication, which I shall attach to this note, so that you can foster its success.' The actual supplication contains a list of various amounts of money he has been asked to pay: there are questions about cutting down and planting trees, etc, etc.

(7) Though it has been merged with the Blundo charities, the Maria SS Immacolata, and the Lo Truglio Hospital foundation by Presidential Decree, n.428 of 28th November 1997.

(8) These simple agrarian credit organizations had been in existence for a long time, but they flourished particularly in the period from the middle of the eighteenth century until the unification of Italy, although mostly on the east coast: a survey carried out in 1854 revealed that around a hundred were operating, of which more than two-thirds were concentrated in the provinces of Messina and Catania, and only four in the province of Trapani of which one was, of course, in Calatafimi (*Banche e Banchieri in Sicilia*, Fondazione Culturale Lauro Chiazzese, 1992, pp.212-13).

(9) The 1859 war, the Second War of Italian Independence, in which France helped Piedmont to oust the Austrians from Lombardy, in return for the territory of Savoy and Nice (Garibaldi's birthplace). Napoleon III's *volte face* and the resultant Treaty of Villafranca went a long way to reinforcing Cavour's innate prudence and evident distrust for Garibaldi, not least because Napoleon III thought that Orsini's attempt on his life in 1858 was connected with the Italian revolutionary movement inspired by Mazzini. It was, incidentally, the heavy casualties at the battle of Solferino, which brought

the war to an end, that motivated Henri Dumont to establish the International Red Cross. Apparently, there were no claims from Calatafimi combatants: hardly surprising as the war was extremely short and Calatafimi was a long way away.

(10) In *Beneficenza del Cav. Sig. Domenico Saccaro di Calatafimi*, a nine-page booklet written by G.S and published in Trapani on 6th February 1874, the anonymous author wrote that Saccaro had set up in 1864 a *bottega di paragone* (a 'parallel shop') which sold basic necessities (bread, pasta, rice and legumes) with better quality and lower prices than other shops.

12. Underground Activity (pages 167 to 175)

(1) Bitumen was mentioned in connection with the 1693 earthquake and crops up on various occasions in descriptions of Calatafimi. I must qualify my statement that there is only one industry in Calatafimi. I notice in the telephone book that there is a company called 'Bitumedil', which, as the name suggests, produces bituminous conglomerate.

(2) A doctor cousin, Franco Trapani, has written an introductory study, *Oleum Petronicum. Un Antico Rimedio Galenico delle Falde Settentrionale della Maiella* (*Oleum Petronicum. An Ancient Galenic Remedy from the Northern Slopes of the Maiella Mountains*), unpublished but written in 2003. He notes references to this from the early 11th century onwards. It contains or is linked to bitumen, petroleum, asphalt, sulphur, grease and stones. It was used to treat scabies, psoriasis, eczema, coughs and catarrh, and as an antiseptic. Bitumen, it must be remembered, was used in mummification, and also for lighting.

(3) J.H. von Riedesel, *Voyage en Sicile et dans la Grande Grèce*, Lausanne 1773.

(4) Leandro Alberti, *Descrittione di Tutta Italia...*(*Description of All Italy...*), Venice, 1561.

(5) *The Travels of Ibn Jubayr*, translated by Roland Broadhurst, and originally published, London, 1952. Recently republished by Goodwood, New Delhi, 2003.

(6) M. Savonarola, *De Balneis e Thermis Naturalibus Omnibus Italiae*, p.914. Quoted by Longo, note 100 on p.136. I do not know which edition he had, as there were various editions published in Ferrara, Bologna, Venice, etc, in the 1480s and 1490s.

(7) According to Nicotra in his *Dizionario dei Comuni Siciliani* (op.cit.), the waters are thus composed: hydro-sulphuric acid, calcium sulphate, magnesium sulphate, calcium carbonate, magnesium carbonate, hydrochlorate of calcium, hydrochlorate of magnesium, hydrochlorate of soda, silica.

(8) I know of an inland town in Sardinia that after the Second World War

was offered a plan to bring the sea to a land-locked town if it voted for a certain candidate.

(9) What follows depends much on the *Giornale di Sicilia* and Costantino Caldo's *Sottosviluppo e Terremoto: la Valle del Belice*, ed. Manfredi (Palermo, no date: ?1974-5).

(10) In Palermo the pens of the seismographs of the Astronomic Centre in the Archbishopric's seminary were damaged, and the prisoners in the famous Ucciardone gaol were overcome with terror and were later allowed to leave their cells (*Giornale di Sicilia*, 16th January).

(11) Costantino Caldo, op.cit.

(12) From Calcara and Gambino's 1980-1 university thesis (op.cit.), written more than ten years after the disaster: 'In the Sasi area, where the "plan" is to position the urban works, there is a superabundance of main roads, piazzas, parking areas, secondary roads and street lighting, waiting for the day the homes will be built.'

13. Emigration and Immigration (pages 176 to 185)

(1) Capponata is a very rich Sicilian *antipasto* or *hors d'oeuvre*. Apart from the mentioned ingredients, it includes olives, celery, onion, capers, pine-nuts and almonds, together with oil and vinegar.

(2) It was not always like this, however, as we have seen from Ibn Jubayr (op.cit.) in his descriptions of the Sicilian countryside. In his delightful book *The Rare Adventures and Painful Peregrinations of William Lithgow*, 'by himself' (first complete published edition, 1632), on p.223 of the 1974 Folio Society edition, we read that he writes of Sicily: '...I compassed the whole island and thrice traversed the middle parts thereof from sea to sea, I never saw any of that self-negation to beg bread or seek alms, so great is the beatitude of their plenty. And I dare avow it (experience taught me) that the poorest creature in Sicily eateth as good bread as the best prince in Christendom doth.' And he certainly had had the experience. Since I have discussed Homer and the authorship of the *Odyssey* elsewhere, it might be interesting to record Lithgow's views on Odysseus' wanderings. He had arrived (on foot) in Cairo in the first decade of the seventeenth century and described on p.170 a quarter of the town called, among other things, Memphis: '...the furthest place that Ulysses in his travels visited, so well memorized by Homer – yet a voyage of no such estimation as that princely poet accounted it, for his travels were not answerable to the fifteenth part of mine.'

(3) In a note in *Opere* (op.cit.), on p.78, he writes: 'In 1922 Cav. Pasquale Civiletti sculpted an artistic reproduction in marble, which had been requested by emigrant citizens, and it is venerated in the church of Saint Joseph in Brooklyn.'

(4) Sicilian emigrants kept together in America even on a village basis. A well-known son of Castellamare, just down the road from Calatafimi, wrote in his autobiography on p.62: 'The Castellamarese tended to stick together. We had our own distinct neighborhoods, not only in Brooklyn and Manhattan, but also in Detroit, Buffalo and Endicott, New York. Not only did we all know each other, but we were often related to one another. Among ourselves we spoke Sicilian. English was handy but usually unnecessary to our lives. We asked nothing from anybody. We took care of our own. In all our ethnic neighborhoods, we established a branch of the Castellamarese Society of Merit, our version of the Kiwanis or Rotary clubs to help the needy, celebrate feast days and remember our heritage.' The autobiography is called *A Man of Honor* (New York, 1983), and it is by Joseph Bonanno, alias Joe Bananas. Local talk here says that his family actually came from Bruca, a tiny hamlet, half of which depends administratively on Calatafimi and the other on Castellamare, but I have not investigated.

(5) See the interesting book *The Sting of Change: Sicilians in Sicily and Australia* by Constance Cronin (University of Chicago, 1970). She spent nearly a year in 'Nicuportu' (i.e. Partinico, which is quite near Calatafimi) and then rather more than a year in Sydney. Among her many findings is that, although relations outside the family in Australia adapt fairly quickly to the new environment, habits within the family change much more slowly.

(6) Constance Cronin, op.cit., p.252.

14. Some Injustices (pages 186 to 194)

(1) Cicero, *Verrine Orations*, Loeb Classics, Heinemann, 1928, 2 vols., translated by L.H.G. Greenwood, II, iii, 92/93, and II, iv, 73/76.

(2) Rupilian Law. The law regulated relations with slaves and stated that Roman citizens should be tried by a jury of their peers.

(3) There are various sources, particularly the *Difesa dei Singoli di Calatafimi contro Gli Eredi del Conte di Modica per la Causa del Terraggiolo* (this long pamphlet was published by Francesco Nocera, but when or where was not given); it was the case for the citizens of Calatafimi drawn up by the Avvocato Giuseppe Scibona. The local historian Longo, who collected the archive evidence which was the backbone of the case against *terraggiolo*, wrote *Discoprimento dell'Angarico Dazio del Terraggiolo* and *Dimostrazione dell'Angarica Imposizione del Terraggiolo*. The unpublished 1945-6 university thesis by Leonardo Pampalone on this subject is also useful.

(4) Apart from the 1393 Privileges and a 1564 confirmation by Ludovico Enriquez di Caprera (both published together with other relevant documents in Pellegrino), there are various references in many documents attesting the obsolete character of feudal dues. One interesting one was quoted in

Leonardo Pampalone's university thesis, which his son, Gaetano, let me read. It is interesting in that it involves the area where we now live, but also because of its date which was when the *terraggiolo* was beginning to be exacted. A document sworn before the Notary Marcantonio Damiani on 9th August 1555 states that 'Contrada San Giovanne' was 'free from any form of feudal service'. It was not however, enough to escape payment of the *terraggiolo*.

(5) Giovanni Evangelista di Blasi, *Storia Cronologica de' Viceré. Luogotenenti e Presidenti del Regno di Sicilia* (originally published 1790-1, Edizioni della Regione Siciliana, 1974, vol.V, n.75, on p.87.

16. Segesta (pages 200 to 220)

(1) Domenico Lo Faso Pietrasanta, Duca di Serradifalco. He was head of the newly formed *Commissione per le Antichità e Belle Arti*. He began excavating and restoring the theatre in 1822.

(2) Leandro Alberti, a Dominican monk, born in Bologna in 1479. His book has an enormously long title and can be usefully shortened to *Descrittione di Tutta Italia...Isole Appartenenti all'Italia*. It was published in Venice in 1561.

(3) Sebastiano Tusa in a supplement to *Giornale di Sicilia* published in 2000. Tusa is the contemporary authority on Segesta. He was for many years in charge of the excavations at Segesta, and has published a great deal on the site. It was Tusa who 'discovered' the Mango sanctuary.

(4) *Ricerche sulle Antichità di Segesta*, MS in the local library by G. Leonora and published in facsimile by ISSPE in Palermo in 1991. Such was Leonora's dedication to local archaeology that he dictated this MS on his death-bed, when he was suffering from partial paralysis. The MS is divided into nine sections: pre-Hellenic history, Hellenic history, the temple, the theatre, the walls (he noted the defences at different stages), the coins (this was his passion), the pottery, the burials and the inscriptions. He gives some nice descriptions of the opening up of graves, but he discovered very little inside them. G. Nenci found this work of use in his excavations with the Scuola Normale di Pisa (op.cit.).

(5) The article was in the local library, but had been a part of a book or magazine, the title or date of which were missing. The author, however, states that he had a similar article printed in the *Bulletin* of the Istituto di Corrispondenza Archeologica in Rome. 'In fact it can be read in last year's Bulletin on p.170', but which year it was I do not know.

(6) R. Giuffrida, *Fonti Inediti per la Storia della Tutela dei Beni Archaeologici della Sicilia: il 'Plano' del Torremuzza sullo Stato dei Monumenti*, quoted by G.Nenci in *Annali della Classe di Lettere e Filosofia della Scuola Normale Superiore di Pisa*, s.III, XXI, 1991, 3-4.

(7) Robert Fagan (1761-1816) became Consul-General for Sicily and Malta in 1809. He was well known for his collection, some of which is today on view in Palermo's National Archaeological Museum. He also excavated at Tindaris and Selinunte. See note 26 to chapter two of Trevelyan's *Princes Under the Volcano* (op.cit.). He was also the diplomatic go-between in the titanic struggle between Lord William Bentinck and the Royal Family over the imposition of the Westminster-style constitution and in the successful bid to put an end to the Queen's political meddling and get her out of Sicily in 1812 (see Harold Acton, *The Bourbons of Naples*, London, 1998, pp. 608 et seq.).

(8) His books were *Ricerche ed Osservazioni Ultimamente Fatte in Segesta*, Palermo, 1855; *Sopra Cio' che Ultimamente Erasi Incomminciato a Scovrire in Segesta*, Palermo, 1856; *Egesta e i suoi Monumenti*, Palermo, 1859. And finally *Preventivo Sposizione di Taluni Monumenti Segestani Editi e di Talune Nuove Ricerche Archeologiche*, Palermo, 1861.

(9) The pamphlet was in the form of a letter to Giuseppe Bandiera, and was published in Alcamo on 5th January 1860.

(10) MS in my possession.

(11) *Un Tour en Sicile*, p.231.

(12) The Regia Trazzera, a sort of track for allowing animals to pass through other peoples' land to reach legitimate pastures and to take normal road traffic, cannot be ploughed or owned, though the owners of the land which it crosses are not always convinced that this is a good idea.

(13) J.H. von Riedesel, *Voyage en Sicile et dans la Grande Grèce*, Lausanne, 1773.

(14) Sir Richard Colt-Hoare, FRS and FRSA (1758-1838), classical scholar, member of the banking family, historian of Wiltshire. He did his own drawings and wrote Wiltshire history and travel books. He travelled as a result of his grief at widowhood.

(15) 'Girgenti' was an old name for Agrigento.

(16) George Bellas Greenhough (1778-1855), a rich geologist who visited Sicily at the beginning of the nineteenth century. He was a map-maker and organized the Geological Society, of which he was the first President.

(17) The Rev Brian Hill, *Observations and Remarks in a Journey Through Sicily and Calabria in the Year 1791*, London, 1792.

(18) Sir George Cockburn (1772-1853), *A Voyage to Cadiz and Gibraltar, up the Mediterranean to Sicily and Malta in 1810*, London, 1815. Professional soldier, Irish. For a short time in 1810 he commanded a division of the British army of occupation (at Messina), after which he travelled around Sicily and published his book. As a reformist, he became a violent pamphleteer and admirer of Cobbet.

(19) This Lord Valentia (George Annesley, Viscount Valentia, 1770-1844) was an Irishman who travelled to India in 1802 and, on his way back,

surveyed the Red Sea and ended up in Egypt. He published an account of his travels in three volumes and, later in 1808, presented a report to the Foreign Secretary Canning recommending that Britain should wrest control of commerce on the Red Sea by establishing alliances with Abyssinia and the Wahhabis in Arabia. Canning did not act on this recommendation. He was also an energetic antagonist of James Bruce, maintaining that he never got to Abyssinia.

(20) Richard Duppa, *Travels in Italy, Sicily and the Lipari Islands*, London, 1828, p.132.

(21) Richard Plantagenet Temple Nugent Brydges Chandos Grenville, Duke of Buckingham and Chandos (1796-1861). He travelled in 1827-8 and succeeded to the title in 1839. He lived at Stowe and was a notorious spendthrift. In 1847 he was having problems with the bailiffs who occupied Stowe. The house was sold that year when the Duke left England with debts of upwards of £1 million. He was publicly criticized by *The Times*. He published works of modern history and died at the Great Western Hotel at Paddington Station in London in 1861. The *Diaries* were published in three volumes in 1862. He deals with Segesta in vol.2, pp.114-22.

(22) Sayve, Auguste de, *Voyage en Sicile Fait en 1820 et 1821*, pp.106-17.

(23) Marquess of Ormonde, *An Autumn in Sicily*, Dublin, 1850, pp.219-20.

(24) Michal Jan (de) Borch, *Lettres sur la Sicile écrites...Brydonn* (sic), Turin, 1782.

(25) Dominique Vivant Denon, *Voyage Pittoresque...*, Paris, 1781-6, in five vols. (Sicily in vols. 5 and 6).

(26) Jean-Frédéric D'Ostervald (1733-1850), *Voyage pittoresque en Sicile*, Paris, 2 vols., 1822-6. In Italian, *Viaggio Pittorico in Sicilia*, Edizioni Giada, Palermo, 1987, pp.138-47.

(27) Gastone Vuillier, *La Sicile, Impressions du Présent et du Passé*, Hachette, Paris, 1896. Artist and illustrator, he visited Sicily in 1893. He dedicated his book to Pitrè, whom he met in Palermo.

(28) Even Butler got involved in the lizard business. In *Further Extracts from the Note-Books of Samuel Butler*, ed. A.T. Bartholomew, Jonathan Cape, London, 1934, he turns his pen to them at the ruins of Segesta's rival Selinus. 'A man at Selinunte told us that the large green lizards were called "salv" uomine' ("man saver") because when a man was lying asleep on the grass if a serpent came near him they would go up and whisper in his ear.'

(29) *A Man of Honour*, Joseph Bonanno (with Sergio Lalli), Simon and Schuster, New York, 1983.

(30) Jean-Louis-Armand Quatrefages de Bréau, *The Rambles of a Naturalist*, London, 1857. The original source of Quatrefages de Bréau's experiences in Sicily was vol.2 of *Souvenirs d'un Naturaliste*, Paris, 1854.

(31) Francis Chenevix-Trench, *A Ride in Sicily* by Oxoniensis, London, 1851, pp.63-8, British Library, 10131.a.7.

(32) *Sowing: An Autobiography of the Years 1880-1904*, Leonard Woolf, Hogarth Press, London, 1961. p.183.

(33) William Young, *A Journal of a Summer's Excursion, by the Road of Montecasino to Naples, and from thence all over the Southern Parts of Italy, Sicily and Malta in the Year 1772*, London ?, 1773?

17. Living the Land (pages 221 to 235)

(1) The highest temperature ever recorded in Italy was registered in Sicily in August 1886: it was 49.6°C. That, of course, was exceptional.

(2) A brief picture of the Arab character of Norman agriculture in the nearby town of Alcamo in December 1184 is given by Ibn Jubayr (*The Travels of Ibn Jubayr*, translated by Roland Broadhurst. There is a London edition dated 1952, and also a 2003 edition published in New Delhi). He was on his way from Palermo to Trapani to return to Spain after his Hadj. Apart from noting a 'continuous line of villages and farms', which he compared to the land outside Cordova, 'but the soil is choicer and more fertile', he goes on to say: 'We passed one night only on the road, at a place called *Alcamah*, a large and spacious town with markets and mosques: its inhabitants and those of the farms we had passed on our way, were Muslims all.'

(3) Incidentally the word 'admiral' got into European languages through Sicilian from the Arabic word *amir*, meaning a commander.

(4) The dialect original runs as follows:

Palermo tutta cochira e cavaddi
A Murriali li jardina beddi
Calatafimi grossa cascavaddi
A Siacca, bacaruni e bacareddi
Mazzara pigghia grossi li so' saddi
Ed a Marsala vopi ed asineddi
A Trapani sù russi li curaddi
E a lu Munti li picciotti beddi.

Palermo all coaches and horses
At Monreale beautiful gardens
Calatafimi big caciocavallos
At Sciacca big and small terracotta jars
At Mazzara the sardines are big
And at Marsala the small netted fish are tasty
At Trapani red red corals
And beautiful young people at Erice.

Quoted in *Storia e Folklore di Sicilia*, Santi Correnti, Mursia, 1975, among other sources.

(5) This insistence on not living in the country (unless in a *baglio*) is centuries old and was confirmed by a recent piece of research that was carried out in the 1960s and included in Costantino Caldo's book (*Sottosviluppo e Terremoto*, Manfredi, Palermo, no date, but around 1975). The research, pp.52-3, was carried out in the Belice valley – a bit of Calatafimi is actually in the valley – in February 1967 on a sample of 499 rural houses. Of these, 428 had no electricity or water; only 29 were regularly inhabited; and only 100 were lived in just in the summer. They were, and still are, basically toolsheds and a place to rest after lunch.

(6) Until relatively recently, the women only went to the country for harvest, staying at home the rest of the year to cook, spin and weave. The situation is less antiquated now, but the country still considers that the office is the place for most men and that women still look after the home.

(7) I have been through this, indirectly, in a negotiation to buy land in Pantelleria: the correspondence was with Australia, it was voluminous and it took a long time.

(8) Giuseppe Pitrè, *Usi e Costumi*, vol.III, ed. Clio, pp.186-204 (chapter on *vendemmias*).

(9) The cry in dialect was remembered as 'Stassi attentu ca sutta l'arvulu c'è me figghiu ca mi nasciu stanotti'. Her husband's name was Nardo Gandolfo.

18. Calatafimi at Table (pages 236 to 245)

(1) The chiesetta was in front of the carabinieri: hence the phrase that he has 'gone to the chiesetta', meaning he is in prison. Last year it was in another church.

(2) According to Pitrè, *Usi e Costumi*, vol.IV, p.349, the only day on which bread was not baked was Good Friday – for fear of burning Jesus Christ.

(3) The names of vegetables and fish change from place to place all over Italy and give rise to some confusion (this happens not only in Italy but in other Mediterranean countries as well). Alan Davidson has written an excellent book in an attempt to clear up the confusion about fish and to suggest some recipes as well: *Mediterranean Fish* in English, and *Il Mare in Pentola*, a much more evocative title ('The Sea in a Saucepan') in Italian. Both editions were published in 1972, the first in London by Penguin and the second by Mondadori in Milan. Much of his basic linguistic research was based on FAO material (the Food and Agricultural Organization of the United Nations), but it is amusing to hear how the rest of the research was done. I had brief contact with Evelyn Waugh's daughter Margaret, while her husband was Counsellor at the Embassy in Rome. Davidson was a diplomat and she told me he took to visiting the various embassies around the Mediterranean regularly, to the great alarm of the various ambassadors' and

counsellors' wives. They knew painfully well that it was their lot to be woken up every morning at five o'clock to accompany Davidson to the local fish-market and facilitate his research. Apparently he was very dogged, and was not to be put off.

(4) From one of his sister Ann's letters, quoted in Vivian Noakes, *Edward Lear: The Life of a Wanderer*, London, 1968, p.75. The 'aniseed' in the bread was fennel, incidentally.

(5) Ann Radcliffe, *A Sicilian Romance*, originally published in London in 1790. In chapter 5 the Duke experiences a wanton feast held by the superior and friars of a Sicilian monastery, indulged in in the belief that 'the enjoyment of the good things of this life was the surest sign of our gratitude to Heaven.' Compare this with Brydone, vol.2, letter XX, also in a monastery: 'Abstinence (continued he) from all innocent and lawful pleasures, we reckon one of the greatest sins...and I am pretty sure it is a sin that none of us here will ever be damned for.'

19. The Mollica Family (pages 246 to 258)

(1) F. Mugnos (1647-70), *Teatro Genealogico delle famiglie nobili...* (Bologna, 1897). Quoted in Pellegrino, op.cit., p.192.

(2) V. Palizzolo Gravina, *Il Blasone in Sicilia*, Palermo, 1871-5. It is worth noting that even Joe Bananas claims descent (though without apparent justification) from the ancient family of Bonanno, Princes of Cattolica and Dukes of Montalbano, etc, but Palizzolo Gravina says most of the branches of this family were extinct in the nineteenth century and doesn't mention any being active in the Castellamare area.

(3) Quoted in *I Mulini di Calatafimi*, L. Accardo et al., op.cit.

(4) It is also interesting to note that as a result of Napoleon's Egyptian ambitions Marsala wine became known to the world at large. I have mentioned that when Nelson's fleet ran out of wine after the Battle of the Nile during his pursuit of Napoleon to Egypt, he had to turn back to supply his ships with wine, which was provided by John Woodhouse, a Yorkshire winemaker at conveniently-situated Marsala. In 1798, before sailing back to Malta, Nelson's log-book records that he took on board thirty-six pipes and twenty-eight hogsheads of wine, which was only part of the order he had made. This was the basis of the future substantial fortunes of the Ingham, Woodhouse, Whittaker and Florio families, fortunes which influenced the economy and politics of the island – and of Italy in the case of the Florios. (See R. Trevelyan, *Princes Under the Volcano: Two Hundred Years of a British Dynasty in Sicily*, London, 1972.)

(5) *Brevi Notizie Storiche sull' Arciprete Canonico D. Francesco Avila*, by Francesco Moresellino Avila, Mazzara (Grillo), 1941. Francesco Avila was

the hero of Calatafimi's fight against the *terraggiolo*, the illegal feudal due that was owed to the Counts of Modica. He was elected to the Sicilian Parliament in 1848.

(6) Despite all his spending, he did not end up badly when his adoptive mother, Domenico Saccaro's wife, died. From papers in Caterina's family we learn that she left him over 140 million liras, a huge sum. There were 4 pieces of real estate, 105 *emphyteuses* (lands granted permanently in return for an established rent), 507 'simple and landed incomes', 3 'public incomes', 13 debts and furniture. For the question of Sebastiana Saccaro's house see *Pel Comune di Calatafimi contro Cav. Domenico Vivona*, Trapani, 1895: there is a copy of this courtroom document in the local library.

(7) There was also a famous singing cousin. Fernando Autuori was an internationally famous baritone. He was often personally requested by Toscanini and sang in Naples, Malta, the USA, Covent Garden and La Scala. He was also a caricaturist, like many of his cousins. Poetry was another family hobby much indulged in by all the cousins. And also by the paternal side of the family: I am particularly fascinated by Giuliano Mollica, who left his MS poems, dated unusually to the year 1876, to the library. There is one dedicated to a dog called Ebreo (Jew), belonging to Canon Marchese. The poem is forty verses long, of which twenty-seven are missing ('missing' was written by Giuliano on the typed MS he donated to the library). The story was about the Canon collecting a group of thirty-six poor peasants to search (unsuccessfully) for treasure night after night, while he recited invocations against evil spirits. What the upshot was is impossible to say because of the missing verses, but the peasants got so fed up that they were about to kill him. He was saved by Ebreo, though exactly how has been lost. In the preface to the reader Giuliano says Ebreo somehow managed to help the Canon flee. He also wrote an inscription for Ebreo's tombstone: 'Here lies Ebreo, a good hunter, who died at Marzuko towards the hour of 6 pm in the month of April of the <u>anno torto</u> [? after the leap-year].' Giuliano was also a self-taught musician.

(8) For the Florio family, see Raleigh Trevelyan, op.cit.

Index

290